DICK VAN PATTEN'S
Totally Terrific TV
TRIVIA

SQUAREONE
PUBLISHERS

COVER DESIGNER: Jeannie Tudor
COVER PHOTOS: Courtesy of Joe Franklin
BACK COVER PHOTO: Courtesy of Natural Balance Pet Foods, Inc.
INTERIOR PHOTOS: Courtesy of Dick Van Patten
and Natural Balance Pet Foods, Inc.
RESEARCHERS: Anthony Pomes, Gene Friedman,
Dennis Golin, and Dominick Grillo
EDITORS: Marie Caratozzolo and Joanne Abrams
TYPESETTER: Gary A. Rosenberg

Square One Publishers
115 Herricks Road
Garden City Park, New York 11040
www.SquareOnePublishers.com
(516) 535-2010 • (866) 900-BOOK

ISBN 0-7570-0231-5
978-0-7570-0231-1

Printed in the United States of America

10   9   8   7   6   5   4   3   2   1

CONTENTS

To my beautiful wife, Pat,
who has been with me
for over fifty wonderful years.

ACKNOWLEDGMENTS

For their dedication and support in helping me bring this project to life, I'd like thank all the folks at Square One, especially publisher Rudy Shur, series editor Marie Caratozzolo, and research editors Joanne Abrams and Anthony Pomes. I'd also like to thank Ron Simon of the Museum of Television & Radio, and trivia experts Dr. Gene Friedman, Dennis Golin, and Dominick Grillo for their help in assisting with the research and accuracy of the information in this book.

How to Play
the Games

Welcome, friends. Are you ready to put your knowledge of television facts and details to the test? My trivia book is built to challenge, while providing endless hours of fun and enjoyment. The games in this book have been designed in a way that allows you, the reader, to play either alone or with others. In most trivia books, when looking up the answer to a question, the reader is able to see the answers to other questions at the same time. This book doesn't allow that to happen, but you must first understand how to play the games. Ready?

THE BASICS

There are eighty games in this book, each with a dozen questions. Every game is also numbered and has been given a title that reflects the basic category of its questions, such as "TV Firsts," "Prime-Time Soaps," "Spinoffs," and "Made-for-TV Movies." Throughout, you'll also find a number of games titled "Grab Bag," which include a mix and match of questions from various categories.

THE PAGE SETUP

Each page holds four frames that are situated from the top of the page to the bottom (as seen in the example on the next page). Each frame is divided in half. The left half contains a question. The right half contains the answer to the question from a previous page. (Seem a little confusing? Not to worry—it actually sounds more complicated than it really is.) Stay with me . . .

Questions
are always on the
left side of each frame.

Answers
(to questions from previous
pages) are always on the
right side of each frame.

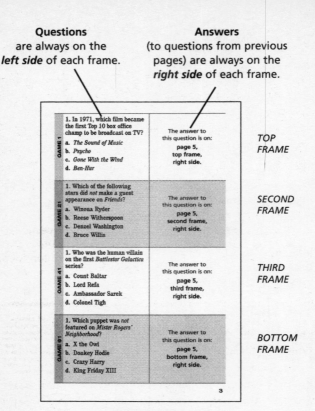

1. In 1971, which film became the first Top 10 box office champ to be broadcast on TV? a. *The Sound of Music* b. *Psycho* c. *Gone With the Wind* d. *Ben-Hur*	The answer to this question is on: page 5, top frame, right side.	*TOP FRAME*
1. Which of the following stars did *not* make a guest appearance on *Friends*? a. Winona Ryder b. Reese Witherspoon c. Denzel Washington d. Bruce Willis	The answer to this question is on: page 5, second frame, right side.	*SECOND FRAME*
1. Who was the human villain on the first *Battlestar Galactica* series? a. Count Baltar b. Lord Refa c. Ambassador Sarek d. Colonel Tigh	The answer to this question is on: page 5, third frame, right side.	*THIRD FRAME*
1. Which puppet was *not* featured on *Mister Rogers' Neighborhood*? a. X the Owl b. Donkey Hodie c. Crazy Harry d. King Friday XIII	The answer to this question is on: page 5, bottom frame, right side.	*BOTTOM FRAME*

3

Typical Page Layout
(four frame levels on each page)

PLAYING THE GAME

The most important point to keep in mind is that the twelve questions for each game are *not* read from the top of the page to the bottom. Rather, they are found on the same frame level on succeeding pages. Let me help make this clearer with an example and some accompanying graphics.

x

Let's start with Game #1, which begins in the *top frame* of page 1—a *right-hand* page. Here, you will find the name and number of the game you are about to play.

Turn the page and look at the next *right-hand* page (page 3) for the game's first question, which is located on the left side of the *top frame* (see graphic below).

So where's the answer to this question? Turn the page again and continue to look at the *top frame* of the next *right-hand* page (page 5). As shown below, the answer is located on the right side of the frame. On the left side of this frame, you'll find the second question of Game #1.

Question #1 is on
***left side* of top frame.**

Answer to Question #1 is
on next right-hand page—
***right side* of top frame.**

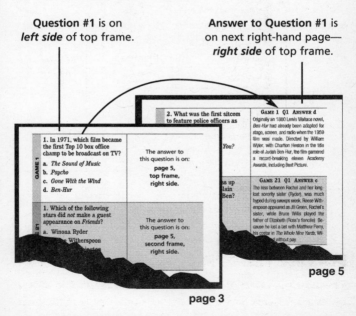

page 3

page 5

The answer to the first question of Game #1 is on the following
right-hand page—and appears on the right side of the top frame.
The left side of the top frame has the game's next question.

And that's how you continue—turning the page for each new question (Q), and finding its answer (A) on the following *right-hand* page (see graphic below).

Beginning with the top frame (*and staying in that top frame*), play the games, which flow from one *right-hand* page to the next until you have reached the last page. Then simply make a U-turn and continue playing the games—still in the top frame—from the back of the book to the front. While going in this direction, however, the answers to the questions will be found on consecutive *left-hand* pages.

Once you've completed the games in the top frame from the front of the book to the back, and then from the back to the front again, you'll find yourself back on page 1. Simply drop down one level to the next frame and begin playing the games found on this new level. Again, questions and answers will flow from one right-hand page to the next. Just be sure to stay on the same frame level.

Individual games are always
played on the same frame level.

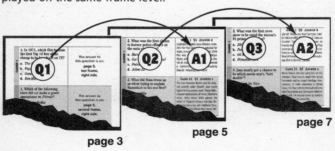

Progression of Questions and Answers

THERE'S HELP ON EVERY PAGE . . .

To be absolutely sure there's no confusion while playing the games, helpful instructions are provided on each and every page. Trust me, once you get the hang of it, you're going to love it. So kick back and get ready to be entertained, amused, and enlightened by these challenging TV questions and their fascinating fact-filled answers.

Have fun,

Dick Van Patten

LET THE GAMES
BEGIN . . .

GAME 1
TV Firsts

Turn to page 3 for the first question of Game 1.

GAME 21
Friends

Turn to page 3 for the first question of Game 21.

GAME 41
Sci-Fi

Turn to page 3 for the first question of Game 41.

GAME 61
Just for Kids

Turn to page 3 for the first question of Game 61.

Game 21 begins on page 1, second frame from the top.	**GAME 20 Q12 ANSWER b** Moose, who played Martin Crane's feisty dog Eddie on *Frasier* (1993–2004), also appeared in the 2000 film *My Dog Skip* as the older version of the title character. Moose's four-year-old son, Enzo, played young Skip. Enzo also appeared as his father's stunt double during the last few seasons of *Frasier*.
Game 41 begins on page 1, third frame from the top.	**GAME 40 Q12 ANSWER c** In the 1970 commercial called the "How Many Licks?" spot, a little boy asks first a turtle and then an owl how many licks it takes to get the center of a Tootsie Pop. Not even wise Mr. Owl knows because he can't eat the pop without taking a bite. But a group of volunteers at Purdue University found that 252 licks will do it.
Game 61 begins on page 1, bottom frame.	**GAME 60 Q12 ANSWER c** During most of the 1995–2004 run of *The Drew Carey Show*, Carey worked in the human resources department of a multinational department store chain called Winfred-Louder. The character was also the founder of Buzz Beer, a fictitious beverage company that manufactured a unique mix of beer and coffee.
Well, that's all, folks! Let's play again sometime . . .	**GAME 80 Q12 ANSWER b** From 1979 to 1984, viewers watched rich and glamorous Jonathan and Jennifer Hart (Robert Wagner and Stefanie Powers) as they traveled the world in their Lear Jet, solving crimes and looking great. Sometimes described as a *Thin Man* for the 1980s, *Hart to Hart* went on to inspire such shows as *Moonlighting* and *Remington Steele*.

1. In 1971, which film became the first Top 10 box office champ to be broadcast on TV?

a. *The Sound of Music*
b. *Psycho*
c. *Gone With the Wind*
d. *Ben-Hur*

The answer to this question is on:

**page 5,
top frame,
right side.**

1. Which of the following stars did *not* make a guest appearance on *Friends*?

a. Winona Ryder
b. Reese Witherspoon
c. Denzel Washington
d. Bruce Willis

The answer to this question is on:

**page 5,
second frame,
right side.**

1. Who was the human villain on the first *Battlestar Galactica* series?

a. Count Baltar
b. Lord Refa
c. Ambassador Sarek
d. Colonel Tigh

The answer to this question is on:

**page 5,
third frame,
right side.**

1. Which puppet was *not* featured on *Mr. Rogers' Neighborhood*?

a. X the Owl
b. Donkey Hodie
c. Crazy Harry
d. King Friday XIII

The answer to this question is on:

**page 5,
bottom frame,
right side.**

12. In which film did Eddie, the Jack Russell terrier on *Frasier*, appear?

a. *Because of Winn-Dixie*

b. *My Dog Skip*

c. *Babe*

d. *Must Love Dogs*

GAME 20 Q11 ANSWER b
The white cockatoo was often perched on the shoulder of Detective Anthony Vincenzo Baretta (Robert Blake) in this popular series, which ran from 1975 to 1978. In 2003, Fred was ranked Number 25 on Animal Planet's list of *50 Greatest TV Animals*. The top three spots went to Lassie, Kermit the Frog, and Flipper.

---

12. In the '70s, what product was advertised by commercials with Mr. Owl and Mr. Turtle?

a. Kool-Aid

b. Honeycomb cereal

c. Tootsie Pop

d. Cheetos

GAME 40 Q11 ANSWER b
Sold in a tube, Brylcreem—the first mass-marketed men's hair product in the United States—was designed to keep men's hair in place and give it a shiny "wet" look. Brylcreem was actually created in England, and during World War II, the product's popularity with Royal Air Force pilots led to their nickname, the Brylcreem Boys.

---

12. In *The Drew Carey Show*, what type of business did Drew Carey work for?

a. Insurance company

b. Toy manufacturer

c. Department store

d. Investment company

GAME 60 Q11 ANSWER b
Played by Harry Anderson, *Night Court's* Judge Harry T. Stone was eccentric, but no more unusual than many of his coworkers, who included Assistant District Attorney Dan Fielding (John Larroquette), a sex-obsessed narcissist; and bailiff Nostradamus "Bull" Shannon (Richard Moll), a seemingly dimwitted hulk who was often childlike.

---

12. Which show featured lead characters living in a Beverly Hills mansion?

a. *Evening Shade*

b. *Hart to Hart*

c. *Charmed*

d. *McMillan and Wife*

GAME 80 Q11 ANSWER a
Played by Aneta Corsaut, *The Andy Griffith Show's* Helen Crump was originally conceived as a one-shot character. But the show's producers liked the chemistry between Corsaut and Andy Griffith, so Crump was made a regular character. When the series ended in 1968, Helen Crump married Andy Taylor.

Answers are in right-hand boxes on page 2.

GAME 1

2. What was the first sitcom to feature police officers as the main characters?

a. *Barney Miller*

b. *Car 54, Where Are You?*

c. *Police Squad!*

d. *Adam-12*

GAME 1 Q1 ANSWER d

Originally an 1880 Lewis Wallace novel, *Ben-Hur* had already been adapted for stage, screen, and radio when the 1959 film was made. Directed by William Wyler, with Charlton Heston in the title role of Judah Ben-Hur, the film garnered a record-breaking eleven Academy Awards, including Best Picture.

GAME 21

2. What did Ross dress up as when trying to explain Hanukkah to his son Ben?

a. Armadillo

b. Skunk

c. Fairy

d. Koala

GAME 21 Q1 ANSWER c

The kiss between Rachel and her long-lost sorority sister (Ryder), was much hyped during sweeps week. Reese Witherspoon appeared as Jill Green, Rachel's sister, while Bruce Willis played the father of Elizabeth (Ross's fiancée). Because he lost a bet with Matthew Perry, his costar in *The Whole Nine Yards*, Willis appeared without pay.

GAME 41

2. Which actress starred in the FOX series *Dark Angel*?

a. Jessica Alba

b. Sarah Michelle Gellar

c. Jennifer Garner

d. Alyssa Milano

GAME 41 Q1 ANSWER a

Count Baltar was played by John Colicos, who was also the first Klingon in the original *Star Trek* TV series. Shown on ABC in 1978 in response to the phenomenal success of *Star Wars*, *Battlestar Galactica* was created by Glen A. Larsons and featured Lorne Greene as Commander Adama and Dirk Benedict as Lieutenant Starbuck.

GAME 61

2. On which series does a puppy send secret messages?

a. *Richie Rich*

b. *Groundling Marsh*

c. *Arthur*

d. *Blue's Clues*

GAME 61 Q1 ANSWER c

Performed by Jerry Nelson, *The Muppet Show's* puppet Crazy Harry had scruffy hair, an unkempt beard, huge baggy eyes—and a fascination with explosives. Crazy Harry usually carried a plunger box that would activate a hidden charge. Besides his TV appearances, the puppet played a role in *The Muppet Movie* (1978).

Answers are in right-hand boxes on page 7.

11. Which TV detective's closest friend was a bird named Fred?

a. Starsky
b. Baretta
c. Toma
d. Columbo

Ross and the capuchin monkey grew uncomfortably close, but Marcel's constant humping of inanimate objects (and people's legs) forced Ross to donate him to the San Diego Zoo. Marcel was actually a female monkey named Katie, who, after only one season on *Friends,* landed the role of the Ebola-spreading animal in the 1995 film *Outbreak.*

---

11. "A little dab'll do ya" is a catchphrase from an old commercial for a:

a. Whipped topping
b. Hair product
c. Perfume
d. Steak sauce

In the 1990s, actor Lucky Vanous played "The Diet Coke Hunk"—a slender but muscular construction worker who's ogled by an office full of admiring women as he removes his shirt and refreshes himself with a Diet Coke. Later, Lucky starred in his own workout video: *The Ultimate Fat-Burning System.*

---

11. Which TV character kept a stuffed armadillo named Clarence on his desk?

a. Merrill Stubing
b. Harry T. Stone
c. Andy Sipowicz
d. Sherman T. Potter

Airing on NBC from 1997 to 2003, the office sitcom *Just Shoot Me!* was originally designed as a vehicle for Laura San Giacomo. Very quickly, though, it became a ticket to stardom for actor-comedian David Spade, who portrayed smart-mouthed assistant Dennis Finch.

---

11. Which sitcom character had a girlfriend named Helen Crump?

a. Andy Taylor
b. Jack Tripper
c. Clinton Judd
d. J.R. Ewing

Cybill Shepherd won a 1996 Golden Globe Award for playing the title role in *Cybill,* a 1995–1998 show based on the British sitcom *Absolutely Fabulous.* Shepherd portrayed Cybill Sheridan, a somewhat faded television actress whose age had relegated her to playing bit parts and character roles.

3. What was the first news show to be rated the season's #1 prime-time series?

a. *20/20*

b. *Person to Person*

c. *60 Minutes*

d. *Primetime Live*

GAME 1 Q2 ANSWER b
Car 54, Where Are You? ran from 1961 to 1963 on NBC. Starring Joe E. Ross as Gunther Toody and Fred Gwynne as Francis Muldoon, the series followed the madcap adventures of the two NYPD officers in a fictional precinct of the Bronx. Most of the episodes, though, were actually shot in Toronto, Canada.

3. Joey nearly got a chance to be which movie star's "butt double"?

a. Robert De Niro

b. Al Pacino

c. Marlon Brando

d. Joe Pesci

GAME 21 Q2 ANSWER a
When Ross's son Ben joins him for the holidays, Ross tries to teach him about Hanukkah and his Jewish heritage. Ben, however, is more interested in Santa Claus. So Ross runs to the local costume store for a Santa suit, but has to settle for what's left. He returns home as Santa's holiday friend, the armadillo.

3. Which character is *not* from a *Star Trek* TV series?

a. Worf

b. Weyoun

c. Vir Cotto

d. B'Elanna Torres

GAME 41 Q2 ANSWER a
Sarah Michelle Gellar was the star of UPN's *Buffy the Vampire Slayer,* while Jennifer Garner played a secret agent in ABC's *Alias* and Alyssa Milano was one of a trio of witchin' sisters in The WB's *Charmed.* Jessica Alba was only nineteen when she starred as Max Guevara in this sci-fi series from filmmaker James Cameron.

3. *The Smurfs* was based on a comic strip from which country?

a. Canada

b. Holland

c. Belgium

d. Singapore

GAME 61 Q2 ANSWER d
The Nickelodeon show *Blue's Clues* follows a dog named Blue through her everyday life. In each show, Blue leaves three clues, which are searched for by the show's host. The host then sits in his "thinking chair" and puts the clues together, while kids at home help him decode the secret messages.

10. On *Friends,* Ross's friend gave him Marcel the monkey, after:

a. Finding him at the park

b. Buying him from a circus

c. Rescuing him from a lab

d. Winning him in a card game

GAME 20 Q9 ANSWER a
Salem Saberhagen (voiced by Nick Bakay) was a warlock, sentenced by the Witches' Council to spend 100 years as an American shorthair with no magical powers. The black cat's witty jokes, delivered in a deadpan manner, provided much of the show's humor. The TV series (1996–2003) was based on the Archie Comics series of the same name.

---

10. What soft drink was advertised by a sexy construction worker taking a break?

a. Diet Coke

b. Diet Pepsi

c. Diet 7UP

d. Tab

GAME 40 Q9 ANSWER c
Keebler's history can be traced to Godfrey Keebler's small Philadelphia bake shop of 1853. Later, several bake shops came together into a union, and finally the Keebler Company was born in 1966. The Elves weren't introduced until 1970, when the world learned that Keebler's "Uncommonly Good" products are made in a magic elvish oven.

---

10. What was Laura San Giacomo's character in *Just Shoot Me*?

a. Maya Gallo

b. Nina Van Horn

c. Vicki Costa

d. Heather Hammerman

GAME 60 Q9 ANSWER d
Nancy Marchand won four Emmys for her role as the autocratic *LA Tribune* owner-publisher on *Lou Grant.* Her other notable TV appearances have included the 1953 original version of *Marty,* the miniseries *North and South, Book II,* and HBO's *The Sopranos,* for which she earned a Golden Globe as Livia, Tony Soprano's belligerent mother.

---

10. What sitcom concerned a wisecracking actress living in Los Angeles?

a. *Alice*

b. *Maude*

c. *Cybill*

d. *Rhoda*

GAME 80 Q9 ANSWER b
Maury Chaykin played fictional detective Nero Wolfe in *A Nero Wolfe Mystery,* which aired on the A&E Network for two seasons, starting in 2001. The creation of novelist Rex Stout, Wolfe is a 286-pound eccentric who dislikes women, loves beer and gourmet food, and, whenever possible, conducts business without leaving his brownstone.

Answers are in right-hand boxes on page 6.

4. Which was the first TV Western to be broadcast in color?

a. *Gunsmoke*

b. *The Big Valley*

c. *Bonanza*

d. *Wagon Train*

GAME 1 Q3 ANSWER c
The investigative news magazine *60 Minutes* was introduced on CBS in 1968, and in the 1979–1980 season, the show beat out *Three's Company*, *M*A*S*H*, and *Dallas*. The show was so successful that during that same season, Australia licensed a spinoff. Ten years later, New Zealand followed suit.

4. Who played Chandler's cross-dressing father?

a. Glenn Close

b. Camryn Mannheim

c. Kathleen Turner

d. Sharon Stone

GAME 21 Q3 ANSWER b
Joey's new agent, the gravelly voiced Estelle Leonard, gets him his first big job in a movie playing Al Pacino's butt double during a shower scene. (To help get into character, Joey even borrows Monica's moisturizer on the day of the shoot.) Unfortunately, the striving actor was fired for "acting too much with it."

4. Which actor was the first doctor on the BBC sci-fi series *Doctor Who*?

a. Tom Baker

b. William Hartnell

c. Jon Pertwee

d. David Tennant

GAME 41 Q3 ANSWER c
Vir Cotto, played by Stephen Furst, is a character from the 1990s sci-fi series *Babylon 5*. Although Furst may be best remembered as Kent "Flounder" Dorfman from the 1978 movie *National Lampoon's Animal House*, he gained sci-fi acclaim with his portrayal of Vir Cotto, a member of the Centauri race who goes on to become an emperor.

4. Which *Sesame Street* resident cuddles a teddy bear named Radar?

a. Big Bird

b. Grover

c. Ernie

d. Elmo

GAME 61 Q3 ANSWER c
The Smurfs—*Les Schtroumpfs* in French—were created by Belgian cartoonist Peyo. Originally, they were simply new characters in Peyo's late-1950s Franco-Belgian comic serial *Johan & Pirlouit*. But the figures were an enormous success, and in 1959, the first independent Schtroumpfs stories were born.

9. On *Sabrina the Teenage Witch*, Salem was turned into a cat because he:

a. Tried taking over the world
b. Stole a rose
c. Hurt Sabrina
d. Started a fire

GAME 20 Q8 ANSWER c
A basset hound named Bernadette was Cleo (Cleopatra)—the droopy-eared pet of Socrates "Sock" Miller (Jackie Cooper). Cleo never actually spoke, but her amusing sarcastic thoughts (voiced by Mary Jan Croft) were heard loud and clear by the audience. Other TV basset hounds include Socrates (*Judging Amy*), Quincy (*Coach*), and Dog (*Columbo*).

9. What brand of cookies is advertised by an elf named Ernie?

a. Hydrox
b. Nabisco
c. Keebler
d. Pepperidge Farm

GAME 40 Q8 ANSWER a
The marketing mascot of Energizer batteries, the Energizer Bunny has been seen in TV ads since 1989—but only in North America, as it is a parody of Europe's Duracell Bunny. In the campaign's first commercial, technicians tested out Energizer batteries in a pink toy bunny, and since then it's been going and going and going. . . .

9. What owner of the *Los Angeles Tribune* often crossed swords with Lou Grant?

a. Carla Mardigian
b. Lucille Bates
c. Celeste Patterson
d. Margaret Pynchon

GAME 60 Q8 ANSWER c
This series about employees of a San Francisco magazine was actually inspired by Brooke Shields' performance in a 1996 *Friends* episode called "The One After the Super Bowl, Part One." NBC executives were so impressed by Shields' portrayal of stalker Erika Ford that they created the sitcom *Suddenly Susan* for her.

9. Which TV crime solver lived in a lavish New York City brownstone?

a. Sonny Crockett
b. Nero Wolfe
c. Theo Kojak
d. Amos Burke

GAME 80 Q8 ANSWER c
In 1960, widower Steve Douglas (Fred MacMurray) began the show with three sons: Mike (Tim Considine), Robbie (Don Grady), and Chip (Stanley Livingston). In 1965, he adopted Ernie (Barry Livingston). Steve then married Barbara Harper (Beverly Garland), who had a daughter, Dodie (Dawn Lynn). For Steve, five was enough.

5. Who appeared on the first cover of *TV Guide*?

a. Jackie Gleason
b. Milton Berle
c. Lucille Ball and Desi Arnaz, Jr.
d. Howdy Doody

GAME 1 Q4 ANSWER c
Broadcast from 1959 to 1973, *Bonanza* was the first network TV series to film all of its episodes in color. Although it was #1 in the Nielsen ratings from 1964 to 1967, the show was not the most popular Western in the history of TV. That honor belongs to *Gunsmoke,* with *Bonanza* enjoying the #2 spot.

5. The *Friends* characters are responsible for how many offspring?

a. Three
b. Four
c. Five
d. Six

GAME 21 Q4 ANSWER c
Perhaps best known as a film actor for her roles in such blockbuster hits as *Body Heat* and *Peggy Sue Got Married,* Kathleen Turner has made her mark on stage and television as well. On *Friends,* she appeared in the recurring role of Chandler's transvestite father (and Vegas burlesque star)—a part that was enhanced by her low, husky voice.

5. On *Buck Rogers in the 25th Century,* who played Colonel Wilma Deering?

a. Barbara Bain
b. Maren Jensen
c. Kirstie Alley
d. Erin Gray

GAME 41 Q4 ANSWER b
Doctor Who debuted in the UK on November 23, 1963—a day after President Kennedy's assassination. The show's initial run was from 1963 to 1989, then a new incarnation of the series was launched in 2005. To date, Doctor Who has been played by ten different actors, including Tom Baker, whose portrayal of the character was parodied on *The Simpsons.*

5. Which kids show featured Phineas T. Bluster, Dilly Dally, and Flub-a-Dub?

a. *Mickey Mouse Club*
b. *Howdy Doody*
c. *Captain Kangaroo*
d. *Mr. Rogers' Neighborhood*

GAME 61 Q4 ANSWER a
The towering (eight feet, two inches) full-body puppet Big Bird can roller skate, ice skate, dance, sing, write poetry, and more. Despite these accomplishments, he still needs his teddy bear Radar—a nod to *M*A*S*H's* Walter "Radar" O'Reilly, who had a teddy bear of his own.

GAME 20

8. What was the dog's name on the 1950s show *The People's Choice*?

a. Chelsea
b. Toni
c. Cleo
d. Trixie

GAME 20 Q7 ANSWER b
Murray was played by a lovable border collie mix named Maui–the offspring of two dogs that were rescued from a Castaic, California animal shelter. During the first few episodes of the series, Murray, who often chased imaginary mice before crashing into walls, was simply called "The Dog." *Mad About You* ran from 1992 to 1999.

GAME 40

8. Which TV ad character wears flip-flops and sunglasses?

a. Energizer Bunny
b. Little Caesar
c. Jolly Green Giant
d. Hawaiian Punch Guy

GAME 40 Q7 ANSWER b
Named for the Greek muse of heroic poetry and history, the Clio Awards were first given in 1959. The Clios are intended to reward creative excellence in advertising and design, and are given in a number of fields, including that of television. The ADDY Awards were also established to recognize superior advertising.

GAME 60

8. Who played the title role on *Suddenly Susan*?

a. Kathy Griffin
b. Barbara Barrie
c. Brooke Shields
d. Courtney Thorne-Smith

GAME 60 Q7 ANSWER b
Elaine Vassal was Ally McBeal's (Calista Flockhart's) nosy yet lovable secretary. The office gossip, Elaine could always be found hovering nearby when other characters were talking. She was also something of a crackpot inventor, who, among other things, created the face-bra in an attempt to prevent wrinkles.

GAME 80

8. How many children did Steve Douglas have by the end of *My Three Sons*?

a. Three
b. Four
c. Five
d. Six

GAME 80 Q7 ANSWER a
Captain Francis Furillo (Daniel J. Travanti) oversaw the troubled precinct on *Hill Street Blues* (1981–1987), an award-winning series created by Steven Bochco and Michael Kozoll. Sergeant Phil Esterhaus (Michael Conrad) is best remembered for the line he always delivered at the end of his morning briefing: "Hey, let's be careful out there."

GAME 1

6. What was the first American TV show to appear in mainland China?

a. *Columbo*

b. *Man from Atlantis*

c. *Kung Fu*

d. *Happy Days*

GAME 1 Q5 ANSWER c
Lucy and her new son graced the premiere edition of *TV Guide*, dated the week of April 3, 1953. The publication, which cost just fifteen cents, was almost an instant success, and in the 1960s, *TV Guide* was the most read and circulated magazine in the country. Today, its TV-shaped logo remains one of the most recognized publication logos.

GAME 21

6. Which statement about Phoebe is false?

a. Neglected by her father

b. Once married to a lawyer

c. Lived on the streets

d. Is a vegetarian

GAME 21 Q5 ANSWER d
Ross and his first wife, Susan, had two children (one through artificial insemination); Phoebe was the surrogate mother of her brother's triplets; and Rachel gave birth to Emma (also Ross's child) at the end the Season Eight. During the show's final season Monica and Chandler became the proud parents of adopted twins.

GAME 41

6. What was the name of the spaceship on *Lost in Space*?

a. Mars One

b. Jupiter 2

c. Phoenix Five

d. Mercury 7

GAME 41 Q5 ANSWER d
As Wilma Deering, Erin Gray played the first female colonel in a TV series. Barbara Bain starred in 1975 with then-husband Martin Landau in TV's *Space: 1999*, while Maren Jensen appeared as Athena in ABC's *Battlestar Galactica*. Kirstie Alley portrayed a Vulcan in the 1982 movie *Star Trek II: The Wrath of Khan*.

GAME 61

6. Which actor provided the voice of Clifford the Big Red Dog for the animated series?

a. Robin Williams

b. Jonathan Winters

c. Louie Anderson

d. John Ritter

GAME 61 Q5 ANSWER b
Howdy Doody aired on NBC from 1947 to 1960. Hosted by Bob Smith, who was dubbed "Buffalo Bob," the show featured the freckle-faced boy marionette called Howdy Doody as well as the puppets Mr. Bluster, Dilly Dally, Princess Summerfall Winterspring, and Flub-a-Dub—a combination of eight animals.

7. Who was Jamie and Paul Buchman's dog on *Mad About You*?

a. Marty
b. Murray
c. Mitchell
d. Marcel

GAME 20 Q6 ANSWER a
In this '60s children's adventure series, the famous dolphin helped ranger Porter Ricks (Brian Kelly) and his two sons (Luke Halpin and Tommy Norden) at Coral Key Park in Florida. Flipper was played mainly by female dolphins, but a male, Mr. Gipper, was needed for scenes involving the dolphin's famous tail walk, which the females couldn't master.

---

7. Which awards are given to recognize excellence in advertising?

a. People's Choice
b. Clio
c. S.A.G.
d. Emmy

GAME 40 Q6 ANSWER d
The "Aaron Burr" ad, showing a man who loses a phone-in radio contest because of a lack of milk, launched the now-famous Got Milk? campaign developed at the request of the California Milk Processor Board in 1993. This campaign helped revive milk sales after a twenty-year slump.

---

7. What office worker did Jane Krakowski play on the comedy *Ally McBeal*?

a. Georgia Thomas
b. Elaine Vassal
c. Renee Raddick
d. Nelle Porter

GAME 60 Q6 ANSWER d
Based on the Colombian telenovela (soap opera) *Yo Soy Betty, La Fea* ("I am Betty, the Ugly One"), ABC's *Ugly Betty* stars America Ferrera as a frumpy young woman who lands a job at New York's *Mode* fashion magazine. Although *Ugly Betty* is not written as a soap opera, tempting bits of a fictional telenovela are seen on the TV in Betty's home.

---

7. Which TV law enforcer took orders from Captain Frank Furillo?

a. Phil Esterhaus
b. Pepper Anderson
c. Phil Fish
d. T.J. Hooker

GAME 80 Q6 ANSWER d
Dr. Heathcliff Huxtable, called "Cliff" by his attorney wife Clair (Phylicia Rashad), was TV's number-one dad from 1984 to 1992. Cosby's character was a wise, funny, and caring father who provided practical advice to his five children—Sondra, Denise, Theo, Vanessa, and Rudy—as well as to his very large viewing audience

---

7. What was the very first nighttime television soap opera?

a. *Soap*

b. *I Remember Mama*

c. *Peyton Place*

d. *Rich Man, Poor Man*

GAME 1 Q6 ANSWER b
The Man from Atlantis starred Patrick Duffy as the not-entirely human Mark Harris—a mystery man who possessed superhuman strength and speed, and who was able to survive underwater. In 1980, the show became the first American TV series to be aired in the People's Republic of China, where it was called *The Man from the Bottom of Atlantic.*

7. Which inappropriate hit song did Ross sing to baby Emma?

a. "Roses"

b. "Baby Got Back"

c. "Bootylicious"

d. "Sexual Healing"

GAME 21 Q6 ANSWER b
Phoebe's character is certainly fascinating. She believed in Santa until Joey told her otherwise; the woman she thought was her mom committed suicide when Phoebe was fourteen; and her twin sister, Ursula, was a porn star. Phoebe also married Duncan, a gay Canadian ice dancer (who turned out to be straight) to help him get his green card.

7. Which TV show followed the adventures of Dr. Samuel Beckett?

a. *The Time Tunnel*

b. *Out of This World*

c. *Alien Nation*

d. *Quantum Leap*

GAME 41 Q6 ANSWER b
Created in 1965 by producer Irwin Allen, *Lost in Space* aired on CBS from 1965 to 1968—and had higher ratings than *Star Trek*. Based partially on the novel *Swiss Family Robinson,* this show followed the adventures of the Robinson family aboard Jupiter 2 during their mission to reach the star Alpha Centauri.

7. Which series introduced kids to Interplanet Janet?

a. *The Jetsons*

b. *Sesame Street*

c. *Schoolhouse Rock!*

d. *Captain Kangaroo*

GAME 61 Q6 ANSWER d
Based on a series of children's books written by Norman Bridwell, *Clifford the Big Red Dog* was one of several PBS Kids shows designed to teach children a number of life lessons. The show aired from 2000 to 2003, with the last cartoons being completed shortly before John Ritter's death on September 11, 2003.

GAME 20

6. The two brothers on *Flipper* were Sandy and:

a. Bud

b. Buzz

c. Bob

d. Bill

GAME 20 Q5 ANSWER d

After he was orphaned in an Indian raid, Rusty and his German shepherd were adopted by the troops at Fort Apache in *The Adventures of Rin Tin Tin* (1954–1959). Flash was Roscoe's basset hound on *The Dukes of Hazzard;* Buck was the Bundy's family pet on *Married with Children;* and Bandit belonged to the Ingalls family on *Little House on the Prairie.*

GAME 40

6. What product was the focus of an ad featuring a peanut butter eater who can't enunciate "Aaron Burr"?

a. Mouthwash

b. Marshmallow spread

c. White bread

d. Milk

GAME 40 Q5 ANSWER d

The California Raisins first appeared in 1987 in a series of commercials for the California Raisin Board. Soon, the dancing raisins were everywhere, including boxes of breakfast cereal. The talented fruit even had their own Saturday morning cartoon series and appeared in holiday specials such as *A Claymation Christmas Celebration.*

GAME 60

6. What magazine is turned out by Betty Suarez—aka "Ugly Betty"—and her coworkers?

a. *Blush*

b. *Glam*

c. *Posh*

d. *Mode*

GAME 60 Q5 ANSWER c

Based on the British series of the same name, the NBC sitcom *The Office* examines the day-to-day lives of people working for the fictitious Dunder-Mifflin Paper Company in Scranton, Pennsylvania. Although the show is scripted, it takes the form of a documentary and often acknowledges the presence of the audience and the camera.

GAME 80

6. What was Dr. Huxtable's first name on *The Cosby Show*?

a. Radcliff

b. Chet

c. Clifford

d. Heathcliff

GAME 80 Q5 ANSWER a

The popular game show *Concentration* ran for over fourteen years (1958–1973). Over time, its hosts included Jack Barry, Hugh Downs, Bob Clayton, Jack Narz, Ed McMahon, and Orson Bean. Then the show was resurrected in 1987 under the name *Classic Concentration,* and ran until 1991, this time hosted by Alex Trebek.

GAME 1

8. The first televised _____ occurred in 1960.

a. Emmy ceremony
b. Presidential debate
c. Oscar ceremony
d. World Series

GAME 1 Q7 ANSWER c
Adapted from the 1956 Grace Matalious novel of the same name, _Peyton Place_ aired from 1964 to 1969, first running in black and white, and then in color. Cast members orginally included Mia Farrow as Allison MacKenzie, Ryan O'Neal as Rodney Harrington, Barbara Parkins as Betty Anderson, and Ed Nelson as Dr. Michael Rossi.

GAME 21

8. What did Chandler tell Janice to discourage her romantic advances?

a. He was becoming a priest
b. He "joined the other team"
c. He was moving to Yemen
d. He was engaged to Phoebe

GAME 21 Q7 ANSWER b
"Baby Got Back" by Sir Mix-a-Lot is hardly a lullaby. But while Ross was babysitting for daughter Emma, he discovered that its bouncy beat made her laugh for the first time. Initially, the song's racy lyrics mortified Rachel; but she eventually joined in the singing after realizing it was the only way to make Emma laugh.

GAME 41

8. Which _Star Trek_ spinoff featured scenes from the first _Star Trek_ TV series?

a. _The Next Generation_
b. _Deep Space Nine_
c. _Enterprise_
d. _Voyager_

GAME 41 Q7 ANSWER d
Scott Bakula starred as Beckett in this popular NBC sci-fi drama that aired from 1989 to 1993. One of the better time-travel TV shows, _Quantum Leap_ also starred Dean Stockwell as Bakula's friend and fellow time traveler Albert Calavicci. The show won five Emmys, including two in 1990 and 1991 for Best Cinematography in a Series.

GAME 61

8. What children's show host was suspended for asking kids to send him their parents' money ?

a. Soupy Sales
b. Andy Devine
c. Mister Rogers
d. Sandy Becker

GAME 61 Q7 ANSWER c
Conceived by Thomas G. Yohe and airing from 1973 to 1986, _Schoolhouse Rock!_ was a series of forty-six short films featuring songs about schoolhouse topics such as grammar, science, economics, history, and politics. The song _Interplanet Janet_, about a "galaxy girl" who flies from planet to planet, taught kids about the solar system.

5. Which TV dog had a master named Rusty?

a. Flash

b. Buck

c. Bandit

d. Rin Tin Tin

Pal, who played Lassie in the 1943 movie *Lassie Come Home,* was also in the TV series pilot. (Nine direct descendants of Pal played the role during the 1954–1974 series.) Although the role was female, all Lassies were male. Females periodically shed much of their coats, making them unfit to film all year, plus males tended to be impressively larger.

---

5. Which manufacturer of raisin bran cereal featured the California Raisins in its ads?

a. Kellogg's

b. Nabisco

c. Quaker

d. Post

The first "Where's the beef?" commercial aired in 1984, and featured actress Clara Peller angrily commenting on a competitor's burger, which had a huge bun but a small patty. Soon, "Where's the beef?" became a popular all-purpose phrase used to question the substance of a product, idea, or event.

---

5. What type of company is run from *The Office*?

a. Clothing

b. Publishing

c. Paper supplies

d. Cosmetics

NewsRadio's Joe Garelli (Joe Rogan) was the station's electrician and general fix-it guy. Rather than buying what he needed for the job, Joe made everything himself, right down to fabricating his own duct tape. Although a self-proclaimed ladies' man, he was unable to approach Catherine Duke (Khandi Alexander), the love of his life.

---

5. Which popular game show featured contestants solving a picture puzzle?

a. *Concentration*

b. *The Joker's Wild*

c. *Password*

d. *Wheel of Fortune*

The Sopranos' turf was Jersey, the nanny nurtured kids in Manhattan, and Murphy Brown worked out of DC. It was the Barone family that lived in Lynbrook, Long Island. Although the show was based on the real-life experiences of its star, Ray Romano, Romano was born and grew up in the borough of Queens—not in the Nassau County town of Lynbrook.

---

9. Which company aired the first official TV ad in 1941?

a. Bulova

b. Texaco

c. Camel

d. Chevrolet

John F. Kennedy and Richard M. Nixon squared off in a debate that was a major factor in JFK's victory. Kennedy—who, unlike Nixon, wore some makeup for his TV appearance—appeared smooth and relaxed, and spoke directly to the viewers by looking into the camera. Many Americans felt that JFK was the runaway winner of the event.

---

9. Who did Danny DeVito appear as in a 2004 _Friends_ episode?

a. Roy, the stripper

b. Chef Charlie

c. Guido, the pizza delivery guy

d. Joey's Uncle Bob

Janice Litman Goralnik née Hosenstein (Maggie Wheeler) was Chandler's on-again off-again girlfriend with the big hair, nasal voice, and New York accent. In a final breakup attempt, he claimed to be moving to Yemen, and actually boarded a plane and flew there as Janice saw him off at the airport. He wanted to prove to her that he wasn't lying!

---

9. In _Early Edition_, which newspaper appeared on Gary Hobson's doorstep each morning?

a. _Chicago Sun-Times_

b. _The New York Times_

c. _Washington Post_

d. _The Oregonian_

In 1996—as a thirtieth-anniversary tribute to the original series—the _Deep Space Nine_ producers aired an episode called "Trials and Tribble-ations" in which the DS9 crew goes back in time and (through digital effects) interacts with events that took place in the original series' second-season episode "The Trouble with Tribbles."

---

9. What did kids learn about when visiting _Beakman's World_?

a. Art

b. History

c. Science

d. Geography

Soupy Sales, whose real name was Milton Supman, began his work in kids shows in the 1950s. On New Year's Day 1965, Soupy—angry about having to work on the holiday—concluded his broadcast by telling his viewers to send him those "funny green pieces of paper" found in their parents' pockets. They did, and Soupy was suspended for two weeks.

GAME 20

4. What breed of dog starred on *Lassie*?

a. German shepherd
b. Cocker spaniel
c. Collie
d. St. Bernard

GAME 40

4. What fast food chain was advertised in the "Where's the beef?" commercial?

a. Wendy's
b. Burger King
c. McDonalds
d. Arby's

GAME 60

4. What was Joe Garelli's job on *NewsRadio*?

a. Weather guy
b. Electrician
c. Anchor
d. Mailroom clerk

GAME 80

4. Which TV show was set on Long Island?

a. *The Sopranos*
b. *Everybody Loves Raymond*
c. *The Nanny*
d. *Murphy Brown*

GAME 20 Q3 ANSWER b
Wilbur Post (Alan Young) lent his ear to Mr. Ed—an American Saddlebred named Bamboo Harvester. It is often said that peanut butter was put on the horse's gums to get him to move his lips when "talking," but it was actually a nylon bit that was pulled by a handler. Allan "Rocky" Lane was the voice of Mr. Ed, but didn't want his name on the credits.

GAME 40 Q3 ANSWER d
The "Mikey" ad campaign ran from 1972 to 1984, becoming one of the most popular and long-running commercials of all time. The TV ads showed older kids persuading the picky four year old, played by John Gilchrist, to sample a bowl of Life cereal. Needless to say, Mikey liked it.

GAME 60 Q3 ANSWER d
Loni Anderson's Jennifer Marlowe was the secretary of Arthur Carlson, WKRP's inept general manager. A gorgeous blond with many wealthy boyfriends, Jennifer was nevertheless very smart and able to handle nearly any situation. Moreover, she was the station's highest paid employee.

GAME 80 Q3 ANSWER d
The Michael Mann-produced drama *Crime Story* (1986–1988) centered on the personal war between Detective Mike Torello, played by Dennis Farina, and mob boss Ray Luca, portrayed by Anthony Denison. The 1961 Del Shannon classic "Runaway" was reworked and rerecorded in 1986 to capture the edgy mood of the series.

GAME 1

10. Which series aired TV's first interracial kiss?

a. *The Jeffersons*

b. *All in the Family*

c. *Star Trek*

d. *Soap*

GAME 1 Q9 ANSWER a

Bulova, a New York-based producer of watches and clocks, paid $9 for the ten-second spot that was broadcast on WNBT (now WNBC) during a baseball game between the Brooklyn Dodgers and the Philadelphia Phillies. The voice-over declared, "America Runs on Bulova Time!"

GAME 21

10. Monica's parents admit spending her wedding fund on which luxury item?

a. A Winnebago

b. A new beach house

c. A trip to Tahiti

d. A cottage in the Hamptons

GAME 21 Q9 ANSWER a

Danny DeVito plays Roy, an unlikely stripper who is hired (sight unseen) at the last minute to perform at Phoebe's bachelorette party. When Phoebe doesn't want to see a short, old fat guy dance around "in a child's Halloween costume," he cries. The hilarious role earned DeVito an Emmy nomination as Best Guest Actor in a Comedy Series.

GAME 41

10. Which character did Roddy McDowall play in the 1974 *Planet of the Apes* TV series?

a. Caesar

b. Galen

c. Cornelius

d. Milo

GAME 41 Q9 ANSWER a

The 1990s CBS show *Early Edition* was partly inspired by the *Back to the Future* time-travel movies. In it, a mysterious cat delivers the newspaper to Gary Hobson (played by actor Kyle Chandler) and it's always a day early. Hobson then spends each episode trying to stop a terrible event that was reported in that newspaper from happening.

GAME 61

10. What was the game show *Where in the World Is Carmen Sandiego?* based on?

a. Board game

b. Computer game

c. Card game

d. Arcade game

GAME 61 Q9 ANSWER c

Based on the Universal Press Syndicate comic strip *You Can With Beakman and Jax*, *The Beakman Show* premiered in September 1992, ran until 1998, and then returned to syndication in 2006. The show starred Paul Zaloom as Beakman, an eccentric scientist who performed comical experiments in response to viewer mail.

3. Who is the only person Mr. Ed, TV's talking horse, spoke to?

a. Rocky

b. Wilbur

c. Orville

d. Roger

GAME 20 Q2 ANSWER c
Jed's old bloodhound was actually a canine actor named Stretch. In one episode, Duke fathered the puppies of a French poodle, much to the dismay of snooty neighbor Mrs. Drysdale, who had wanted her own poodle, Claude, to sire the litter. Stretch, who also appeared in the film *No Time for Sergeants* (1958), retired from the series at age 13.

---

3. Which product was popularized by an ad campaign featuring the finicky "Mikey"?

a. Kraft Macaroni and Cheese

b. Hershey's Syrup

c. Heinz Ketchup

d. Life Cereal

GAME 40 Q2 ANSWER b
From 1954 to 1959, the character on the Trix box was a stick figure boy. Then in 1959, Joe Harris created an anthropomorphic cartoon rabbit who was always trying to trick kids into giving him a bowl of the fruit-flavored cereal. Soon, Trix became one of General Mills' best sellers.

---

3. What was the name of Loni Anderson's character on *WKRP in Cincinnati*?

a. Claire Hartline

b. Mona Loveland

c. Bailey Quarters

d. Jennifer Marlowe

GAME 60 Q2 ANSWER c
Played by Grant Shaud, Miles Silverberg was a mere twenty-five years old, and no match for veteran journalist Murphy Brown (Candice Bergen). Although Miles tried to get his way, he rarely if ever did. When Shaud left the show in 1996, he was replaced by Lily Tomlin, who played producer Kay Carter-Shepley.

---

3. Which 1980s series had the theme song "Runaway," sung by Del Shannon?

a. *Jake and the Fatman*

b. *The Insiders*

c. *Hooperman*

d. *Crime Story*

GAME 80 Q2 ANSWER c
*M*A*S*H* was set in the early 1950s during the Korean War; *Brooklyn Bridge* was set in the mid-'50s; and *Happy Days*, in the late '50s. *The Wonder Years*, though, tackled the social issues and historic events of the '60s—as well as typical teenage issues—as experienced by young Kevin Arnold (Fred Savage).

---

11. Who played TV's first Beatnik, Maynard G. Krebs, of *The Many Loves of Dobie Gillis*?

a. Wally Cox
b. Bob Denver
c. Dwayne Hickman
d. Jim Nabors

GAME 1 Q10 ANSWER c
The kiss, which occurred between Captain Kirk (William Shatner) and Lieutenant Uhura (Nichelle Nichols), aired on November 22, 1968. Although the event led to major protests in the Southern states, with some Southern stations first refusing to air the episode, the bulk of the feedback received by the network was quite positive.

11. After she marries Mike, Phoebe changes her name to Princess:

a. Walkie Talkie Doggiedoor
b. Regina Falange II
c. Consuela Banana Hammock
d. Ava Cado Guacamole

GAME 21 Q10 ANSWER b
When Monica discovers that her parents spent her wedding fund on a beach house, she thinks she'll have to give up her plans for a dream wedding. Chandler, who had wanted to save his money for their future, offers it to her. When Monica realizes he had been saving for their life together, she decides to forego the big wedding.

11. Which series featured aliens called Ebonites, Chromoites, and Megasoids?

a. *One Step Beyond*
b. *The Twilight Zone*
c. *The X-Files*
d. *The Outer Limits*

GAME 41 Q10 ANSWER b
In the CBS series, McDowall played Galen, the chimpanzee. He first appeared as Cornelius in the classic 1968 film *Planet of the Apes,* and again in the 1971 sequel, *Escape From the Planet of the Apes.* In 1972's *Conquest for the Planet of the Apes,* MacDowall played Cornelius's grown son, Milo, who changes his name to Caesar.

11. What colorful blobs were invented by *Teletubbies* creator Anne Wood?

a. Huffenpuffs
b. Dinky Dorks
c. Rumdums
d. Boohbahs

GAME 61 Q10 ANSWER b
Based on a computer game of the same name, *Where in the World Is Carmen Sandiego?* aired on PBS from 1991 to 1996. Contestants were given 50 ACME Crime Bucks to begin each round. Then, through comedy sketches, a Lightning Round, and other features, clues were provided to the geographical location of criminal Carmen Sandiego.

2. Which TV family owned a bloodhound named Duke?

a. Waltons

b. Bradfords

c. Clampetts

d. Ingalls

GAME 20 Q1 ANSWER d
The shaggy dog belonged to the boys, while the girls had a cat named Fluffy. The pets were introduced in the first episode during Mike and Carol's wedding. Tiger got loose and chased the cat, causing lots of chaos. Fluffy never appeared in another episode and Tiger, who showed up periodically during the first season, was never seen after that.

---

2. "Silly rabbit, ___ are for kids!" is a well-known line from a TV commercial.

a. Corn Pops

b. Trix

c. Cheerios

d. Cocoa Puffs

GAME 40 Q1 ANSWER c
The Pillsbury Doughboy was created in 1965 by Rudy Perz, a copywriter for ad executive Leo Burnett. The first Doughboy was a $16 doll of clay whose voice was provided by Paul Frees—the same actor who supplied the voice of *Rocky and His Friends'* villain Boris Badenov.

---

2. What was the name of Murphy Brown's boss?

a. Frank Fontana

b. Corky Sherwood

c. Miles Silverberg

d. Eldin Bernecky

GAME 60 Q1 ANSWER a
Running from 1996 to 2002, ABC's *Spin City* focused on a fictitious mayor of New York City—Randall Winston, played by Barry Bostwick—and his staff. Although Winston was the mayor, the person who was *truly* in charge was the Deputy Mayor, who was portrayed first by Michael J. Fox and then by Charlie Sheen

---

2. Which of these TV shows was *not* set in the 1950s?

a. *M*A*S*H*

b. *Brooklyn Bridge*

c. *The Wonder Years*

d. *Happy Days*

GAME 80 Q1 ANSWER a
Bobby Simone (Jimmy Smits) died of heart failure. Sam Beckett (Scott Bakula) leapt back to help his friend Al but "never returned home." Due to an expected series cancellation, Magnum (Tom Selleck) "died" at the end of Season 7. When the show came back for another (final) season, so did Magnum, who (the writers decided) had just been in a coma.

---

12. What was Jackie Gleason's first attempt at TV situation comedy?

a. *The Life of Riley*

b. *The Honeymooners*

c. *The Great One*

d. *Mr. Peepers*

GAME 1 Q11 ANSWER b
Viewers of the show may remember that Maynard played the bongos, loved the horror movie *The Monster That Devoured Cleveland*, and spent a good deal of time watching the wrecking ball swing at the "Old Endicott Building." What did Maynard hate? Work!

12. Monica and Rachel lose their apartment to Joey and Chandler because they don't know:

a. What Chandler's job is

b. The duck's name

c. Joey's favorite TV show

d. Where Chandler was born

GAME 21 Q11 ANSWER c
When Phoebe realizes she can change her name to anything, she opts for "Princess Consuela Banana Hammock," unaware that a banana hammock is a type of men's bikini swimwear. To get her to change it back, Mike tells her he is changing his name to "Crap Bag." This prompts Phoebe to once again change her name—to Phoebe Buffay-Hannigan.

12. On *The Six Million Dollar Man*, who was Steve Austin's government-agency boss?

a. Charlie

b. Oscar

c. Rudy

d. Higgins

GAME 41 Q11 ANSWER d
Following in the footsteps of Rod Serling's *Twilight Zone*, *The Outer Limits* aired on ABC from 1963 to 1965. Episodes were written by such acclaimed scriptwriters as Joseph Stefano (best-known for writing Hitchcock's *Psycho* in 1960) and sci-fi writing legend Harlan Ellison, who later wrote for *Star Trek*.

12. On which show was each Wednesday "Anything Can Happen Day"?

a. *Captain Kangaroo*

b. *Bozo the Clown*

c. *Mickey Mouse Club*

d. *Pee-wee's Playhouse*

GAME 61 Q11 ANSWER d
Boobahs are furry, gumdrop-shaped, brightly colored creatures played by actors in full-body suits. Their thick fur sparkles with tiny lights, and a row of lights form the eyebrows above the huge eyes in their Kewpie-doll-style heads. As if that isn't creepy enough, Boobahs can retract their heads into their furry necks.

1. What was the dog's name on *The Brady Bunch*?

a. Rags
b. Tramp
c. Moptop
d. Tiger

The answer to this question is on:

**page 24,
top frame,
right side.**

1. What is the more familiar name of ad icon Poppin' Fresh?

a. Orkin Man
b. Little Squirt
c. Pillsbury Doughboy
d. Campbell Kid

The answer to this question is on:

**page 24,
second frame,
right side.**

1. Which sitcom was *not* set in a broadcast industry office?

a. *Spin City*
b. *Murphy Brown*
c. *Mary Tyler Moore Show*
d. *Good Morning Miami*

The answer to this question is on:

**page 24,
third frame,
right side.**

1. Which of the following characters did *not* die during its TV series?

a. Barnaby Jones/*Barnaby Jones*
b. Bobby Simone/*NYPD Blue*
c. Sam Beckett/*Quantum Leap*
d. Thomas Magnum/*Magnum, P.I.*

The answer to this question is on:

**page 24,
bottom frame,
right side.**

GAME 2

Soap Operas

Turn to page 29 for the first question.

GAME 1 Q12 ANSWER a
Initially an NBC radio comedy starring William Bendix, *The Life of Riley* was then adapted for TV. Because Bendix had other commitments, the show starred Jackie Gleason, with Rosemary DeCamp playing his wife, Peg. *The Life of Riley* ran from 1949 to 1950, and then was canceled, but not before winning television's first Emmy.

GAME 22

Spinoffs

Turn to page 29 for the first question.

GAME 21 Q12 ANSWER a
From the show's onset, Chandler's job (in Statistical Analysis and Data Reconfiguration) is never clear. During a trivia game in which Joey and Chandler try to prove they know the girls better than Monica and Rachel know the guys, the girls can't come up with Chandler's job. Rachel guesses "transponster," which Monica reminds her isn't even a word!

GAME 42

Relatively Speaking

Turn to page 29 for the first question.

GAME 41 Q12 ANSWER b
In this 1970s ABC series, actor Richard Anderson played Oscar Goldman, the man responsible for repairing much of Steve Austin's body with bionic parts, which gave him superhuman ability and strength. Austin was played by actor Lee Majors, who became world-famous in the role. In the 1980s, Majors starred in another ABC hit series *The Fall Guy*.

GAME 62

Cameos and Crossovers

Turn to page 29 for the first question.

GAME 61 Q12 ANSWER c
Produced and televised by Walt Disney Productions, the original 1950s *Mickey Mouse Club* was intended to help finance and promote the building of the Disneyland theme park in Anaheim, California. Although Walt Disney called an end to the series in 1959, audience demand resulted in syndicated reruns from 1962 to 1965.

GAME 20

Love Those Animals

Turn to page 26
for the first question.

Turn to page 26
for the first question.

GAME 19 Q12 ANSWER c

At the end of their "Rock Your Body" performance during the 2004 Super Bowl halftime show, Timberlake ripped a piece of Jackson's costume, exposing her breast. They claimed the incident (called "Nipplegate") was unintentional, but lawsuits and FCC fines ensued. It also caused stronger FCC decency guidelines within the communications industry.

GAME 40

TV Commercials

Turn to page 26
for the first question.

Turn to page 26
for the first question.

GAME 39 Q12 ANSWER d

Airing on NBC from 1970 to 1977, *McCloud* starred Dennis Weaver as a law officer from New Mexico who was on "special assignment" with the New York City Police Department. Although he received Emmy nominations in 1974 and 1975 for his work on the series, Weaver did not actually win an Emmy for the role.

GAME 60

At the Office

Turn to page 26
for the first question.

Turn to page 26
for the first question.

GAME 59 Q12 ANSWER b

Borgnine joined the US Navy right after graduating from high school and served for ten years. After winning a Best Actor Oscar in 1955 for *Marty,* Borgnine went on to win a Best Actor Emmy in 1963 for the ABC sitcom *McHale's Navy.* He was also the first center square on *The Hollywood Squares* when it debuted in October 1966.

GAME 80

GRAB BAG

Turn to page 26
for the first question.

Turn to page 26
for the first question.

GAME 79 Q12 ANSWER b

With an acting career that has spanned stage, screen, and television, my younger sister, Joyce, first appeared at age eight in the Broadway production of *Love's Old Sweet Song.* Since the 1950s, she has had roles in over 100 TV shows, including *As the World Turns* (the original cast), *Perry Mason, Judging Amy,* and *Desperate Housewives.*

1. Whose *General Hospital* wedding was one of daytime TV's highest-rated episodes?

a. Phil and Tara's

b. Luke and Laura's

c. Charles and Patsy's

d. Tad and Dixie's

The answer to this question is on:

page 31, top frame, right side.

---

1. What was the first network television spinoff?

a. *Pete and Gladys*

b. *Our Miss Brooks*

c. *Petticoat Junction*

d. *The Andy Griffith Show*

The answer to this question is on:

page 31, second frame, right side.

---

1. Which shows feature a real-life sister and brother?

a. *Cagney & Lacey/Wings*

b. *Punky Brewster/Facts of Life*

c. *Twin Peaks/Boston Public*

d. *That Girl/Murphy Brown*

The answer to this question is on:

page 31, third frame, right side.

---

1. Which *Golden Girl* played Sue Ann Nivens on *The Mary Tyler Moore Show*?

a. Bea Arthur

b. Betty White

c. Estelle Getty

d. Rue McClanahan

The answer to this question is on:

page 31, bottom frame, right side.

12. Who was Janet Jackson's partner during her famous "wardrobe malfunction"?

a. Steven Tyler
b. Kid Rock
c. Justin Timberlake
d. Jon Bon Jovi

GAME 19 Q11 ANSWER a
During her 1995 appearance, the carefree Barrymore shocked the bewildered host by dancing on top of his desk and pulling up her shirt (with her back to the audience). The "for-Dave's-eyes-only" flashing was her birthday gift to him. Shortly after, Courtney Love flashed Letterman in the same manner (but he appeared unimpressed).

---

12. Which detective role never won the actor an Emmy?

a. Theo Kojak
b. Thomas Magnum
c. Lieutenant Columbo
d. Sam McCloud

GAME 39 Q11 ANSWER d
Elizabeth Hubbard played Althea Davis on *The Doctors* from 1964 to 1969, and again from 1970 until the show's cancellation in 1982. It was for this role that she won the 1974 Daytime Emmy Award for outstanding actress. Later, she received nine Emmy nominations for her role of Lucinda Walsh in *As the World Turns*.

---

12. Which of these *McHale's Navy* stars was himself a WWII Navy veteran?

a. Bob Newhart
b. Ernest Borgnine
c. James Garner
d. Hal Holbrook

GAME 59 Q11 ANSWER b
This intense WWII drama followed soldiers in a frontline American infantry squad as they battled their way across war-torn France. The ABC series ran from 1962 to 1967, and starred Vic Morrow and Rick Jason. Only the show's fifth (and final) season aired in color. Noted filmmaker Robert Altman was one of its original producers.

---

12. Actress Joyce Van Patten is:

a. My cousin
b. My sister
c. My niece
d. No relation

GAME 79 Q11 ANSWER c
In the April 2005 "Spring Breakout" episode of *Arrested Development*, I played Cal Cullen, an investor from whom the Bluths hoped to get some money. Showing good sense, I refused to do business with the Bluths, saying that I "couldn't afford to end up on *Scandalmakers*"— an entertainment show that frequently featured the dysfunctional family.

2. Which popular comedian was a regular on *Soap*, a satire of daytime soap operas?

a. Billy Crystal

b. Tim Allen

c. Jamie Foxx

d. Drew Carey

GAME 2 Q1 ANSWER b

Played by Anthony Geary and Genie Francis, the wildly popular Luke and Laura were the first "supercouple" of daytime soaps. When they wed on November 16, 1981, 30 million viewers watched breathlessly. The couple stayed married for an impressive two decades.

2. The character played by Wayne Rogers in TV's *M*A*S*H* had a spinoff called:

a. *Hogan's Heroes*

b. *Gideon's Crossing*

c. *Trapper John, MD*

d. *Ben Casey*

GAME 22 Q1 ANSWER a

A spinoff of *December Bride, Pete and Gladys* (1960–1962) focused on the lives of Pete Porter (Harry Morgan) and his ditzy wife Gladys (Cara Williams). Williams earned a 1962 Emmy nomination for the role. Morgan's extensive TV and film career includes such roles as *M*A*S*H's* Colonel Potter and *Dragnet's* Captain Gannon.

2. Which shows feature a real-life aunt and niece?

a. *Captain Video/Dragnet*

b. *Gunsmoke/Secret Storm*

c. *Police Story/Police Woman*

d. *Your Show of Shows/Coach*

GAME 42 Q1 ANSWER a

A talented stage and screen actress, Tyne Daly played detective Mary Beth Lacey in the CBS drama *Cagney & Lacey* from 1982 to 1988. Tyne's younger brother, Timothy Daly, is perhaps best known for his portrayal of pilot Joe Hackett in the NBC sitcom *Wings,* which aired from 1990 to 1997. Father James Daly was also an actor.

2. Which supermodel had a 1998 cameo on NBC's *3rd Rock from the Sun*?

a. Christie Brinkley

b. Kathy Ireland

c. Carol Alt

d. Cindy Crawford

GAME 62 Q1 ANSWER b

Rose Nylund, Betty White's character on *The Golden Girls,* was soft spoken, naïve, and a bit dimwitted. She was also the complete opposite of Sue Ann Nivens—White's *Mary Tyler Moore* character. Sue Ann, WJM's Happy Homemaker, was bold and flirty—and always chasing Lou Grant (Ed Asner). White won Emmys for both characters.

GAME 19

11. Who performed a semi-striptease on *Late Show with David Letterman*?

a. Drew Barrymore

b. Sharon Stone

c. Demi Moore

d. Madonna

GAME 19 Q10 ANSWER b
David Niven was announcing award nominees when Robert Opal ran across the stage wearing nothing but a grin. After the historic "run," which ended with security guards ushering Opal away, Niven said to the shocked audience, "Probably the only laugh that man will ever get in his life is by stripping off his clothes and showing his shortcomings."

GAME 39

11. Who was the first woman to receive a Daytime Emmy for Outstanding Actress in a Daytime Drama?

a. Brenda Dickson

b. Jeannie Cooper

c. Susan Flannery

d. Elizabeth Hubbard

GAME 39 Q10 ANSWER a
Duke, who had played Hellen Keller in the 1962 film of the same name, received her 1980 Emmy for Outstanding Lead Actress in a Limited Series or Special. Also appearing in the made-for-TV movie were Melissa Gilbert as Helen Keller and Diana Muldaur as Kate Keller, Helen's mother. Anne Bancroft played Sullivan in the 1962 movie.

GAME 59

11. In which country did *Combat!* take place?

a. Italy

b. France

c. Belgium

d. Germany

GAME 59 Q10 ANSWER c
Kim Delaney's character Alex Devlin was a wire service reporter covering the war in Vietnam. Debuting on CBS in 1987, *Tour of Duty* was the first TV series that focused on the Vietnam War. The show's opening credits were set to The Rolling Stones' song "Paint It Black," also used in Stanley Kubrick's Vietnam epic *Full Metal Jacket.*

GAME 79

11. In what TV show did I play investor Cal Cullen?

a. *Scrubs*

b. *King of Queens*

c. *Arrested Development*

d. *Will & Grace*

GAME 79 Q10 ANSWER a
Vince, my talented youngest son, made his TV debut in a Colgate commercial as a child. This was followed by roles in scores of commercials and TV shows, as well as a career in professional tennis. The *World Poker Tour,* which he hosts along with poker pro Mike Sexton, has been credited with fueling a nationwide boom in Texas hold 'em poker.

Answers are in right-hand boxes on page 30.

GAME 2

3. Which family was never associated with *The Young and the Restless*?

a. The Brooks

b. The Chancellors

c. The Abbotts

d. The Scorpios

GAME 22

3. *Mork & Mindy* was a spinoff of which show?

a. *Welcome Back, Kotter*

b. *Laverne & Shirley*

c. *Happy Days*

d. *Alf*

GAME 42

3. Which shows feature a real-life husband and wife?

a. *Ellen/Hawiian Eye*

b. *Cheers/Joan of Arcadia*

c. *McMillan & Wife/McCloud*

d. *The FBI/Remington Steele*

GAME 62

3. Which famous pop star had a part in the CBS sitcom *Good Times*?

a. Janet Jackson

b. Whitney Houston

c. Mariah Carey

d. Paula Abdul

GAME 2 Q2 ANSWER a
Crystal played Jodie Dallas, Mary Campbell's gay son who married and raised a baby. In fact, *Soap,* which ran from 1977 to 1981, was one of the earliest American prime-time shows to have a regular gay character. The show was also noteworthy for openly dealing with topics such as marital infidelity, impotence, and interracial marriage.

GAME 22 Q2 ANSWER c
Pernell Roberts played Trapper John, Chief of Surgery at San Francisco Memorial Hospital. Not wanting to play a TV doctor again, Wayne Rogers turned down the role. (Ironically, he later played one on *House Calls.*) In a court case involving royalty recipients, the show was legally considered a spinoff of the original film, *not* the TV series.

GAME 42 Q2 ANSWER d
Actress Nanette Fabray was first seen by TV viewers in the 1950–1954 hit *Your Show of Shows.* Born with the last name *Fabares,* she switched to a phonetic spelling when Ed Sullivan pronounced it *Fa-bare-ass.* The original spelling was kept by niece Shelley Fabares, who played Christine in the 1989–1997 ABC sitcom *Coach.*

GAME 62 Q2 ANSWER d
Along with the *3rd Rock* episode entitled "36! 24! 36! Dick!," Cindy Crawford— the supermodel with the trademark facial beauty mark—has appeared on NBC's *Frasier* and ABC's *According to Jim.* Crawford has made childhood leukemia the primary focus of her extensive charity work in memory of her brother, who died from the blood disorder at age four.

10. When a streaker showed up at the 1974 Oscars, what gesture did he give?

a. A wave

b. The peace sign

c. The middle finger

d. A thumbs up

At a 1990 Cincinnati Reds/San Diego Padres game, Barr screeched an off-key version of the song in a failed attempt to get laughs. She further infuriated fans by spitting and grabbing her crotch to mimic clichéd baseball behavior. Barr was booed off the field. Even President George HW Bush called her performance "disgusting" and a "disgrace."

10. Who won a 1980 Emmy for portraying Anne Sullivan in the made-for-TV movie *The Miracle Worker*?

a. Patty Duke

b. Anne Bancroft

c. Melissa Gilbert

d. Diana Muldaur

McNichol won the Emmy for her portrayal of Letitia "Buddy" Lawrence on ABC's *Family*, which aired from 1976 to 1980. After the series' run, the actress appeared in several films, and then returned to television in 1988, playing Barbara Weston on NBC's *Empty Nest*. Unfortunately, health issues forced McNichol to leave the show in 1992.

10. Which *NYPD Blue* actress was in *Tour of Duty* in the late '80s?

a. Sharon Lawrence

b. Andrea Thompson

c. Kim Delaney

d. Sherry Stringfield

Airing only a year after *M*A*S*H* debuted (also on CBS), *Roll Out* was about a group of mostly-black servicemen who delivered supplies to the French army during WWII. Garrett Morris starred as the fast-talking trucker known as Wheels, along with Ed Begley Jr. as Lieutenant Robert W. Chapman and Teddy Wilson as High Strung.

10. Which member of my family hosts the Travel Channel's *World Poker Tour*?

a. Vince

b. Dick

c. James

d. Nels

Played by Grant Goodeve, David was the eldest Bradford son, but not the eldest child. (That honor belonged to Mary.) After *Eight Is Enough*, Grant had a recurring role in *Northern Exposure* and won guest spots in several other series. He now appears on Home & Garden Television (HGTV), hosting *If Walls Could Talk* and *Homes of Our Heritage*.

4. On *All My Children*, Erica Kane has been married to all of the following men except:

a. Jeff Martin

b. Travis Montgomery

c. Trevor Dillon

d. Adam Chandler

GAME 2 Q3 ANSWER d
The Scorpio family has its home in *General Hospital*, television's longest running daytime soap opera, having debuted in 1963. *The Young and the Restless* didn't appear on the TV scene until 1973. For many years, though, *Y&R* was television's highest-rated daytime serial.

---

4. Which TV spinoff was set on Manhattan's East Side?

a. *Good Times*

b. *The Jeffersons*

c. *One Day at a Time*

d. *All in the Family*

GAME 22 Q3 ANSWER c
Starring Robin Williams as the beloved alien from Ork, *Mork & Mindy* ran from 1978 to 1982. Many of the show's gags were on-the-spot improvisations by Williams, who won the Golden Globe in 1979 for Best TV Actor in a Musical/Comedy.

---

4. Which shows feature a real-life father and daughter?

a. *Twin Peaks/Joan of Arcadia*

b. *Wyatt Earp/Alice*

c. *Longstreet/Felicity*

d. *Star Trek/Boston Legal*

GAME 42 Q3 ANSWER b
Ted Danson is best known for his role as barkeeper Sam Malone in the NBC hit sitcom *Cheers* (1982–1993). In 1995, Danson wed his third wife, actress Mary Steenburgen, who would later play Helen Girardi in the CBS fantasy/drama *Joan of Arcadia* (2003–2005). Husband and wife worked together on the short-lived 1996 CBS sitcom *Ink*.

---

4. Who played Murray's daughter on *The Mary Tyler Moore Show*?

a. Jamie Lee Curtis

b. Helen Hunt

c. Courteney Cox

d. Melanie Griffith

GAME 62 Q3 ANSWER a
Eleven-year-old Janet Jackson joined the cast in 1977 for the last two seasons of this series, which focused on the Evans family. She played Penny Gordon Woods, a young girl who followed JJ (Jimmie Walker) home from school. When it was discovered that Penny was being abused by her mom, Willona (the Evans' neighbor) legally adopted her.

---

9. Whose performance of *The Star Spangled Banner* caused a national uproar?

a. Whitney Houston

b. Roseanne Barr

c. Madonna

d. Linda Ronstadt

GAME 19 Q8 ANSWER c

Madonna (dressed as a groom) kissed both pop stars (dressed as brides) during a performance at the 2003 Video Music Awards. But it was her prolonged, open-mouth kiss with Spears that garnered the most attention. During the song, Missy Elliot represented the priest, while Madonna's young daughter, Lourdes, briefly appeared as a flower girl.

9. Which member of TV's *Family* won best supporting actress Emmys in 1977 and 1979?

a. Quinn Cummings

b. Sada Thompson

c. Kristy McNichol

d. Meredith Baxter

GAME 39 Q8 ANSWER b

Although *Three's Company* didn't win the coveted Emmy Award for best comedy series, in 1984, star John Ritter won an Emmy for Outstanding Actor in a Comedy Series, and also garnered a Golden Globe Award. And in 1979, Norman Fell—another cast member—won a Golden Globe Award for Best TV Actor in a Supporting Role.

9. Which *SNL* cast member appeared in the 1973 CBS sitcom *Roll Out*?

a. Dan Aykroyd

b. Garrett Morris

c. John Belushi

d. Chevy Chase

GAME 59 Q8 ANSWER c

Set in the Vietnam city of Danang on the South China Sea, *China Beach* was unique in that it told the story of Vietnam through the perspective of the women who were there. As Lieutenant McMurphy, Dana Delany became a household name and won two Best Actress Emmys for her work in that role. *China Beach* ran on ABC from 1988 to 1991.

9. What was the name of my eldest son on *Eight Is Enough*?

a. Tommy

b. Nicholas

c. Grant

d. David

GAME 79 Q8 ANSWER d

Based on the radio serial of the same name, TV's *Young Doctor Malone* aired on ABC from 1958 through 1963. Both my sister, Joyce, and I worked on the soap for a time, as did many young actors. In fact, both Joan Hackett and Kathleen Widdoes had their TV debuts on *Young Doctor Malone*.

5. What was the name of Marlena's identical twin sister on *On Days of Our Lives*?

a. Danielle
b. Samantha
c. Suzanne
d. Cynthia

GAME 2 Q4 ANSWER c
All My Children's Erica Kane has been played by Susan Lucci since the soap's premiere in 1970. In addition to being married ten times—which is not, by the way, a record on daytime soaps—Erica has had relationships with a variety of other men, including three generations of the same family.

---

5. Who was the only Cosby kid to get a spinoff series?

a. Sondra
b. Theo
c. Denise
d. Vanessa

GAME 22 Q4 ANSWER b
In this *All in the Family* spinoff, newly successful businessman George Jefferson (Sherman Hemsly) moves his family from Queens to a ritzy Manhattan apartment. The hit sitcom ran from 1975 to 1985, and was the first to feature an interracial married couple.

---

5. Which shows feature a real-life father and daughter?

a. *Quincy, ME/Hotel*
b. *Another World/Baywatch*
c. *Days of Our Lives/Friends*
d. *Bonanza/7th Heaven*

GAME 42 Q4 ANSWER a
Although actor/dancer Russ Tamblyn's breakout role was in the 1954 film *Seven Brides for Seven Brothers,* many TV viewers remember his portrayal of the eccentric psychiatrist in the '90s show *Twin Peaks.* Daughter Amber Tamblyn is best known for playing the title role in the 2003–2005 CBS series *Joan of Arcadia.*

---

5. Harold Hecuba (Phil Silvers), one of the visitors to *Gilligan's Island*, was a:

a. Movie producer
b. World War II pilot
c. Mad scientist
d. Detective

GAME 62 Q4 ANSWER b
Hunt appeared in the *Mary Tyler Moore* episode as Laurie Slaughter when she was just thirteen. (She was only nine when cast in *Pioneer,* her first TV movie.) In the 1980s, she joined the *St. Elsewhere* cast as Clancy Williams, but her best-known TV role—for which she won four Emmys—was Jamie Buchman in the 1990s hit sitcom *Mad About You.*

---

8. Whose MTV kiss with Madonna was overshadowed by Britney's?

a. Gwen Stefani

b. Pink

c. Christina Aguilera

d. Courtney Love

Early in his career, the TV journalist hosted the much-hyped live opening of the gangster's vault in Chicago's Lexington Hotel. Accompanied by a medical examiner (in case human remains were found), Rivera fired a submachine gun at the wall to break it down. But instead of money and jewels, the vault held only a dusty liquor bottle.

---

8. Which of these TV shows did *not* win at least one Emmy for best comedy series?

a. *Sex and the City*

b. *Three's Company*

c. *M*A*S*H*

d. *Arrested Development*

Created by Hanna-Barbera, and airing from 1958 to 1962, *The Huckleberry Hound Show* was most likely the series that made Hanna-Barbera a household name. It should not have been a surprise, then, when this animated series about a blue-haired Southern dog won the 1959 Emmy Award for Outstanding Achievement in Children's Programs.

---

8. What was the rank of Colleen McMurphy (Dana Delany) on *China Beach*?

a. Major

b. Private

c. Lieutenant

d. Captain

A spinoff character of *The Andy Griffith Show*, Gomer Pyle (Jim Nabors) never rose above his PFC ranking. This made for several amusing run-ins between Gomer and his drill instructor, Gunnery Sergeant Vince Carter (Frank Sutton). *Gomer Pyle, USMC* debuted on CBS in 1964 and ended in 1970, during the height of the Vietnam War.

---

8. On which soap opera did I have a regular role?

a. *As the World Turns*

b. *Search for Tomorrow*

c. *The Secret Storm*

d. *Young Doctor Malone*

Believe it or not, Mark Hamill—*Star Wars'* heroic Jedi Knight Luke Skywalker—was originally cast as eldest son David Bradford on *Eight Is Enough*. But having just completed the first *Star Wars* movie, Hamill wanted to focus on his film career, so Grant Goodeave took over the role.

GAME 2

6. Which specialist in soap villains played David Rinaldi on *One Life to Live*?

a. Michael Zaslow

b. Anthony Herrera

c. Maurice Benard

d. Eric Braeden

GAME 2

GAME 2 Q5 ANSWER b

The character of Samantha was played by Deidre Hall's identical twin sister, Andrea Hall-Lovell. After her stint on *Days,* Andrea pursued other business interests, and eventually returned to her earlier profession as a special education teacher.

GAME 22

6. Which show was a spinoff of the popular television comedy *Diff'rent Strokes*?

a. *Webster*

b. *Punky Brewster*

c. *The Facts of Life*

d. *Growing Pains*

GAME 22 Q5 ANSWER c

Set at Hillman College, *A Different World* (1987–1983) focused on the college life of Cosby kid Denise Huxtable, played by Lisa Bonet. The sitcom, which offered an exceptional number of opportunities to young black actors, writers, producers, and directors, gave America its first look at life on a predominantly black college campus.

GAME 42

6. Which shows feature a real-life husband and wife?

a. *Barney Miller/China Beach*

b. *Major Dad/Charlie's Angels*

c. *A-Team/Bionic Woman*

d. *Simon & Simon/Designing Women*

GAME 42 Q5 ANSWER c

Greek-born John Aniston—originally, Ioannis Anastassakis—has appeared in several soap operas, and has long portrayed Victor Kiriakas in NBC's *Days of Our Lives*. His daughter, Jennifer Aniston, rose to fame playing Rachel Green in NBC's long-running sitcom *Friends*. Jennifer's godfather was the late Greek-American actor Telly Savalas.

GAME 62

6. Which comic actor played Theo's friend Smitty on *The Cosby Show*?

a. Eddie Murphy

b. Adam Sandler

c. Chris Rock

d. Luke Wilson

GAME 62 Q5 ANSWER a

When Hollywood producer Harold Hecuba appeared on the island during his world-wide talent search, the castaways tried to impress him with a musical adaptation of *Hamlet*. They hoped Hecuba would take them back to Hollywood. This 1966 third-season episode called "The Producer" is hailed as one of the series favorites (and funniest).

---

7. Who came up empty after opening up Al Capone's secret vault in 1986?

a. Larry King
b. Peter Jennings
c. Walter Cronkite
d. Geraldo Rivera

During the 1994 show (the most censored in talk-show history), Madonna's crude language was also peppered with double entendres. She also gave Dave a pair of her panties. She refused to leave the set, but was finally removed during a commercial break. The next night, when guest Charles Grodin came out, he presented Dave with a pair of his briefs!

---

7. What was the first animated TV cartoon series to win an Emmy Award?

a. *The Jetsons*
b. *The Flintstones*
c. *Huckleberry Hound*
d. *The Bugs Bunny Show*

Drea De Matteo hoped to be a director when she first entered New York University's Tisch School of the Arts. But in 2004, De Matteo won an Emmy Award for Best Supporting Actress for her role of Adriana La Cerva in *The Sopranos*. The actress also played Joey Tribbiani's sister Gina on the NBC sitcom *Joey*.

---

7. At the end of *Gomer Pyle, USMC*, what was Gomer's military rank?

a. General
b. Sergeant
c. Lance Corporal
d. Private First Class

Phil Silvers played Sergeant Ernie Bilko on CBS's *The Phil Silvers Show* from 1955 to 1959. The series was created by Nat Hiken, one of TV's first producer/writers and the man who wrote the theme song to the early '60s NBC sitcom *Car 54, Where Are You? The Phil Silvers Show* won three consecutive Emmys for Best Comedy Series.

---

7. Which *Star Wars* actor played one of the kids in the *Eight Is Enough* pilot?

a. Mark Hamill
b. Harrison Ford
c. Carrie Fisher
d. Anthony Daniels

Created by Mel Brooks, the 1975 series *When Things Were Rotten* parodied the Robin Hood legend, with me playing Friar Tuck. Despite critical acclaim, the series failed to find an audience and was canceled after thirteen episodes. Mel had a better reception with the 1993 film *Robin Hood: Men in Tights,* in which I played an abbot.

GAME 2

7. *Texas* was a spinoff of which soap?

a. *Dallas*
b. *Dynasty*
c. *Falcon Crest*
d. *Another World*

GAME 2 Q6 ANSWER a
Michael Zaslow was also famous for his work on *Guiding Light,* where he played the evil Roger Thorpe from 1971 to 1980, and then again from 1989 to 1997. His final television work, though, was on *One Life to Live.* The book *Not That Man Anymore,* written by wife Susan Hufford, chronicles the actor's struggle with Lou Gehrig's disease.

GAME 22

7. Which popular TV series spun off the award-winning *Boston Legal*?

a. *The Practice*
b. *Ally McBeal*
c. *L.A. Law*
d. *Law & Order*

GAME 22 Q6 ANSWER c
In *The Facts of Life* (1979–1988), Mrs. Garrett (Charlotte Rae) left her job as housekeeper for the Drummond family to become housemother at the all-girl Eastland Academy. The series began with poor ratings and the replacement of four cast members, including Molly Ringwald, but went on to become one of the longest-running sitcoms of the '80s.

GAME 42

7. Which shows feature a real-life father and son?

a. *Knots Landing/Dallas*
b. *Hawaii Five-O/The Fugitive*
c. *Bosom Buddies/Roswell*
d. *Happy Days/Kojak*

GAME 42 Q6 ANSWER d
Gerald McRaney got his first professional break playing Rick Simon in the CBS drama *Simon & Simon* from 1981 to 1985. In 1989, he married Delta Burke, who is best remembered for her 1986–1991 role of Suzanne Sugarbaker in the CBS sitcom *Designing Women.* The two met when they were seated together at a Hollywood awards luncheon.

GAME 62

7. In an *I Dream of Jeannie* episode, what entertainer does Jeannie make a double of?

a. Vic Damone
b. Tom Jones
c. Sammy Davis, Jr.
d. Dean Martin

GAME 62 Q6 ANSWER b
In 1987, Sandler appeared on four *Cosby Show* episodes. By 1990, he was a *Saturday Night Live* writer and cast regular. He left the show in 1995 to focus on his acting career. Although many of his movies fell into the "goofball humor" genre, his roles in such films as *Punch Drunk Love* and *Spanglish* have highlighted his talent as a serious actor.

---

6. On which show did Madonna repeatedly use the "F" word?

a. *Larry King Live*

b. *Late Show with David Letterman*

c. *Saturday Night Live*

d. *Prime Time Live*

GAME 19 Q5 ANSWER a
After singing Bob Marley's "War," the controversial Irish singer said, "Fight the real enemy," then tore the picture. Although NBC had no knowledge of her intention, it was flooded with angry calls. On the next show, Joe Pesci held up the photo, which had been taped back together. When Madonna appeared next, she tore up a picture of Joey Buttafuoco!

6. Which cast member of *The Sopranos'* won a 2004 Emmy?

a. Drea De Matteo

b. James Gandolfini

c. Edie Falco

d. Tony Sirico

GAME 39 Q5 ANSWER d
Playing *Mission: Impossible's* Cinnamon Carter, Bain won her best actress Emmys in 1967, 1968, and 1969. After accepting the third award, Bain and husband Martin Landau (who played Rollin Hand) left the popular show due to a contract dispute.

6. In what branch of the service did Sergeant Bilko serve?

a. Coast Guard

b. Army

c. Marines

d. Navy

GAME 59 Q5 ANSWER c
MacLeod played Joseph "Happy" Hanes on this ABC series from 1962 to 1964, and also appeared as the character in two feature films—*McHale's Navy* in 1964, and *McHale's Navy Joins the Air Force* in 1965. MacLeod would take to the high seas again as Captain Merrill Stubing on ABC's kitsch-classic show *The Love Boat.*

6. Which legend was explored in *When Things Were Rotten*?

a. Cinderella

b. King Arthur

c. Robin Hood

d. Sleeping Beauty

GAME 79 Q5 ANSWER a
Over the years, I've been lucky enough to guest star in dozens of wonderful television shows, including *McMillan & Wife*, *The Streets of San Francisco*, *Maude*, *Happy Days*, *One Day at a Time*, *The Facts of Life*, *Murder, She Wrote*, *Boy Meets World*, *Touched by an Angel*, and many many more.

8. *Ryan's Hope,* which debuted in 1975, was named for a fictional Manhattan:

a. Hospital
b. Tavern
c. School
d. Airport

GAME 2 Q7 ANSWER d
Sometimes called *Another World in Texas,* the show aired from 1980 to 1982, and was the first soap opera to have hour-long episodes from its inception. *Texas* struggled to find viewers from the beginning, and at one point, renamed itself *Texas: The New Generation* to attract a younger audience. It didn't work.

---

8. Which of the following sitcoms had the greatest number of "direct" spinoffs?

a. *Make Room for Daddy*
b. *The Mary Tyler Moore Show*
c. *Three's Company*
d. *Happy Days*

GAME 22 Q7 ANSWER a
The Practice's eighth and final season introduced the unethical character Alan Shore, for which James Spader earned the 2004 Best Lead Actor Emmy. Spader continued the role in the spinoff *Boston Legal* and won another Emmy in 2005. Costar William Shatner won a Best Supporting Actor Emmy for his role as Denny Crane.

---

8. Which shows feature real-life siblings?

a. *Family Ties/A-Team*
b. *Ally McBeal/Grey's Anatomy*
c. *Judging Amy/Cold Case*
d. *Eight Is Enough/As the World Turns*

GAME 42 Q7 ANSWER c
Tom Hanks made his TV debut in the ABC 1980–1982 sitcom *Bosom Buddies,* but soon moved on to fame on the big screen. Tom's son Colin Hanks (by first wife Samantha Lewes) appeared not only in the 1999–2002 WB series *Roswell,* but also in HBO's 2001 series *Band of Brothers*—an episode of which was directed by his dad.

---

8. Which first lady made a cameo appearance on *The Mary Tyler Moore Show*?

a. Pat Nixon
b. Betty Ford
c. Rosalynn Carter
d. Nancy Reagan

GAME 62 Q7 ANSWER c
In this classic 1967 episode, Tony (Larry Hagman) is in charge of entertainment for General Peterson's birthday party. He learns the General's favorite entertainer is Sammy Davis, Jr., but is unable to book him. With a blink and a nod, Jeannie (Barbara Eden) creates a double of the legendary song-and-dance man, who then appears at the party.

---

5. In 1992, whose picture did Sinead O'Connor rip up on *Saturday Night Live*?

a. Pope John Paul II

b. Uncle Sam

c. Jesus Christ

d. Queen Elizabeth

GAME 19 Q4 ANSWER b
When a production glitch caught her lip-synching what was supposed to be a "live" song, the embarrassed Simpson hopped around on the stage a bit before scurrying off. Later, she explained that she had lost her voice due to severe acid reflux, so she used a guide track for the song. Shortly after, she admitted, "I made a complete fool of myself."

---

5. Which TV series earned Barbara Bain three consecutive Emmys?

a. *Space: 1999*

b. *Perry Mason*

c. *The Fugitive*

d. *Mission: Impossible*

GAME 39 Q4 ANSWER a
Airing on CBS from 1970 to 1977, *The Mary Tyler Moore Show* is one of the most critically acclaimed series in television history. In addition to garnering a total of twenty-nine Emmy Awards in the seven years it was on the air, it won three Golden Globe Awards as well as a long list of honors.

---

5. Which *Mary Tyler Moore Show* regular was *McHale's Navy's* "Happy" Hanes?

a. Ted Knight

b. Ed Asner

c. Gavin MacLeod

d. John Amos

GAME 59 Q4 ANSWER b
Hogan's Heroes aired on CBS from 1965 to 1971 and starred Bob Crane as Air Force POW Robert E. Hogan. Werner Klemperer, who played Colonel Klink, was half-Jewish and had fled Nazi Germany along with his family in 1933. For his work in the role of Klink, Klemperer won Best Supporting Actor Emmys in 1968 and 1969.

---

5. On which of these series was I *not* a guest star?

a. *St. Elsewhere*

b. *Lois & Clark*

c. *The Love Boat*

d. *Barnaby Jones*

GAME 79 Q4 ANSWER b
Brando's acting debut was in this 1944 Broadway production. An eight-time Oscar nominee, Brando won the award for his roles in *On the Waterfront* and *The Godfather*. The American Film Institute ranked him fourth on its list of top fifty stars of the American cinema. The top three spots went to Humphrey Bogart, Cary Grant, and James Stewart.

 Answers are in right-hand boxes on page 42.

9. These stars were all in soaps before hitting it big. Which one was on *General Hospital*?

a. Sarah Michelle Gellar

b. Kevin Bacon

c. Kelly Ripa

d. Ricky Martin

GAME 2 Q8 ANSWER b

The story line centered on a large Irish-American family whose patriarch, Johnny Ryan, owned a bar. At the end of the show's first season, *Ryan's Hope* ranked last among all the soaps. But by the end of the second season, ratings had jumped, and they continued to be steady until 1982. In 1989, the show was finally canceled.

9. Which detective from the *Barney Miller* crew got his own spinoff show?

a. Phil Fish

b. Ron Harris

c. Stan "Wojo" Wojciehowicz

d. Nick Yemana

GAME 22 Q8 ANSWER d

Garry Marshall's *Happy Days* (1974–1984), spun off five sitcoms—*Laverne & Shirley, Blansky's Beauties, Mork & Mindy, Fonz and the Happy Days Gang,* and *Joanie Loves Chachi.* Norman Lear's *All in the Family* (1971–1979) also spun off five new shows. They were *The Jeffersons, Archie Bunker's Place, Maude, Gloria,* and *704 Hauser.*

9. Which shows feature real-life cousins?

a. *Perry Mason/ Bordertown*

b. *Bob Newhart Show/Knots Landing*

c. *Rockford File /Adam-12*

d. *Night Stalker/Addams Family*

GAME 42 Q8 ANSWER d

Joyce and Dick Van Patten's mom advertised them as "the Van Patten Kids," available for any role, and it paid off. After working on both stage and screen, Joyce had her first regular TV stint in the '50s on the soap *As The World Turns.* Dick, too, enjoyed a varied career before his long run in the 1977–1981 "dramedy" *Eight Is Enough.*

9. What was the occupation of George Clooney's character on *Roseanne*?

a. Factory supervisor

b. Truck driver

c. Short-order cook

d. Teacher

GAME 62 Q8 ANSWER b

In this memorable 1976 episode, Mary and Lou are at a seminar in Washington, DC, where Lou was once a news correspondent. When he tells her of all the VIP contacts he has, Mary thinks he is exaggerating. Refusing to believe she is on the phone with then-First Lady Betty Ford, Mary tells her, "Yeah, and this is Mary . . . Queen of Scots."

GAME 19

4. Which singer's "live" vocals started without her on *Saturday Night Live*?

a. Britney Spears
b. Ashlee Simpson
c. Mandy Moore
d. Avril Lavigne

GAME 19 Q3 ANSWER a
The well-publicized brawl occurred during a 1988 taping of *The Geraldo Rivera Show* that featured white supremacists, black and Jewish activists, and an audience filled with neo-Nazi skinheads. When the inevitable violence erupted, Rivera was hit in the face with a chair. The incident prompted *Newsweek* to characterize his show as "Trash TV."

GAME 39

4. Of these TV series, which won the most Emmy Awards?

a. *The Mary Tyler Moore Show*
b. *Cheers*
c. *All in the Family*
d. *M*A*S*H*

GAME 39 Q3 ANSWER b
Debuting in 2004, the ABC drama *Lost* has been both a critical and ratings success. In addition to winning several industry awards, *Lost* has become a staple of popular culture, with references to the series appearing in commercials, comic books, song lyrics, magazines, and other television shows.

GAME 59

4. On *Hogan's Heroes*, the listening device in Colonel Klink's office was hidden in a:

a. Tobacco jar
b. Picture of Hitler
c. Chess set
d. Desk lamp

GAME 59 Q3 ANSWER d
Steven Bochco, creator of shows like *Hill Street Blues, L.A. Law,* and *NYPD Blue,* was the executive producer of this FX Network series. Criticized for its violence, this was the first American TV show to depict a war while it was still being fought. Aired in July 1995, the show lasted only thirteen episodes.

GAME 79

4. I played Nels on TV's *I Remember Mama*. Who had the original role on Broadway?

a. Karl Malden
b. Marlon Brando
c. Burt Lancaster
d. Laurence Olivier

GAME 79 Q3 ANSWER c
I appeared in *I Remember Mama* for eight years, from 1949 to 1957. Based on the charming Kathryn Forbes' book *Mama's Bank Account,* this early TV series told the story of a Norwegian-American family living in San Francisco in the early 1900s. Unfortunately, most of the series was telecast live, leaving no taped record of the show.

---

10. Which veteran actor starred in the 1983 premiere of the soap opera *Loving*?

a. Martin Sheen
b. Lloyd Bridges
c. Fernando Lamas
d. Anthony Franciosa

GAME 2 Q9 ANSWER d
Born in San Juan, Puerto Rico, as Enrique Martin Morales, Martin got his first acting experience when living in Mexico City, where he performed in theater productions. He won the *General Hospital* role of bartender Miguel Morez shortly after moving to Los Angeles in 1994.

10. Which TV show originated in a 1960 episode of *The Danny Thomas Show*?

a. *My Three Sons*
b. *The Andy Griffith Show*
c. *Love, American Style*
d. *Petticoat Junction*

GAME 22 Q9 ANSWER a
Abe Vigoda starred in the short-lived sitcom called *Fish* (1977–1978) in which he and wife Bernice (Florence Stanley) became the foster parents of five racially mixed kids. During the early days of the series, Fish's character continued to make appearances at *Barney Miller's* 12th precinct; but eventually he retired from the NYC Police Department.

10. Which shows feature a real-life mother and son?

a. *Partridge Family/Hardy Boys*
b. *Get Smart/Hart to Hart*
c. *M*A*S*H/Roseanne*
d. *Doogie Howser/MacGyver*

GAME 42 Q9 ANSWER b
From 1972 to 1978, Suzanne Pleshette played wife Emily Hartley in CBS's *The Bob Newhart Show*—a show sometimes confused with the later series *Newhart*, which starred Mary Frann as Newhart's wife. Suzanne's cousin John Pleshette was an original cast member of CBS's 1979–1993 show *Knots Landing*, in which he played Richard Avery.

10. Which *Barney Miller* star appeared as a refrigerator repairman on *All in the Family*?

a. Abe Vigoda
b. Ron Glass
c. Ron Carey
d. Steve Landesberg

GAME 62 Q9 ANSWER a
Award-winning actor and *People* magazine's two-time Sexiest Man of the Year, George Clooney had a one-season stint on *Roseanne* as Booker Brooks, the handsome supervisor at the plastics factory. Although Clooney found steady work early in his career, it was his role as Dr. Doug Ross on *ER* that launched him into stardom.

3. Which talk show host had his nose broken in an on-air altercation?

a. Geraldo Rivera
b. Jerry Springer
c. Morton Downey, Jr.
d. Richard Bey

GAME 19 Q2 ANSWER c
A live TV broadcast captured both Dan Rather and Mike Wallace being shoved to the convention floor by security guards. Clashes between Vietnam War protesters and police added to the chaotic atmosphere. In addition to growing anger over the war, the tumultuous year had seen the assassinations of Martin Luther King and Robert F. Kennedy.

3. What show won the Emmy for Outstanding Drama Series in 2005?

a. *Cold Case*
b. *Lost*
c. *Six Feet Under*
d. *C.S.I.*

GAME 39 Q2 ANSWER b
In 1978, Susan Lucci, who appears on *All My Children,* began receiving Emmy nominations for Outstanding Lead Actress in a Drama Series. When the actress failed to win the award after several nominations, she was lampooned in the press. Both she and the viewing audience were shocked when she finally captured the Emmy in 1999.

3. Which TV drama was about US soldiers fighting in the Iraq War?

a. *Jarhead*
b. *Three Kings*
c. *Courage Under Fire*
d. *Over There*

GAME 59 Q2 ANSWER d
While working together on the Oscar-winning WWII movie *Saving Private Ryan,* Tom Hanks and Steven Spielberg decided to co-produce *Band of Brothers*—a ten-hour HBO miniseries based on the book by Stephen Ambrose. The miniseries aired in 2001 and won six of its nineteen Emmy Award nominations, as well as a Golden Globe for Outstanding Miniseries.

3. What character did I play in the 1950s series *I Remember Mama*?

a. Lars Hansen
b. Dr. Johnson
c. Nels Hansen
d. Peter Thorkelson

GAME 79 Q2 ANSWER c
The series *Eight Is Enough* was loosely based on the 1975 book of the same name—an autobiography written by journalist Thomas Braden. But aside from including a family with a similar last name and a father with a job in journalism, the sitcom bore little relationship to Tom Braden's book.

11. What grande dame of soaps played Bert Bauer on *Guiding Light* for nearly thirty-five years?

a. Charita Bauer

b. Ruth Warrick

c. Frances Heflin

d. Wendy Drew

GAME 2 Q10 ANSWER b
Loving aired from 1983 to 1995. Lloyd Bridges, best known by long-time TV viewers for his role in *Sea Hunt* (1957 to 1961), was joined in the premiere by another veteran actor—Geraldine Fitzgerald. Eventually, cast members also included Luke Perry and John O'Hurley. Kirsten Dunst had an uncredited role as a young child.

11. Vicki Lawrence starred in which spinoff of *The Carol Burnett Show*?

a. *Mama's Family*

b. *The Golden Girls*

c. *Growing Pains*

d. *The Facts of Life*

GAME 22 Q10 ANSWER b
The Andy Griffith Show (1960–1968) is one of TV's earliest spinoffs. It came from a *Danny Thomas Show* episode in which Danny is arrested in Mayberry by Sheriff Andy Taylor (Griffith) for running a stop sign. While Danny waits in the courthouse, we meet some of Mayberry citizens who wander in, including Aunt Bee (Frances Bavier).

11. Which shows feature a real-life father and son?

a. *Brady Bunch/Lost*

b. *Show of Shows/All in the Family*

c. *Sea Hunt/TJ Hooker*

d. *Monk/Prison Break*

GAME 42 Q10 ANSWER a
Singer-actress Shirley Jones starred on stage and screen before portraying *The Partridge Family's* mom from 1970 to 1974. Inspired by the success of Shirley's stepson David Cassidy, also of *Partridge Family* fame, Shirley's son Shaun Cassidy then entered show business, and in 1978, Shaun landed a role in *The Hardy Boys*.

11. On what game show is *I Dream of Jeannie's* Jeannie asked to appear?

a. *Laugh-In*

b. *The Dating Game*

c. *The Ed Sullivan Show*

d. *Candid Camera*

GAME 62 Q10 ANSWER b
Ron Glass portrayed Ron Harris, the dapper black detective of *Barney Miller's* 12th Precinct. One of Glass's first career roles was in an *All in the Family* episode as Jack, a refrigerator repairman's apprentice. Always the bigot, Archie claimed Jack pulled a knife on him, prompting the insulted repairman and his assistant to leave.

2. Which journalist was "roughed up" at the 1968 Democratic Convention?

a. Peter Jennings

b. Ted Koppel

c. Dan Rather

d. Sam Donaldson

GAME 19 Q1 ANSWER a
During a 1995 taping of a *Jenny Jones Show* episode on secret crushes, Scott Amedure professed his love for Jonathan Schmitz, who had a history of mental illness and killed Amedure three days later. Amedure's family sued the show's producers for their negligent role in Scott's death and won, but the Michigan Appellate Court overturned the verdict.

2. Which daytime actress was nominated for nineteen Emmys before winning one?

a. Ruth Warrick

b. Susan Lucci

c. Finola Hughes

d. Deidre Hall

GAME 39 Q1 ANSWER c
Olmos won the 1985 Emmy Award, as well as a 1986 Golden Globe Award, for the role of *Miami Vice's* authoritative police Lieutenant Martin Castillo. Many critics found Castillo—distant, imposing, and utterly professional—to be the most interesting and complex character in the popular series.

2. Which WWII miniseries focused on the soldiers of Easy Company?

a. *The Winds of War*

b. *A Rumor of War*

c. *War and Remembrance*

d. *Band of Brothers*

GAME 59 Q1 ANSWER c
Debuting on ABC in 1977, this short-lived sitcom was based on the 1959 movie starring Cary Grant and Tony Curtis. The series actually featured Curtis's daughter Jamie Lee Curtis. *McHale's Navy,* which aired during the 1960s, was also set in the South Pacific during WWII. *China Beach* and *Tour of Duty* took place in Vietnam.

2. What was the last name of my family on *Eight Is Enough*?

a. Anderson

b. Braden

c. Bradford

d. Lawrence

GAME 79 Q1 ANSWER b
I was born in New York City in 1928, and for a kid who was being primed for show business, that was a perfect place to start. At age seven, I made my Broadway debut in *Tapestry in Gray,* and before I reached adulthood, I would appear in a total of twelve plays. This was a great way to learn my craft before jumping into TV and films.

GAME 2

12. What Texas ranch was the setting for the hit prime-time soap *Dallas*?

a. The Lone Pine
b. The Triple E
c. The Southfork
d. The King

GAME 2 Q11 ANSWER a
Charita Bauer played the headstrong Bertha "Bert" Miller Bauer on radio from 1950 to 1956, and on TV from 1952 to 1984. Supposedly to avoid confusion, Bauer named her real-life children Ed and Mike after Bert's children on *The Guiding Light*. She died in 1985, only a few weeks before her thirty-fifth anniversary on the show.

GAME 22

12. *Rhoda* and *Phyllis* were both spinoffs of which show?

a. *That Girl*
b. *The Mary Tyler Moore Show*
c. *Alice*
d. *Maude*

GAME 22 Q11 ANSWER a
Lawrence played Thelma "Mama" Crowley Harper, a feisty old widow and head of a Southern blue-collar family in Raytown, Missouri. The comedy, which premiered in 1983 and ran for six seasons, also starred Ken Berry and Dorothy Lyman. Carol Burnett was originally slated for the role of Mama, while Lawrence was to play her daughter Eunice.

GAME 42

12. Which shows feature a real-life father and son?

a. *West Wing/Two and Half Men*
b. *Paladin/Combat*
c. *Lost in Space/X-Files*
d. *Mr. Ed/Kung-Fu*

GAME 42 Q11 ANSWER b
Born to comedian Carl Reiner of *Your Show of Shows* and *The Dick Van Dyke Show*, Rob Reiner began his career by acting in one of his father's films—1967's *Enter Laughing*. But it was his portrayal of Michael "Meathead" Stivic in the 1971–1979 comedy *All in the Family* that made him a household name.

GAME 62

12. Which *Dick Van Dyke Show* regular had a recurring role on *Leave It to Beaver*?

a. Richard Deacon
b. Morey Amsterdam
c. Jerry Paris
d. Carl Reiner

GAME 62 Q11 ANSWER a
Tony (Larry Hagman) goes to Hollywood in this 1969 episode, so Jeannie prepares a special good-bye for him that appears in a mirror. Producers of *Laugh-In* see Jeannie's image and think it's a magic trick. They're so impressed, they invite Jeannie to be on the show. *Laugh-In's* Gary Owens, Judy Carne, and Arte Johnson appear in the episode.

GAME 19	**1.** Which talk show host took the stand at the murder trial of Jonathan Schmitz? **a.** Jenny Jones **b.** Sally Jessy Raphael **c.** Ricki Lake **d.** Oprah	The answer to this question is on: **page 50,** **top frame,** **right side.**
GAME 39	**1.** Which TV show earned Edward James Olmos an Emmy Award? **a.** *The West Wing* **b.** *Hill Street Blues* **c.** *Miami Vice* **d.** *Battlestar Galactica*	The answer to this question is on: **page 50,** **second frame,** **right side.**
GAME 59	**1.** Which 1970s show was set in the South Pacific during World War II? **a.** *McHale's Navy* **b.** *China Beach* **c.** *Operation Petticoat* **d.** *Tour of Duty*	The answer to this question is on: **page 50,** **third frame,** **right side.**
GAME 79	**1.** Where was I born? **a.** Seattle **b.** New York City **c.** Minneapolis **d.** Los Angeles	The answer to this question is on: **page 50,** **bottom frame,** **right side.**

GAME 3

Game Shows

*Turn to page 55
for the first question.*

*Turn to page 55
for the first question.*

GAME 2 Q12 ANSWER c

Dallas aired on CBS from 1978 to 1991, and centered on the Ewings, a wealthy Texas oil family. Although the most popular character was the greedy, scheming J.R. Ewing, played by Larry Hagman, the show's creators had initially intended the focus to be on Bobby and Pam Ewing, portrayed by Patrick Duffy and Victoria Principal.

GAME 23

Talk Shows

*Turn to page 55
for the first question.*

GAME 22 Q12 ANSWER b

The Betty White Show and *Lou Grant* were also spinoffs of *The Mary Tyler Moore Show*, which began its seven-year run in 1970. With Moore cast as the associate producer of a small TV newsroom, the show reflected the country's emergence of working women. The show and cast earned many Emmys, including three for Outstanding Comedy Series.

GAME 43

The Honeymooners

*Turn to page 55
for the first question.*

GAME 42 Q12 ANSWER a

Martin Sheen played *West Wing* president Josiah Bartlett from 1999 to 2006. Sheen's real-life children include not only actor Charlie Sheen from *Two and a Half Men*, but also actors Emilio Estevez of the movie *The Breakfast Club*; Ramon Estevez of the movie *The Dead Zone*; and Renee Estevez, who often guest-starred on Dad's show.

GAME 63

Relatively Speaking II

*Turn to page 55
for the first question.*

GAME 62 Q12 ANSWER a

A balding character actor with a somber face and authoritative voice, Richard Deacon was known for his role on the *Dick Van Dyke Show* as Mel Cooley, producer of the fictional *Alan Brady Show* and brother-in-law of Brady (Carl Reiner). Deacon's other notable TV role was Fred Rutherford (Lumpy's father) on *Leave It to Beaver*.

GAME 19

Controversies and Embarrassments

Turn to page 52 for the first question.

Turn to page 52 for the first question.

According to William Shatner's voiceover during the show's opening credits, the Enterprise was on a five-year mission to explore the furthest reaches of space. Of course, the original series fulfilled only three of those five years—something that *Saturday Night Live* made fun of during an Emmy-winning *Star Trek* parody skit in 1976.

GAME 39

Emmy Winners and Losers

Turn to page 52 for the first question.

In this 1973 *Brady Bunch* episode, Marcia becomes enamored of the family dentist. Worst of all, she thinks that he's interested in her, too. He certainly is, but only as a baby-sitter for his son so that he and his wife can go out on the town. As sister Jan would say, "Marcia, Marcia, Marcia!"

GAME 59

War!

Turn to page 52 for the first question.

Norm (George Wendt) is the last person to walk out of the Cheers bar *on screen* in the show's finale. But Sam (Ted Danson)—the owner of the bar—is seen walking into the back room to close it up. This brought the series full circle, as in the show's pilot episode, the first scene had Sam walking out of the back room to open the bar.

GAME 79

All About ME— Dick Van Patten

Turn to page 52 for the first question.

Based on Benchley's 1991 best-selling novel, *The Beast* did not measure up to Benchley's mega-hit *Jaws*. Set in a harbor town, the miniseries concerned three men who set out to battle a sea creature—this time, a giant squid that had been terrifying the townfolk. But the lack of dramatic impact watered down the experience.

54

GAME 3

1. "Hole in One" and "Cliff Hangers" are contests on which TV game show?

a. *Beat the Clock*

b. *Let's Make a Deal*

c. *Double Dare*

d. *The Price Is Right*

The answer to this question is on:

page 57, top frame, right side.

GAME 23

1. Whose late-night talk show featured a comedy segment called "If They Mated"?

a. David Letterman

b. Jay Leno

c. Conan O'Brien

d. Greg Kinnear

The answer to this question is on:

page 57, second frame, right side.

GAME 43

1. What was Ralph Kramden's job in *The Honeymooners*?

a. Sewer worker

b. Bus driver

c. Band leader

d. Insurance salesman

The answer to this question is on:

page 57, third frame, right side.

GAME 63

1. Which shows featured a real-life father and daughter?

a. *Bonanza/High Chaparral*

b. *Punky Brewster/Facts of Life*

c. *Twin Peaks/Boston Public*

d. *Make Room for Daddy/That Girl*

The answer to this question is on:

page 57, bottom frame, right side.

12. In the original *Star Trek* series, how long was the Enterprise's mission supposed to last?

a. Three years
b. Five years
c. Seven years
d. Nine years

GAME 18 Q11 ANSWER a
In this early 1966 episode, a space virus affects several members of the crew and breaks down their collective ability to control their emotions. This affords Sulu (George Takei) some shirtless fun while frolicking about the ship with a fencing sword, but it leads Spock (Leonard Nimoy) to a total breakdown—shouting out math theorems while sobbing.

---

12. In "Love and the Older Man," on whom does Marcia Brady get a crush?

a. Her teacher
b. Her pediatrician
c. Her neighbor
d. Her dentist

GAME 38 Q11 ANSWER c
In this 1971 episode, a producer sees the Bradys shopping in a supermarket, and decides they'd be the perfect family to represent his client's laundry soap. After trying the product, the Bradys agree, but when acting teacher Myrna Carter gets into the act and starts giving the family advice, the results are disastrous.

---

12. In the *Cheers* series finale, who is the last regular to exit the bar?

a. Cliff
b. Norm
c. Frasier
d. Carla

GAME 58 Q11 ANSWER a
In the eighth season *Cheers'* episode "What is . . . Cliff Clavin?," know-it-all Cliff (John Ratzenberger) realizes his dream to appear on *Jeopardy!* After gaining an untouchable lead, Cliff gets cocky and loses all his money on the final Jeopardy question. This episode was unusual in that the bulk of the action took place outside the bar.

---

12. On whose story was the 1996 miniseries *The Beast* based?

a. Robert Heinlein
b. Robert Ludlum
c. Peter Benchley
d. Michael Crichton

GAME 78 Q11 ANSWER d
After the unprecedented success of the 1977 miniseries *Roots,* many well-known actors stepped forward to play roles in the 1979 sequel, *Roots: The Next Generation.* In fact, for his portrayal of George Lincoln Rockwell, leader of the American Nazi Party, Marlon Brandon won an Emmy for Outstanding Supporting Actor in a Limited Series.

Answers are in right-hand boxes on page 54.

2. What lifeline helps contestants find the answers on *Who Wants to Be a Millionaire*?

a. 50-50
b. Wipeout
c. Get a Clue
d. Ask the Expert

Originally created in the 1950s by the Mark Goodson-Bill Todman team, *The Price Is Right* was hosted by Bill Cullen when it appeared in 1956. A new version of the show was presented in 1972, this time hosted by Bob Barker. The 1972 version has the distinction of being the longest-running game show in North American television history.

---

2. After her opening monologue, what does Ellen Degeneres always do?

a. Dance
b. Whistle "Dixie"
c. Bow to the audience
d. Sign the word "welcome"

This hilarious *Late Night with Conan O'Brien* segment merges the headshots of two celebrities to create odd-looking offspring. When O'Brien first appeared as David Letterman's successor in 1993, the show met with unfavorable reviews; but by 1997, its writing team began earning a string of Emmy nominations and Writers Guild Award wins.

---

2. To which lodge did *Honeymooners'* Ralph Kramden and Ed Norton belong?

a. The Beavers
b. The Owls
c. The Water Buffaloes
d. The Raccoons

Audiences first met Ralph Kramden in the early 1950s on Jackie Gleason's variety show, which was first called *Cavalcade of Stars*, but renamed *The Jackie Gleason Show* when it moved from the DuMont Television Network to CBS. The show's most popular recurring character was bus driver Ralph Kramden.

---

2. Which shows featured real-life brothers?

a. *Captain Video/Dragnet*
b. *Gunsmoke/Mission: Impossible*
c. *Police Story/Bosom Buddies*
d. *Combat/Rat Patrol*

Playing nightclub comedian Danny Williams, Danny Thomas starred in *Make Room for Daddy* from 1953 to 1957. When ABC lost interest, CBS picked the series up as *The Danny Thomas Show*, where it was a hit for its 1957 to 1964 run. Daughter Marlo Thomas's series *That Girl* also enjoyed great popularity, airing from 1966 to 1971.

---

11. In which episode did Spock break down in a fit of tears?

a. "The Naked Time"

b. "The Enemy Within"

c. "The Savage Curtain"

d. "The Immunity Syndrome"

GAME 18 Q10 ANSWER b

In what many still consider a mediocre third season, this final episode presented William Shatner with the challenge of portraying Captain Kirk after a vengeful ex-lover takes over his mind and inhabits his body. This was the same season that saw Shatner dressed as an Indian chief in "The Paradise Syndrome."

---

11. What product are the Bradys hired to advertise in "And Now, a Word from Our Sponsor"?

a. Hot dogs

b. Dog food

c. Laundry soap

d. Toothpaste

GAME 38 Q10 ANSWER b

In the 1972 episode "Dough Re Mi," Peter suggests that the Brady kids provide the vocals for Greg's new song, but the plan goes awry when Peter's voice starts to change. The result is the hastily-written song "Time to Change," into which Peter injects some humor with his off-key "Sha Na Na" chorus.

---

11. Which *Cheers* character appears on the game show *Jeopardy*?

a. Cliff

b. Woody

c. Sam

d. Diane

GAME 58 Q10 ANSWER c

Known by everyone as "Coach," Ernie Pantusso—the Cheers bar's assistant bartender—was portrayed by Nicholas Colasanto. Although genial, warm, and caring, Coach was slow and forgetful, and often didn't quite "get" what was going on around him. Colasanto died in 1985, only a few years into the show's run.

---

11. Which famous actor did *not* appear in *Roots: The Next Generation*?

a. Henry Fonda

b. Andy Griffith

c. Marlon Brando

d. Fred Astaire

GAME 78 Q10 ANSWER c

Based on the steamy 1978 novel by Judith Krantz, *Scruples* was set in trendy Beverly Hills. The theme was simple: Marry a sick old billionaire, and you might have a shot at happiness. On the upside, the cast included Lindsay Wagner, Barry Boswick, Efrem Zimbalist Jr., Connie Stevens, Nick Mancuso, Gene Tierney, and Kim Cattrall.

GAME 3

3. Who hosted the December 2005 premiere of the nighttime game show *Deal or No Deal*?

a. Howie Mandel

b. Jon Stewart

c. Chuck Woolery

d. David Spade

GAME 3 Q2 ANSWER a

Debuting in the United States in 1999, *Who Wants to Be a Millionaire?* offers a maximum cash prize of $1 million for correctly answering multiple-choice questions of increasing difficulty. Contestants unsure of an answer can use one or more "lifelines." The 50-50 Lifeline randomly eliminates two wrong answers, narrowing the player's choices.

GAME 23

3. What is the title of Jay Leno's 1997 autobiography?

a. *Victory Begins at Home*

b. *I Kid You Not*

c. *America (The Book)*

d. *Leading with My Chin*

GAME 23 Q2 ANSWER a

Since its launch in 2003, *The Ellen DeGeneres Show* has received widespread critical praise. In its first year, the show received eleven Daytime Emmy nominations and won four. It made TV history as the first talk show to win the Outstanding Talk Show Emmy during its first three seasons. To date, the show has won fifteen Daytime Emmys.

GAME 43

3. Who played Ralph Kramden's wife in *The Honeymooners* series?

a. Shirley Booth

b. Audrey Meadows

c. Eve Arden

d. Jayne Meadows

GAME 43 Q2 ANSWER d

Ralph and Ed belonged to a fraternal order that was referred to at different times as the International Order of Friendly Sons of Raccoons, the International Order of Loyal Raccoons, and the Royal Order of Raccoons. The motto of the fraternity was "E Pluribus Raccoon," and the leader was the Grand High Exalted Mystic Ruler.

GAME 63

3. Which shows featured a real-life father and daughter?

a. *Highway Patrol/Roseanne*

b. *Wonderama/Facts of Life*

c. *McMillan & Wife/McCloud*

d. *77 Sunset Strip/Remington Steele*

GAME 63 Q2 ANSWER b

James Arness (originally James Aurness) is best known for his role of Marshal Matt Dillon on *Gunsmoke,* which ran from 1955 to 1975. Although an accomplished film actor, younger brother Peter Graves (born Peter Aurness) is also known for playing Jim Phelps on *Mission: Impossible* from 1967 to 1973, and again from 1988 to 1990.

---

10. What was the last original *Star Trek* episode to be aired?

a. "Assignment Earth"
b. "Turnabout Intruder"
c. "Operation: Annihilate!"
d. "Spock's Brain"

GAME 18 Q9 ANSWER c
Although he first appeared on the show as a Romulan commander in the 1967 episode "Balance of Terror," actor Mark Lenard would go on to portray Spock's father Sarek that same year in the episode "Journey to Babel." Sarek also appeared in the *Star Trek* movies, as well as the television *Star Trek: The Next Generation*.

10. What event prompted the *Brady Bunch* song "Time to Change"?

a. Greg's smoking habit
b. Peter's voice change
c. Jan's mental issues
d. Bobby's growth spurt

GAME 38 Q9 ANSWER a
Although younger audiences know Ann B. Davis as the Brady's housekeeper Alice, older viewers may remember that her first big TV role was that of "Schultzy" (Charmaine Schultz) in the '50s sitcom *The Bob Cummings Show*. Later in life, Davis, a born-again Christian, began giving lectures to church groups around the country.

10. What was Coach's actual first name on *Cheers*?

a. Joe
b. Danny
c. Ernie
d. Bert

GAME 58 Q9 ANSWER d
Played by John Ratzenberger, *Cheers'* Cifford Clavin was known for being a storehouse of useless trivia, which he would often recite apropos of nothing. Although Cliff lived with his mother for a long, long time, he did finally make a commitment to girlfriend Margaret O'-Keefe (Annie Golden), a fellow postal worker.

10. The title of the 1980 miniseries *Scruples* refers to:

a. A cosmetic line
b. An art gallery
c. A boutique shop
d. A beauty magazine

GAME 78 Q9 ANSWER a
The Thorn Birds (1983) was, in its time, the second highest rated miniseries, right behind Roots (1977), and won the Golden Globe Award for Best Miniseries. *Thorn Birds* was nominated for sixteen Emmys and won four, but lost the Emmy's top prize to British-produced *The Life and Adventures of Nicholas Nickleby*.

GAME 3

4. Which game show added its "Before and After" category in 1989?

a. *Jeopardy!*

b. *The Price Is Right*

c. *Wheel of Fortune*

d. *The Hollywood Squares*

Before each game, a third party randomly places winnings ranging from a cent to $1 million in twenty-six briefcases. The cases are then distributed to twenty-six models. Contestants choose a case, after which "The Banker"—a mysterious figure—makes an offer to buy the case. If the contestant accepts the "Deal," the game is over.

GAME 23

4. Of the following, who holds the record for most hours before a TV camera?

a. Johnny Carson

b. Regis Philbin

c. Steve Allen

d. Merv Griffin

This title is another example of *The Tonight Show* host making fun of his large chin. Every year on a hot summer day, he broadcasts a sketch in which he climbs to the top of the NBC Studios and uses his chin to eclipse the sun, providing shade to the people below. He is also the voice of the Crimson Chin on *The Fairly Odd Parents* animated series.

GAME 43

4. In which New York borough was the classic *Honeymooners* set?

a. Brooklyn

b. Manhattan

c. Bronx

d. Staten Island

The original Honeymooners skits, shown on Jackie Gleason's variety show, featured veteran actress Pert Kelton as Ralph's wife, Alice. When Kelton was blacklisted and forced off the show, she was replaced by Audrey Meadows, who had to make herself look plainer and older to convince Gleason that she could play the part.

GAME 63

4. What shows featured real-life brothers?

a. *Gentle Ben/ The Waltons*

b. *Wyatt Earp/Bat Masterson*

c. *Diagnosis: Murder/Coach*

d. *Star Trek/Boston Legal*

Efrem Zimbalist, Jr. is known for his starring role of Stuart Bailey in *77 Sunset Strip* (1958–1964), and his role of Inspector Louis Erskine in *The FBI* (1965–1974). His daughter Stephanie starred in *Remington Steele,* playing Laura Holt from 1982 to 1986. Stephanie's dad appeared often in the show, portraying Daniel Chalmers.

---

9. What is the name of Spock's father?

a. Valeris
b. Saavik
c. Sarek
d. Surak

Renegade from an army of genetically superior supermen who began a Third World War on Earth in the 1990s, Khan (Ricardo Montalbán) is awakened in the 23rd century by the Enterprise crew. He tries to murder Kirk and take the ship. Khan's life is spared by Kirk, who offers him and his few followers the planet Ceti Alpha V to have as their own.

9. Who played *Brady Bunch* housekeeper, Alice Nelson?

a. Ann B. Davis
b. Ann Sothern
c. Ann Miller
d. Anne Archer

In Season One, thanks to an essay written by Marcia, Mike wins a Father of the Year contest sponsored by the local newspaper. Later that season, the newspaper names Peter a hero when he saves a little girl from a falling shelf at a toy store. In Season Three, Cindy and Bobby get media attention when trying to break a teeter-totter record.

9. What did Cheers regular Cliff Clavin collect?

a. Model trains
b. Post office memorabilia
c. Beer mugs
d. Useless trivia

The first husband of Cheers waitress Carla (Rhea Perlman), sleazy Nick Tortelli occasionally visited the Cheers bar during the show's run. Referred to in one episode as the "missing link," Nick was sometimes accompanied by his tall blond trophy wife, Loretta (Jean Kasem).

9. Which of the following did *not* win the Emmy for Outstanding miniseries?

a. *The Thorn Birds*
b. *Roots*
c. *Holocaust*
d. *War and Remembrance*

Randall Flagg is a recurring villain who appears in several of Stephen King's works. In the 1994 miniseries *The Stand,* based on the 1978 novel of the same name, Flagg (Jamey Sheridan) is a shape-shifting demon who tries to stop civilization from being rebuilt after the Superflu wipes out most of the world's population.

5. Which game show's trade-mark joke answers were dubbed "Zingers"?

a. *The Dating Game*

b. *Liars Club*

c. *The Newlywed Game*

d. *The Hollywood Squares*

GAME 3 Q4 ANSWER c

In *Wheel of Fortune,* contestants compete against each other to solve a word puzzle similar to Hangman. Every round has a category such as "Person/People," "Proper Name," "On the Map," and "On the Menu." The name of the game comes from the large wheel that's spun to determine the money award for each correct letter in the puzzle.

---

5. Which talk show host was also a writer/producer for *The Simpsons*?

a. Morton Downey, Jr.

b. Conan O'Brien

c. Geraldo Rivera

d. Dennis Miller

GAME 23 Q4 ANSWER b

On August 20, 2004, Philbin set a Guinness World record (passing Hugh Downs) for the most hours before a TV camera—15,188. Before gaining national exposure on *The Joey Bishop Show,* Philbin was a *Tonight Show* page and regional southern California newscaster. During his career, he has hosted numerous talk shows and game shows.

---

5. What was the name of Ed Norton's wife on *The Honeymooners*?

a. Mabel

b. Marge

c. Trixie

d. Madge

GAME 43 Q4 ANSWER a

Ralph and Alice Kramden lived in Brooklyn at 358 Chauncey Street—Gleason's actual childhood address. So popular was the show that in 1988, the New York Transit Authority renamed the Brooklyn Fifth Avenue Bus Depot, calling it The Jackie Gleason Bus Depot.

---

5. What shows featured a real-life daughter, father, and mother?

a. *Buffy/Mission: Impossible*

b. *Quincy, ME/Hotel*

c. *Lone Ranger/Supernatural*

d. *Sgt. Bilko/Another World*

GAME 63 Q4 ANSWER c

Despite many movie roles, Dick Van Dyke is best known for his roles in TV's *The Dick Van Dyke Show* (1961–1966) and *Diagnosis: Murder* (1993–2001). Dick's younger brother, Jerry Van Dyke, made his acting debut on *The Dick Van Dyke Show,* but is better remembered for playing the befuddled Luther on *Coach* (1989–1997).

GAME 18

8. What is the middle name of Kirk's arch nemesis Khan Singh?

a. Ceti

b. Noonien

c. Alpha

d. Mutara

GAME 18 Q7 ANSWER c

This pinch, usually delivered to the neck, was created by Leonard Nimoy as the proper retaliatory response for the logical Spock. Nimoy brought nuance to the Spock character that wasn't always in the script. For example, in the first episode of the series, Spock was much more intense and even grabbed a laser gun in one scene.

GAME 38

8. How many times did *Brady Bunch* family members appear in the newspaper?

a. One

b. Two

c. Three

d. Four

GAME 38 Q7 ANSWER b

In the 1971 episode "Juliet is the Sun," Marcia at first doubts that she's suitable for the role of Juliet. But after receiving family support, she grows confident—too confident. Finally, the unmanageable Marcia gets the boot from her drama teacher, grows humble, and accepts a bit part in the play.

GAME 58

8. Which recurring character on *Cheers* was played by Dan Hedaya?

a. Robin Colcord

b. Eddie Le Bec

c. Nick Tortelli

d. Evan Drake

GAME 58 Q7 ANSWER a

In the "Bar Wars" episode of *Cheers,* a war of practical jokes rages on between the Cheers staff and the staff of rival bar Gary's Olde Towne Tavern, resulting in damaged property. When bar owner Gary tries to make amends by sending Wade Boggs to Cheers for an autograph session, the Cheers gang thinks that he's an imposter.

GAME 78

8. Which Stephen King miniseries featured villain Randall Flagg?

a. *Needful Things*

b. *The Stand*

c. *The Tommyknockers*

d. *Storm of the Century*

GAME 78 Q7 ANSWER a

Band of Brothers told the story of soldiers who served in Easy Company of the US Army Airborne Paratrooper division. The series followed these men from their basic training in the US to battles in Europe and a journey to Hitler's Eagle's Nest. Produced by Tom Hanks and Steven Spielberg, *Band of Brothers* won six Emmy Awards.

GAME 3

6. What TV game show has been hosted by both Dick Clark and Donny Osmond?

a. *Pyramid*

b. *Tic Tac Dough*

c. *American Bandstand*

d. *The Price Is Right*

GAME 3 Q5 ANSWER d

Center square Paul Lynde was the master of these quips, which were so popular that they resulted in at least two books and one LP of zingers in the 1970s. In reality, the "spontaneous" one-liners were not ad-libs, but were written for the celebrities in advance.

GAME 23

6. Who was MTV's first talk show host?

a. Jon Stewart

b. Howard Stern

c. Bill Maher

d. Craig Kilborn

GAME 23 Q5 ANSWER b

After a three-year stint writing for *Saturday Night Live,* Conan joined FOX in 1991, and worked as a writer for *The Simpsons.* He eventually became a supervising producer for the show as well. O'Brien is credited for creating the character of the sea captain Horatio McCallister, and for naming Patty and Selma Bouvier's iguana Jub-Jub.

GAME 43

6. In what pungent location did *Honeymooners* character Ed Norton spend his workday?

a. Sewer

b. Locker room

c. City subway

d. Men's room

GAME 43 Q5 ANSWER c

In the original Honeymooners skits, Trixie Norton—whose real name was Thelma—was first played by Elaine Stritch. Long before *The Honeymooners* became an independent series, though, Stritch was replaced by Joyce Randolph, who portrayed Trixie throughout the taping of the show.

GAME 63

6. What shows featured a real-life husband and wife?

a. *Addams Family/Flying Nun*

b. *Combat!/Girl From Uncle*

c. *Sea Hunt/Honey West*

d. *Six Million Dollar Man/Charlie's Angels*

GAME 63 Q5 ANSWER a

Buffy the Vampire Slayer fans well remember Juliet Laundau's portrayal of deranged vampire Drusilla on both *Buffy* and the spinoff *Angel.* Juliet is the daughter of Martin Landau and Barbara Bain, who both starred in the 1960s hit series *Mission:Impossible* for three seasons, playing Rollin Hand and Cinnamon Carter, respectively.

---

7. Which Vulcan technique did Spock first perform in the episode "Dagger of the Mind"?

a. Hand salute
b. Death grip
c. Nerve pinch
d. Mind meld

GAME 18 Q6 ANSWER a
Although it received fourteen Emmy nominations during its three-year run (1966–1969), *Star Trek* never won an Emmy. The series was also nominated for eight Hugo Awards from the prestigious World Science Fiction Convention. It won the award in 1968 for "The City on the Edge of Forever" written by master sci-fi writer Harlan Ellison.

---

7. In which school play did Marcia of *The Brady Bunch* win the lead role?

a. *Our Town*
b. *Romeo and Juliet*
c. *Cat on a Hot Tin Roof*
d. *West Side Story*

GAME 38 Q6 ANSWER a
In the 1973 episode "Miss Popularity," Jan Brady tries to overcome middle child syndrome by being voted most popular girl at Fillmore Junior High. But when Jan wins the title, she regens on her impossible-to-keep campaign promises and becomes an insufferable snob.

---

7. Which Red Sox legend visited the bar in a 1988 *Cheers* episode?

a. Wade Boggs
b. Roger Clemens
c. Ted Williams
d. Carlton Fisk

GAME 58 Q6 ANSWER c
In the 1985 episode "Bar Bet," Michael Richards—*Seinfeld's* future Kramer—plays Eddie Gordon, Sam Malone's (Ted Danson's) old bar buddy. Eddie visits Sam's bar to collect a debt. It seems that Sam bet that he would marry actress Jacqueline Bisset within a year. Since Sam failed to win Bisset's hand, the Cheers bar belongs to Eddie.

---

7. What 2001 miniseries was based on Stephen Ambrose's book about World War II?

a. *Band of Brothers*
b. *Saving Private Ryan*
c. *Winds of War*
d. *Combat*

GAME 78 Q6 ANSWER d
Based on the Stephen King novella of the same name, this 1995 miniseries focused on ten airline passengers who awaken to find all other passengers missing and the world they know gone. The series starred Kate Maberly, Patricia Wettig, Dean Stockwell, David Morse, and Bronson Pinchot, with Stephen King making a cameo appearance.

---

7. On the 1970s game show *Name That Tune* what was a round called?

a. Mystery Composer

b. Sing-a-Long

c. Fact or Fiction

d. Bid-a-Note

GAME 3 Q6 ANSWER a
Pyramid debuted in 1973 with Dirk Clark as host, and Clark hosted several versions of the show throughout the 1970s and 1980s. In fact, Clark has appeared in almost all versions of the show, either as host or as celebrity player. Other *Pyramid* hosts have included Bill Cullen, John Davidson, and Donny Osmond.

7. Which of the following interviewers is one of the faces of PBS?

a. Charlie Rose

b. Lou Dobbs

c. Geraldo Rivera

d. Aaron Brown

GAME 23 Q6 ANSWER a
Talented comic, author, actor, and producer, Jon Stewart may be best known as the Emmy Award-winning host of Comedy Central's *The Daily Show,* which he took over when Craig Kilborn left in 1999. Earlier he had hosted *Short Attention Span Theater* for that network. In 1993, he became MTV's first talk show host with *The Jon Stewart Show.*

7. What did *Honeymooners* friends Ralph Kramden and Ed Norton often get caught up in?

a. Extramarital affairs

b. Get-rich-quick schemes

c. Run-ins with police

d. Gambling binges

GAME 43 Q6 ANSWER a
Art Carney gained lifelong fame for his portrayal of sewer worker and upstairs neighbor Ed Norton on *The Honeymooners.* (Norton referred to his occupation as an "underground maintenance specialist.") Later, Carney had many stage and screen roles, including that of neurotic Felix Unger in the Broadway production of Neil Simon's *The Odd Couple.*

7. What shows featured a real-life sister and brother?

a. *Knots Landing/Dallas*

b. *Hawaii Five-O/Fugitive*

c. *Full House/Growing Pains*

d. *Happy Days/Kojak*

GAME 63 Q6 ANSWER d
In 1976, Lee Majors and Farrah Fawcett became the first husband and wife to simultaneously star in separate TV hits, with Majors portraying Steven Austin in *The Six Million Dollar Man,* and Fawcett playing Jill Munroe in *Charlie's Angels.* Eventually, the demands of their careers became too great, and the two separated in 1979.

6. How many Emmys did the original *Star Trek* series win?

a. None
b. One
c. Eight
d. Fourteen

GAME 18 Q5 ANSWER b
"Scotty" is a nickname for the Enterprise's chief engineer Montgomery Scott, played by James Doohan. Third in command after Kirk and Spock, Scotty is obsessed with technical journals and taking care of the Enterprise. Although we all say "Beam me up, Scotty," that phrase was never actually said on the show.

6. Which junior high school did *Brady Bunch* kids Greg, Peter, Marcia, and Jan attend?

a. Fillmore
b. Buchanan
c. Lincoln
d. Washington

GAME 38 Q5 ANSWER d
In the 1970 episode "The Hero," Peter gets an inflated ego when he saves a little girl from a falling shelf at Mr. Driscoll's toy store, and is honored by the local newspaper. Eventually, Peter sees the error of his ways—but not before he lets the little girl's mother buy him several boxes of toys as a reward.

6. Which *Seinfeld* regular was one of Sam's drinking buddies on *Cheers*?

a. Wayne Knight
b. Jason Alexander
c. Michael Richards
d. Jerry Stiller

GAME 58 Q5 ANSWER d
During the run of *Cheers,* Sam and Diane decided to get married three separate times, but never actually made it to the altar—probably because the lowbrow pub owner and the highbrow waitress were too different from each other to live together. At the end of the series, the two characters agreed to part for good.

6. Which miniseries featured creatures resembling flying cannonballs with sharp teeth?

a. *The Stand*
b. *Fatal Vision*
c. *The Beast*
d. *The Langoliers*

GAME 78 Q5 ANSWER c
Originally planned as a four-hour special to be aired over two nights, *Roots* turned into an eight-night epic. In 1977, the miniseries was nominated for thirty-seven Emmys and won nine. Its Sunday-night finale was the highest rated single TV broadcast, surpassing *Gone With the Wind,* which held the previous record.

8. A point value scale of 1 to 11 was a trademark of what game show?

a. *The $64,000 Question*

b. *The Joker's Wild*

c. *Twenty One*

d. *Concentration*

GAME 3 Q7 ANSWER d
Name That Tune pitted two contestants against each other to test their knowledge of songs. Bid-a-Note was the show's signature game in which the host would read a clue to a song, and the players would bid as to how few notes they needed to name that tune.

---

8. Which talk show host interviewed guests while seated on a large sofa?

a. Alan Thicke

b. Phil Donahue

c. Sally Jessy Raphael

d. Arsenio Hall

GAME 23 Q7 ANSWER a
Before appearing before a camera, this noted interviewer produced *Bill Moyer's Journal* on PBS in the mid 1970s. He worked at a number of networks during his career, and in 1987, he won an Emmy for his interview with Charles Manson on *CBS News Nightwatch*. In 1991, *Charlie Rose* aired on PBS and became nationally syndicated in 1993.

---

8. What cartoon was based on *The Honeymooners*?

a. *The Family Guy*

b. *The Jetsons*

c. *The Simpsons*

d. *The Flintstones*

GAME 43 Q7 ANSWER b
The Honeymooners' Ralph Kramden was always searching for schemes that would make him wealthy, and best friend Ed, while full of encouragement, was not all that helpful. Predictably, their get-rich-quick schemes never worked out, causing friction between Ralph and his practical wife, Alice.

---

8. What shows featured a real-life brother and sister?

a. *The Bionic Woman/Soap*

b. *Family Ties/Hogan Family*

c. *Providence/Cold Case*

d. *Ally McBeal/Grey's Anatomy*

GAME 63 Q7 ANSWER c
Candace Cameron got her big break when she landed the role of Donna Jo Tanner in *Full House* (1987–1995), while brother Kirk Cameron got his break playing Mike Seaver in *Growing Pains* (1985–1992). Both siblings eventually became born-again Christians, and now steer clear of roles that they feel would violate their religious principles.

---

5. Which full character name from the *Star Trek* series is incorrect?

a. Leonard McCoy

b. Scotty Montgomery

c. Hikaru Sulu

d. Janice Rand

GAME 18 Q3 ANSWER a
Walter Koenig first appeared as Ensign Pavel Chekhov in "Mirror, Mirror," the first episode of the show's second season. In addition to his perfect Russian accent, Koenig was picked to play Chekhov because he looked a lot like teen heartthrob Davy Jones from the fellow NBC show *The Monkees*.

---

5. On *The Brady Bunch*, what type of business did Mr. Driscoll own?

a. Bicycle repair shop

b. Barbershop

c. Gas station

d. Toy store

GAME 38 Q4 ANSWER c
Mike Brady, played by Robert Reed, had a home office that included a drafting table, a bookcase of reference books, and other items needed by a 1970s architect. The arrangement was intended to explain how the head of the Brady household managed to earn a good living while always being at home.

---

5. Where did Sam propose to Diane in the fifth season premiere of *Cheers*?

a. Empire State Building

b. A private jet

c. Fenway Park

d. A boat

GAME 58 Q4 ANSWER a
Played by Woody Harrelson, Woodrow "Woody" Tiberius Boyd was a big-hearted but rather dimwitted young man, who usually failed to understand what was going on around him. Nevertheless, the bartender managed to win the love and eventually marry the wealthy Kelly Gaines, played by Jackie Swanson.

---

5. How many nights did the 1977 miniseries *Roots* air?

a. Four

b. Six

c. Eight

d. Ten

GAME 78 Q4 ANSWER d
Kingpin centered on Mexican drug lord Miguel Cadena (Yancey Arias) and his family. NBC's answer to the highly popular *Sopranos*, the miniseries was to be followed by a full television series. Unfortunately, *Kingpin* failed to win an audience, and the series never materialized.

---

9. Which game show producer was host of *The Gong Show*?

a. Chuck Barris

b. Mark Goodson

c. Bill Todman

d. Merv Griffin

GAME 3 Q8 ANSWER c

Twenty One aired from 1956 to 1958. Infamous for being rigged—contestants not only were provided with answers, but were told exactly how to dress, what to say to the host, and even when to mop their brow—the show's run ended in scandal. The story of *Twenty One's* downfall inspired the 1994 movie *Quiz Show*.

---

9. Whose first TV talk show was aired during the day?

a. Jon Stewart

b. Dennis Miller

c. Jay Leno

d. David Letterman

GAME 23 Q8 ANSWER d

After costarring with Eddie Murphy in *Coming to America*, Hall became host of *The Arsenio Hall Show* (1989–1984). In addition to the huge sofa, which made his interviews "homey," the show was also known for its audience's chanting of "Whoop Whoop Whoop" while pumping their fists—inspired by fans of the Cleveland Browns football team.

---

9. In the *Honeymooners* episode "The Man From Space," Ralph wants money to:

a. Buy a costume

b. Tour NASA

c. View a space launch

d. Invest in land

GAME 43 Q8 ANSWER d

The Flintstones drew on *The Honeymooners* for its four main characters: the blustering Fred Flintstone; Fred's wife, the ever-patient Wilma; Fred's friend and neighbor, Barney Rubble; and Barney's wife, Betty. Voice actor Alan Reed actually modeled Fred's voice after Jackie Gleason's interpretation of Ralph Kramden.

---

9. What shows featured a real-life mother and son?

a. *Perry Mason/Greatest American Hero*

b. *Rhoda/Partridge Family*

c. *CSI/Rockford Files*

d. *Crossing Jordan/Friends*

GAME 63 Q8 ANSWER b

Justine Bateman is most identified with her role of the superficial Mallory Keaton in the hit sitcom *Family Ties* (1982–1989). Younger brother Jason Bateman began his career in 1981 with a role in *Little House on the Prairie*, but is better known for playing David Hogan on the 1986–1991 sitcom *The Hogan Family*.

---

4. Who was last to join the Enterprise crew on the original *Star Trek* series?

a. Chekhov
b. Uhura
c. Sulu
d. McCoy

GAME 18 Q3 ANSWER a
The first pilot episode of *Star Trek* ("The Cage") featured actor Geoffrey Hunter as Captain Christopher Pike. When the pilot failed, a second pilot was shot with William Shatner as Captain Kirk. Portions of "The Cage" featuring Captain Pike were used in a two-part episode called "The Menagerie," aired later that first season.

4. What was *Brady Bunch* dad Mike Brady's occupation?

a. Doctor
b. Ad man
c. Architect
d. Househusband

GAME 38 Q3 ANSWER d
Played by Allan Melvin, butcher Sam Franklin was mentioned frequently in *Brady Bunch* dialogue, and made it onto the screen in eight episodes. Although Sam and Alice didn't marry during the show's run, they were husband and wife when the made-for-TV movie *The Brady Girls Get Married* aired in 1981.

4. In 1992, whom did *Cheers* character Woody marry?

a. Kelly
b. Lilith
c. Esther
d. Carla

GAME 58 Q3 ANSWER b
Played by Shelley Long, Diane Chambers first enters the Cheers bar with her fiancé, who soon abandons her, prompting Diane to get a job at the pub. But pub life is at first unpleasant for the prim, self-important Diane, who acts superior to the bar's staff and customers, and spends a good deal of time bemoaning her fate.

4. What 2003 miniseries told the story of a family-run drug cartel?

a. *Traffic*
b. *The Gangster Chronicles*
c. *Crime and Punishment*
d. *Kingpin*

GAME 78 Q3 ANSWER a
Originally a short story in *Playboy*, Shaw's 1969 novel quickly became an international bestseller, and in 1976, it was adapted for TV. The story revolves around the two Jorache brothers—Tom (Nick Nolte), the troublesome son, and Rudy (Peter Strauss), the good son. The highly popular series garnered twenty Emmy nominations, winning four.

10. In 2006, the only nominees for a Best Game Show Host Emmy were Alex Trebek and:

a. Tom Kennedy

b. Meredith Vieira

c. Bob Barker

d. Pat Sajak

Barris's first game show creation was *The Dating Game*, which debuted in 1965. The next year, Barris produced *The Newlywed Game*. But he did not appear as host of one of his creations until 1976. On *The Gong Show*, viewers found Barris's bumbling personality a good fit for the show's goofy amateur performers.

---

10. Which show is *not* taped in New York?

a. *Late Night with Conan O'Brien*

b. *The Montel Williams Show*

c. *The Late Show with David Letterman*

d. *The Oprah Winfrey Show*

After becoming a favorite guest and guest host on *The Tonight Show*, NBC gave Letterman his own weekday morning comedy show in 1980. Interestingly, in spite of the show's critical praise, poor ratings caused its cancellation after a four-month run. Apparently, the morning audience was more interested in game shows and soap operas.

---

10. What was Ralph's catch phrase on *The Honeymooners*?

a. "Stifle, Alice."

b. "The devil made me do it."

c. "Who loves ya, baby?"

d. "To the moon, Alice!"

In the fourteenth episode of *The Honeymooners*, Ralph wants $10 to purchase a costume for the Raccoon Lodge ball, and win the prize for most original costume. Unable to get the money, Ralph dresses as a "Man From Space" by putting together junk found around the apartment. In the end, Norton wins the prize—wearing his work outfit.

---

10. Which shows featured a real-life father and son?

a. *Get Smart/Hart to Hart*

b. *Three's Company/Joan of Arcadia*

c. *Baywatch/The Pretender*

d. *Babylon 5/Bosom Buddies*

Barbara Hale played Della Street, Perry Mason's loyal secretary, from 1957 to 1966. Her son William Katt is most famous for the role of superhero Ralph Hinkley in the 1981–1983 show *The Greatest American Hero*. Later, the two worked together in the periodic *Perry Mason* TV movies, with Katt playing Paul Drake and Hale portraying Della Street.

---

3. In *Star Trek's* first pilot episode, who was the captain of the Enterprise?

a. Captain Pike
b. Captain Kidd
c. Captain Hunter
d. Captain Kirk

GAME 18 Q2 ANSWER c
Joan Collins starred as visionary Edith Keeler. Kirk and Spock meet her when they are thrown through time into the Great Depression era while in search of McCoy. Since saving Keeler from being fatally struck by a car would alter world history and result in the Nazis winning WWII, Kirk has to let the woman he loves die.

3. Alice, the Brady's housekeeper, frequently dated Sam, the neighborhood:

a. Cop
b. Mechanic
c. Mailman
d. Butcher

GAME 38 Q2 ANSWER a
Because Barry Williams played Greg, the oldest of the Brady kids, his storylines often involved romance. As the character reached his mid-teens, *Brady Bunch* producers began promoting the actor as a teen idol, and in 1971, three years into the show's run, Williams was receiving some 6,500 fan letters a week.

3. When Diane Chambers first enters the bar in the *Cheers* pilot, she's:

a. Feeling ill
b. Left there by her fiancé
c. Looking for a job
d. Assaulted by a drunk

GAME 58 Q2 ANSWER d
Norm Peterson's wife, Vera, was seen only twice during *Cheers'* 1982–1993 run. The first time, her face was covered in a thrown pie. The second time, viewers could see only Vera's legs. Interestingly, Vera Peterson was played by George Wendt's (Norm's) real-life wife, Bernadette Birkett.

3. Which popular miniseries was based on a novel by Irwin Shaw?

a. *Rich Man, Poor Man*
b. *Winds of War*
c. *Roots*
d. *Shogun*

GAME 78 Q2 ANSWER c
After his stint in *Dr. Kildare* (1961–1966), Richard Chamberlain's acting career took off. In the '70s and '80s, he won many leading roles in made-for-TV movies and miniseries. In 1980, he portrayed John Blackthorne in *Shogun*; in 1983, Father Ralph de Bricassart in *The Thorn Birds*; and in 1986, John Fremont in *Dream West*.

11. Which Wink Martindale-hosted game show had nine categories of questions?

a. *Gambit*

b. *High Rollers*

c. *The Last Word*

d. *Tic Tac Dough*

GAME 3 Q10 ANSWER b
In 2006, Bob Barker was *not* nominated for the daytime Best Game Show Host Emmy for the first time in many, many years. A year earlier, Barker had set a longevity record, having held a television job continuously for an amazing forty-nine years.

---

11. Which show featured the Thrill Cam?

a. *Thicke of the Night*

b. *Late Night with David Letterman*

c. *The Jon Stewart Show*

d. *The Arsenio Hall Show*

GAME 23 Q10 ANSWER d
In 1984, Winfrey was hired to host *AM Chicago*, a low-rated morning talk show. By 1986, it had been renamed *The Oprah Winfrey Show* and began broadcasting in national syndication. It has since become the longest-running daytime TV talk show.

---

11. In 1987, Jackie Gleason pleased *Honeymooners* fans by:

a. Filming new episodes

b. Releasing old episodes

c. Opening a theme museum

d. Driving a Brooklyn bus

GAME 43 Q10 ANSWER d
Ralph Kramden's phrase "To the moon, Alice!" was ranked number two in *TV Guide's* list of TV's Twenty Top Catch Phrases. Although some of Ralph's remarks to his wife would be unacceptable on today's sitcoms, whenever the two made up after an argument, Ralph's voice would fill with love as he said, "Baby, you're the greatest."

---

11. Which shows featured a real-life father and son?

a. *Brady Bunch/Lost*

b. *Show of Shows/TJ Hooker*

c. *Sea Hunt/Stargate SG-1*

d. *Barney Miller/Prison Break*

GAME 63 Q10 ANSWER b
Playing Jack Tripper, John Ritter starred in the sitcom *Three's Company* from 1977 to 1984. Playing Kevin Girardi, John's son Jason Ritter starred in the drama *Joan of Arcadia* from 2003 to 2005 as Joan's paraplegic brother. Of course, the family's show biz tradition began with John's parents—actress Dorothy Fay and singer-actor Tex Ritter.

---

2. In the *Star Trek* episode "The City on the Edge of Forever," which actress does Kirk let die?

a. Sally Kellerman
b. Diana Rigg
c. Joan Collins
d. Jane Fonda

GAME 18 Q1 ANSWER c
Other writers on the first *Trek* series included the show's creator Gene Roddenberry, Gene L. Coon, and novelist Richard Matheson. Rod Serling's contribution to '60s TV was *The Twilight Zone*, which featured an episode written by Richard Matheson called "Nightmare at 20,000 Feet." The star of that episode? William Shatner.

2. Who did Barry Williams play on *The Brady Bunch*?

a. Greg
b. Peter
c. Bobby
d. Max

GAME 38 Q1 ANSWER b
In the classic 1973 episode "The Subject Was Noses," Marcia makes a date with nice guy Charley only to dump him for Doug Simpson, the school hunk. But when Marcia gets accidentally hit in the nose by brother Peter's football, she faces a true dilemma.

2. Who was Norm Peterson's never-seen wife on *Cheers*?

a. Maris
b. Hilda
c. Norma
d. Vera

GAME 58 Q1 ANSWER a
After *Cheers* creators came up with the show's plot, they chose the location—Boston—and decided to style the bar after Boston's Bull & Finch Pub. The owner of the pub allowed shots of the bar's exterior and interior to be used in the series, and eventually made millions by licensing the pub's image and selling *Cheers* memorabilia.

2. Which popular television miniseries did *not* star Richard Chamberlain?

a. *The Thorn Birds*
b. *Dream West*
c. *Lonesome Dove*
d. *Shogun*

GAME 78 Q1 ANSWER b
Based on the best-selling John Jakes novel, *North and South* became a 1985 twelve-hour miniseries. The series followed the events leading up to the Civil War by focusing on two families, the Hazards of Pennsylvania and the Mains of South Carolina. Patrick Swayze played southerner Orry Main and James Read played northerner George Hazard.

12. Who was the first female to host a TV game show by herself?

a. Betty White
b. Arlene Francis
c. Sarah Purcell
d. Meredith Vieira

GAME 3 Q11 ANSWER d
Although best known as a game show host, Wink Martindale began his career as a disc jockey on KFWB radio in Los Angeles in the 1950s, and had many radio jobs into the 1980s. His first TV job was at WHBQ-TV in Memphis, Tennessee, where he hosted the children's program *Mars Patrol*.

12. Which talk show host caused a brouhaha when he wore a dress?

a. Geraldo Rivera
b. Phil Donahue
c. Maury Pauvich
d. Montel Williams

GAME 23 Q11 ANSWER b
NBC's *Late Night with David Letterman* (1982–1993) often had fun with camera angles by mounting mini-cams in odd places. The Thrill Cam ran along a track above the audience and honed in on the people below, while a Monkey Cam was strapped to the back of a chimp. The show also featured such bits as Stupid Pet Tricks and Stupid Human Tricks.

12. Which *Honeymooners* star won five Emmy awards for the show?

a. Jackie Gleason
b. Audrey Meadows
c. Art Carney
d. Joyce Randolph

GAME 43 Q11 ANSWER b
Just a few years before Jackie Gleason's death, he released so-called "lost episodes" of *The Honeymooners*. In reality, these were not lost episodes, but were kinescopes of live CBS shows that included Honeymooners sketches. Now they are available on home video, and also sometimes show up in syndication along with "The Classic 39."

12. Which shows featured a real-life husband and wife?

a. *Addams Family/Patty Duke Show*
b. *Palladin/Dark Shadows*
c. *Fury/Lost in Space*
d. *Mr. Ed/The X-Files*

GAME 63 Q11 ANSWER c
Lloyd Bridges first gained wide recognition playing Mike Neslon in the 1957–1961 adventure series *Sea Hunt*. In 2005, Lloyd's son Beau joined the cast of *Stargate SG-1*, playing Major General Hank Landry. The Bridges family includes other actors as well—namely, Beau's well-known brother, Jeff Bridges, and Beau's son, Jordan Bridges.

1. Who did *not* write an episode of the original *Star Trek* series?

a. Robert Bloch

b. Harlan Ellison

c. Rod Serling

d. Theodore Sturgeon

The answer to this question is on:

page 76, top frame, right side.

---

1. On *The Brady Bunch*, what caused Marcia's date with the school hunk to unravel?

a. A case of the flu

b. A broken nose

c. A sprained ankle

d. A bad haircut

The answer to this question is on:

page 76, second frame, right side.

---

1. On which street in Boston was the *Cheers* bar located?

a. Beacon

b. South Main

c. Charles

d. Newbury

The answer to this question is on:

page 76, third frame, right side.

---

1. Who were the two main characters in the miniseries *North and South*?

a. Sam Greene & Miles Colbert

b. Orry Main & George Hazard

c. Justin Mott & Salem Jones

d. Rhett Butler & Ashley Wilkes

The answer to this question is on:

page 76, bottom frame, right side.

GAME 4
Reality TV

*Turn to page 81
for the first question.*

Turn to page 81
for the first question.

GAME 3 Q12 ANSWER a

In 1977, Sarah Purcell cohosted *The Better Sex* with Bill Anderson, but in 1983, it was Betty White who first hosted a TV game show "solo." *Just Men!* ran only six months, but for her role as "femcee," White won that year's Emmy for Outstanding Game Show Host. Meredith Vieira won the award in 2005 for *Who Wants to Be a Millionaire?*

GAME 24
The Tonight Show

*Turn to page 81
for the first question.*

Turn to page 81
for the first question.

GAME 23 Q12 ANSWER b

The "tabloid" talk show format originated with *The Phil Donahue Show* (1970–1996), which began much like other talk shows of that time. But Donahue's willingness to delve into controversial subject matter—religious, sexual, political—made the show stand apart. It was during a 1986 show on transvestites that he wore a dress over his suit.

GAME 44
TV Theme Songs

*Turn to page 81
for the first question.*

Turn to page 81
for the first question.

GAME 43 Q12 ANSWER c

Art Carney won seven Emmy Awards during his lifetime, five of which were for his portrayal of *Honeymooners* goofball Ed Norton. In 1974, he also won the Academy Award for Best Actor for his performance in the film *Harry and Tonto*. Inexplicably, although Jackie Gleason won both Academy and Golden Globe awards, he gleaned no Emmys.

GAME 64
GRAB BAG

*Turn to page 81
for the first question.*

Turn to page 81
for the first question.

GAME 63 Q12 ANSWER a

Patty Duke was already an Academy Award-winning actress when ABC gave the teenager her own sitcom, *The Patty Duke Show,* which ran from 1963 to 1966. John Astin is best known for his portrayal of Gomez Addams on the 1964–1966 series *The Addams Family.* The two were married from 1972 to 1985, and had two sons together.

GAME 18

Star Trek
The Original Series

Turn to page 78
for the first question.

GAME 17 Q12 ANSWER c
With an IQ of 159 (far higher than her father Homer's IQ of 55), Lisa is the genius
of the Simpson family. Although her favorite instrument is the baritone sax, she
also can play guitar, electric bass, accor-
dion, and the piano. She learned to ap-
preciate jazz from her mentor, the late
alto sax player "Bleeding Gums" Murphy.

GAME 38

The Brady Bunch

Turn to page 78
for the first question.

GAME 37 Q12 ANSWER a
When Lucy was pregnant with Little
Ricky—and, in real life, with Desi, Jr.—
she had to say "expectant" instead of
"pregnant." Moreover, no one on the
show could use the word "lucky," since
sponsor Philip Morris didn't want *I Love
Lucy* viewers to be reminded of the
company's main rival, Lucky Strike cigarettes.

GAME 58

Cheers

Turn to page 78
for the first question.

GAME 57 Q12 ANSWER a
Toledo-born Maxwell Q. Klinger (Jamie
Farr) was proud of his Lebanese heritage
and of his hometown, which he regularly
mentioned, along with references to
Tony Packo's Café—a real-life Toledo
attraction. Klinger also often referred to
his beloved Toledo Mud Hens, a minor
league baseball team.

GAME 78

Miniseries

Turn to page 78
for the first question.

GAME 77 Q12 ANSWER c
Running from 1954 to 1962, *Father
Knows Best* starred Robert Young as Jim
Anderson; Jane Wyatt as his wife, Mar-
garet; Elinor Donahue as eldest daughter
Betty; Billy Gray as son Bud; and Lauren
Chapin as youngest daughter Kathy. Al-
though remembered lovingly by Baby
Boomers, the show has been criticized
for its overly rosy portrayal of family life.

GAME 4	**1.** Which bachelor picked Darva Conger as his wife, only to later be rejected by her? **a.** Rick Rockwell **b.** Dave Davidson **c.** Chris Christian **d.** Frank Fontana	The answer to this question is on: **page 83, top frame, right side.**
GAME 24	**1.** Who was banned from *The Tonight Show* after the live 2004 New Year's Eve telecast? **a.** Kid Rock **b.** The Dixie Chicks **c.** Motley Crue **d.** Limp Bizkit	The answer to this question is on: **page 83, second frame, right side.**
GAME 44	**1.** The theme for *Miami Vice* was a #1 hit single in 1985 for: **a.** Joe Lugnut **b.** Jan Hammer **c.** Paul Screwdriver **d.** Manny Wrench	The answer to this question is on: **page 83, third frame, right side.**
GAME 64	**1.** What was Felix Unger's job on the ABC sitcom *The Odd Couple*? **a.** Musician **b.** Newswriter **c.** Photographer **d.** Librarian	The answer to this question is on: **page 83, bottom frame, right side.**

12. On *The Simpsons*, which brass instrument does Lisa play?

a. Trumpet
b. French horn
c. Saxophone
d. Trombone

GAME 17 Q11 ANSWER a
On the show, Maggie, the youngest of the Simpson kids, is always shown with a pacifier in her mouth. Much of her humor is conveyed through silent gags and gestures. In the 1992 episode "Lisa's First Word," where it was learned that Lisa's first word was "Bart," we also hear Maggie say *her* first word, "Daddy," in the voice of Elizabeth Taylor.

12. What word did network censors not permit anyone to say on *I Love Lucy*?

a. Pregnant
b. Kill
c. Highjack
d. Bomb

GAME 37 Q11 ANSWER c
In a tribute to the famous mirror scene in the Marx Brothers' film *Duck Soup*, Lucy dresses as Harpo Marx and then runs into the real Harpo while hiding in a kitchen doorway. When Harpo confronts his own image, Lucy is forced to mimic his every move to convince him he's looking into a mirror.

12. On *M*A*S*H*, which city was Klinger's hometown?

a. Toledo, Ohio
b. Gary, Indiana
c. Buffalo, New York
d. Springfield, Illinois

GAME 57 Q11 ANSWER d
Walter "Radar" O'Reilly, played by Gary Burghoff, was first a worldly, somewhat sneaky character, who would occasionally drink Colonel Blake's brandy. But the writers decided that a change was needed, and Radar became a naïve farm boy whose favorite beverage was not alcohol, but Nehi's grape-flavored soft drink.

12. Which early sitcom featured the Anderson family?

a. *My Three Sons*
b. *I Remember Mama*
c. *Father Knows Best*
d. *The Donna Reed Show*

GAME 77 Q11 ANSWER a
From 1986 to 1987, the show was called *Valerie*. But due to contract disputes, Valerie Harper left the show to be replaced by Sandy Duncan, and the name was changed to *Valerie's Family*. Finally, in 1988, with Valerie Harper long gone, the producers renamed the show *The Hogan Family*, which it remained until the series' 1991 cancellation.

2. Who won the first season of *American Idol*?

a. Ruben

b. Carrie

c. Fantasia

d. Kelly

An emergency room nurse, Darva Conger was selected as the winner on the 2000 show *Who Wants to Marry a Multi-Millionaire?* Rockwell and Conger were married on the spot, but shortly after the honeymoon, Conger sought an annulment. She claimed that—among other issues—the show went against her sense of morals.

---

2. Which game show did Johnny Carson host before joining *The Tonight Show*?

a. *To Tell the Truth*

b. *I've Got a Secret*

c. *Concentration*

d. *Who Do You Trust*

After Motley Crue's Vince Neil dropped the "F" bomb when yelling out a Happy New Year greeting to bandmate Tommy Lee, NBC decided not to invite the band back, and canceled two of its already scheduled appearances. The band has since filed a lawsuit against the network for violation of free speech and for hindering sales.

---

2. Which hit single was the theme song for *Dawson's Creek*?

a. "Foolish Games"

b. "Building a Mystery"

c. "I Don't Want to Wait"

d. "Give Me One Reason"

Miami Vice was known not only for its memorable theme song, but also for its innovative use of music throughout each episode. The many well-known artists and bands that contributed to the unique style of the show included Jackson Browne, Phil Collins, Bryan Adams, Tina Turner, U2, Laura Branigan, and Billy Idol.

---

2. Which *Desperate Housewives* star played Kirstie Alley's sister on *Cheers*?

a. Marcia Cross

b. Teri Hatcher

c. Nicolette Sheridan

d. Felicity Huffman

A photographer on the series, Felix was a newswriter in the 1965 Neil Simon play, which starred Walter Matthau as Oscar and Art Carney (Ed Norton of *The Honeymooners*) as Felix. Felix's last name is spelled "Ungar" in the play and the '68 film, but spelled "Unger" on the TV show. Actor Tony Randall won the 1975 Emmy for this role.

---

11. On *The Simpsons*, what was Maggie's first spoken word?

a. Daddy

b. Rosebud

c. Bart

d. Krusty

Santa's Little Helper (voiced by Dan "Homer" Castellaneta or Frank Welker) is a greyhound. Bart and Homer brought the canine home after he came in last at the local dog track. Over the course of the series, the dog has fathered twenty-five puppies with fellow greyhound named She's the Fastest, and another litter with a poodle named Rosa Barks.

---

11. Which Marx Brother made an appearance on an *I Love Lucy* episode?

a. Groucho

b. Chico

c. Harpo

d. Zeppo

When the *I Love Lucy* pilot was completed in 1951, everyone assumed that the show would be sponsored by General Foods, which sponsored Lucille Ball's radio show. When General Foods turned it down, Milton Biow bought the show for his client, Philip Morris. Biow is also credited with creating the slogan "Call for Philip Morris."

---

11. What classic 1950s beverage was loved by *M*A*S*H's* Radar?

a. Ovaltine

b. Yoo-hoo

c. Bosco

d. Grape Nehi

Colonel Henry Blake (MacLean Stevenson) hailed from Bloomington, Illinois, and was a graduate of the University of Illinois. When word of this reached the university, one of its signature school sweaters—blue with the large orange letter "I" on the front—was donated to the show. Blake wore the sweater in several episodes.

---

11. After Valerie Harper left *Valerie*, what new name was ultimately given to the series?

a. *The Hogan Family*

b. *The Sandy Duncan Show*

c. *Family Ties*

d. *Full House*

Played by Fred Gwynne, Butch Patrick, and Yvonne De Carlo, respectively, Herman, Eddie, and Lily were all characters in the 1964–1966 sitcom *The Munsters*. But Morticia (Carolyn Jones) was the matriarch on *The Addams Family*—a show that ran during the same two television seasons.

GAME 4

3. Who was *not* a winner on the show *Survivor*?

a. Richard Hatch

b. Brian Heidik

c. Colby Donaldson

d. Ethan Zohn

GAME 4 Q2 ANSWER d

After her 2002 win on *American Idol*, Kelly Brianne Clarkson made her debut under RCA Records. Following the success of her single "A Moment Like This," her album *Thankful* was released in 2003. The album received generally favorable reviews and eventually was certified double platinum.

GAME 24

3. Who sang a song to Johnny Carson on his next to last *Tonight Show* appearance?

a. Liza Minnelli

b. Bette Midler

c. Michelle Pfeiffer

d. Barbra Streisand

GAME 24 Q2 ANSWER d

In 1957, Carson followed Edgar Bergan as host of the popular ABC daytime game show. During the show, Johnny would first chat with two contestants, who then tried to win money by correctly answering questions. It was during Carson's five years with *Who Do You Trust* that he met future *Tonight Show* sidekick Ed McMahon.

GAME 44

3. Which TV show's theme song was whistled?

a. *The Dick Van Dyke Show*

b. *My Three Sons*

c. *Leave It to Beaver*

d. *The Andy Griffith Show*

GAME 44 Q2 ANSWER c

Originally, the producers of *Dawson's Creek* chose Alanis Morissette's "Hand in My Pocket" for the show's theme song. But when Morissette refused to grant them permission to use the song, they decided on Paula Cole's "I Don't Want to Wait," which soon became a #11 pop hit single.

GAME 64

3. On the 1982 NBC series *Voyagers!*, what was the time-travel device called?

a. Flux Capacitor

b. Tipler Cylinder

c. Omni

d. Imaging Chamber

GAME 64 Q2 ANSWER a

While Teri Hatcher was busy playing Lois Lane on ABC's *Lois & Clark: The New Adventures of Superman* and British actress Nicolette Sheridan portrayed Paige Matheson on the CBS drama *Knots Landing*, Marcia Cross played Susan Howe—actress and younger sister to Kirstie Alley's character, Rebecca Howe, on this popular NBC show.

---

10. What's the name of the family dog on *The Simpsons*?

a. Dubya
b. Santa's Little Helper
c. The Anti-Lassie
d. Max

GAME 17 Q9 ANSWER a
As the only son of Abraham and Mona Simpson, Homer learned during the 1991–1992 season about his half-brother Herb Powell (voiced by Danny DeVito). By the 2003–2004 season, Homer learned he also has a half-sister named Abbie, from Abraham's WWII affair with an English woman named Edwina (voiced by Jane Leeves of *Frasier*).

10. During *I Love Lucy*'s heyday, Lucy and Desi appeared in several ads for what product?

a. Oldsmobile
b. Philip Morris cigarettes
c. Morton salt
d. Alpo dog food

GAME 37 Q9 ANSWER b
In the classic 1952 episode "Lucy Does a Commercial," Lucy persuades Ricky to let her be the Vitameatavegamin girl on a TV variety show. Turns out, though, that the bitter-tasting tonic she's hawking contains not only vitamins but also alcohol, and after numerous tastings, Lucy becomes unable to even pronounce the product's name.

10. Colonel Blake often wears a sweater with a large letter "I." What school does it represent?

a. University of Idaho
b. University of Illinois
c. University of Indiana
d. Iowa State

GAME 57 Q9 ANSWER c
When Frank Burns goes AWOL, the MASH unit is in need of another surgeon. Commanding officer Horace Baldwin, who happens to be in debt (from playing cribbage) to Major Charles Emerson Winchester III (played by David Ogden Stiers), volunteers him for the position. Despite his initial arrogance, Winchester ultimately settles in with the unit.

10. Who was *not* a member of the TV family known as The Munsters?

a. Herman
b. Eddie
c. Lily
d. Morticia

GAME 77 Q9 ANSWER d
Played by Michael Fishman throughout the 1988–1997 run of *Roseanne*, David Jacob "D.J." Conner was originally a lonely and unpopular child who was taunted by both his peers and sisters Darlene and Becky. As D.J. grew up, though, he became a bit more normal, and even found a girlfriend who shared his interest in filmmaking.

GAME 4

4. Which reality TV show was hosted by CNN anchor Anderson Cooper?

a. *The Bachelor*

b. *The Amazing Race*

c. *Big Brother*

d. *The Mole*

GAME 24

4. What representative of the San Diego Zoo was a frequent guest on Johnny Carson's *Tonight Show*?

a. Taylor Hawkins

b. Paul Hogan

c. Jim Fowler

d. Joan Embrey

GAME 44

4. Which Beatles tune provided the theme song for the series *Life Goes On*?

a. "Ob-La-Di, Ob-La-Da"

b. "Lady Madonna"

c. "Come Together"

d. "Here Comes the Sun"

GAME 64

4. Which actress did *not* appear on the *Batman* TV show?

a. Lee Meriwether

b. Julie Newmar

c. Eartha Kitt

d. Yvonne Craig

GAME 4 Q3 ANSWER c
Colby Donaldson competed in *Survivor: The Australian Outback,* but was only a runner-up, losing to contestant Tina Wesson. Donaldson then appeared on *Survivor All Stars,* and in an online poll, was voted sexiest male castaway for the first eight seasons.

GAME 24 Q3 ANSWER b
Singer/actress/comedien Bette Midler won a 1992 Emmy for her unforgettable performance on that *Tonight Show* appearance. Her emotionally charged song to Johnny—"One for My Baby (and One More for the Road)"—was a memorable tribute to the show's thirty-year host. It was also considered the high point of his sentimental final week on the show.

GAME 44 Q3 ANSWER d
The Andy Griffith Show's theme song, "The Fishin' Hole," was written by Earle H. Hagen and Herbert Spencer, with unsung lyrics by Everret Sloane. As it played, viewers watched Andy Griffith and Ron Howard amble by what looked like a rural fishing hole, but was actually a manmade lake in Los Angeles.

GAME 64 Q3 ANSWER c
When his Omni malfunctions, time traveler Phineas Bogg (Jon-Erik Hexum) finds himself discovered by young orphan Jeffrey Jones (Meeno Peluce). Drawing on his knowledge of history, Jeffrey travels through time with Phineas to help keep historical events in line. Though critically acclaimed, the NBC series lasted only one season.

9. What is the name of Homer Simpson's father?

a. Abraham
b. Virgil
c. Clancy
d. Plato

GAME 17 Q8 ANSWER a
Aired every Halloween since the show first went on the air in 1990, these specials are made up of three small vignettes rather than one single story. The first "Treehouse" special featured voiceover cameos from James Earl Jones in all three stories, and gave script credit to late author Edgar Allan Poe for the "Raven" segment.

---

9. Lucy got drunk while making a commercial for what product?

a. Wine
b. Vitamins
c. Insurance
d. Chocolate

GAME 37 Q8 ANSWER a
In the sixth and final season of the show, Lucy and Ricky pulled up stakes and moved to a new home in Westport, Connecticut, where they were soon joined by friends Ethel and Fred. As a result, the series started involving country clubs, barbecues, gardens, and even rural pursuits such as raising chickens.

---

9. Which *M*A*S*H* character was born to Boston "bluebloods"?

a. B.J. Hunnicutt
b. Radar O'Reilly
c. Charles Winchester
d. Frank Burns

GAME 57 Q8 ANSWER a
When he accepted the part of *M*A*S*H's* Trapper John McIntyre, Wayne Rogers was told that the characters of Trapper and Hawkeye would be equally important; but that changed when Alan Alda was cast as Hawkeye. Fed up with playing Ethel to Alda's Lucy, Rogers quit at the end of the show's third season.

---

9. Which family TV show had a kid named D.J.?

a. *Eight Is Enough*
b. *7th Heaven*
c. *The Bernie Mac Show*
d. *Roseanne*

GAME 77 Q8 ANSWER a
Inspired by the stand-up routine of comedienne Margaret Cho, the 1994 sitcom *All-American Girl* centered on the clashes between a fully Americanized Asian girl (Cho) and her traditional Korean mother. Although the format of the show was changed several times in an effort to boost ratings, the series was canceled after just one season.

5. Where did the first series of *Big Brother* air?

a. Brazil

b. The Netherlands

c. Australia

d. Canada

Anderson Cooper is the younger son of designer and railroad heiress Gloria Vanderbilt and writer Wyatt Emory Cooper. His two-season stint on *The Mole* was an abrupt departure from his career as a reporter—a career that has taken him to Burma, Vietnam, Somalia, Bosnia, and Rwanda.

---

5. Which *Tonight Show* character would give an answer *before* hearing the question?

a. Carnac the Magnificent

b. Floyd R. Turbo

c. Aunt Blabby

d. Tarmac the Great

Embrey and zoologist Jim Fowler of *Mutual of Omaha's Wild Kingdom* were regular guests. Their appearances (often with wild animals) were both informative and amusing. During one show, Carson got too close to a caged panther, who swiped at him with its claws. Carson bolted across the stage and jumped into the arms of sidekick Ed McMahon.

---

5. The theme song for *The Lone Ranger* TV series was an excerpt from what classic?

a. *Rodeo*

b. *1812 Overture*

c. *William Tell Overture*

d. *Peer Gynt Suite*

"Ob-La-Di, Ob-La-Da" was originally released on the 1968 double-disc album *The Beatles,* also known as *The White Album.* But the version that served as the theme song for the 1989–1993 ABC series *Life Goes On* was sung by star Patti LuPone and the rest of the show's cast.

---

5. Which '70s show introduced viewers to the alien Mork from planet Ork?

a. *Land of the Lost*

b. *Shazam!*

c. *Laverne and Shirley*

d. *Happy Days*

Although she played Catwoman in the 1966 *Batman* feature film, Lee Meriwether never appeared as Catwoman on the ABC series. Crowned Miss America of 1955, Meriwether drove Adam "Batman" West wild in the movie—she nearly got Bruce Wayne to reveal his secret identity while posing as Russian reporter Miss Kitka.

GAME 17

8. What's the title of the annual Halloween special on *The Simpsons*?

a. "The Treehouse of Horror"
b. "The Attic of Horror"
c. "The Bedroom of Horror"
d. "The Tavern of Horror"

GAME 17 Q7 ANSWER b
Marge Simpson (voiced by Julie Kavner) has two older cigarette-smoking sisters, Patty and Selma, who are also voiced by Kavner. On the show, in a joke on Kennedy family history, Marge's maiden name is Bouvier and her mother's first name is Jacqueline. Series creator Matt Groening named Marge after his own mother, Margaret Groening.

GAME 37

8. Where did the Ricardos move during the final season of *I Love Lucy*?

a. Connecticut
b. Utah
c. Hollywood
d. Cuba

GAME 37 Q7 ANSWER c
Born in Cuba and raised in both Cuba and Miami, Florida, Desi Arnaz began his music career in 1936, playing in a Latin orchestra. He eventually formed his own orchestra and became a successful recording artist. In 1946, he had a hit with "Babalu," which was to become his signature song.

GAME 57

8. Who played Trapper John McIntyre on *M*A*S*H*?

a. Wayne Rogers
b. Mike Farrell
c. Elliott Gould
d. Larry Linville

GAME 57 Q7 ANSWER b
Portrayed by Alan Alda, Captain Benjamin Franklyn "Hawkeye" Pierce was born and raised in Maine. His father, Dr. Daniel Pierce, took the nickname "Hawkeye" from the James Fennimore Cooper novel *The Last of the Mohicans*. In one episode, Hawkeye bequeaths his copy of the book to Colonel Potter, whom he regards as a father.

GAME 77

8. *All-American Girl*, a 1990s TV sitcom, was about a _____-American family.

a. Korean
b. Chinese
c. Indian
d. Japanese

GAME 77 Q7 ANSWER c
Keshia Knight Pulliam was just five years old when she began playing Rudy, the youngest of the Huxtables' five children, on *The Cosby Show*. Then at age six, Pulliam became the youngest actress ever nominated for an Emmy Award (best supporting actress) for her role in the sitcom.

6. Host Phil Keoghan regularly says "You're team number one" on which reality TV show?

a. *The Amazing Race*
b. *Fear Factor*
c. *Big Brother*
d. *Survivor*

GAME 4 Q5 ANSWER b
Big Brother was created by Dutchman John De Mol and developed by Endemol, his production company. The show—which got its name from George Orwell's 1949 novel *Nineteen Eighty-Four*—became a prime-time success in over seventy countries, and in 2000, De Mol sold his share of Endemol.

---

6. Who began hosting his own talk show on the same day Johnny Carson took over as host of *The Tonight Show*?

a. Mike Douglas
b. David Frost
c. Dick Cavett
d. Merv Griffin

GAME 24 Q5 ANSWER a
As the turban-wearing psychic, Carson held a sealed envelope that contained a question to his head, then he'd give an answer to the unseen question. For example, after holding the envelope, he'd say "Debate." Then he'd open the envelope to reveal the question: "What do you use to catch fish?" Corny? Yep. But the audience loved it.

---

6. "Believe It or Not" was the theme song for which series?

a. *Greatest American Hero*
b. *That's Incredible*
c. *Beauty and the Beast*
d. *Bosom Buddies*

GAME 44 Q5 ANSWER c
Although it was originally the "cavalry charge" finale of Gioacchino Rossini's *William Tell Overture*, Baby Boomers will always remember it as the theme to the 1949–1957 series *The Lone Ranger*. It certainly provided the perfect accompaniment as the Lone Ranger sped along on his horse, Silver.

---

6. What instrument did Danny Partridge play on *The Partridge Family*?

a. Bass guitar
b. Drums
c. Keyboards
d. Flute

GAME 64 Q5 ANSWER d
In what turned out to be one of Richie Cunningham's dreams, the alien Mork (Robin Williams) tried to abduct Richie and take him back to his planet. Best-friend Fonzie, however, went to battle with Mork and saved Richie. The episode showed comedian Williams in one of his first TV roles, which developed into the spinoff series *Mork and Mindy*.

GAME 17

7. How many sisters does Marge Simpson have?

a. Three

b. Two

c. One

d. None

GAME 17 Q6 ANSWER a
Phil Hartman voiced this vain D-movie actor who hosts infomercials and TV specials. Born in Canada in 1948, Hartman was also an album cover designer—he created the cover for the 1977 Steely Dan album *AJA* before joining *SNL* in the mid-eighties. He was also the voice for recurring *Simpsons* character Lionel Hutz.

GAME 37

7. For what song is Desi Arnaz best known?

a. "Moonlight Serenade"

b. "Stardust"

c. "Babalu"

d. "My Red-Haired Girl"

GAME 37 Q6 ANSWER d
In the 1955 episode "Lucy Visits Grauman's," Lucy discovers that the cement slab bearing John Wayne's footprints has come loose from the sidewalk outside Grauman's Chinese Theatre. She decides to take it home as a souvenir, leaving Ricky to enlist Wayne's help in replacing the block and keeping Lucy out of jail.

GAME 57

7. Which *M*A*S*H* character hailed from Crabapple Cove, Maine?

a. Sherman Potter

b. Hawkeye Pierce

c. Charles E. Winchester

d. Frank Burns

GAME 57 Q6 ANSWER c
Played by Harry Morgan, Colonel Sherman T. Potter was a fine surgeon and an excellent leader, but at heart, he was a family man. For this reason, he kept in frequent contact with his beloved wife, Mildred, and their children and grandchildren. At one point, he was even able to meet Mildred for a two-week reunion in Tokyo.

GAME 77

7. Which character was the baby of his or her TV family?

a. John Boy Walton

b. Mary Ingalls

c. Rudy Huxtable

d. Richie Cunningham

GAME 77 Q6 ANSWER c
Although some people mistakenly think that the *Married . . . with Children* family was named after serial killer Ted Bundy, creators Michael G. Moye and Ron Leavitt actually named the Bundys after their favorite wrestler, King Kong Bundy (born Chris Pallies). In one episode, the wrestler made an appearance as one of Peg's relatives.

---

7. Which TV program was inspired by a Swedish show called *Expedition: Robinson*?

a. *Trading Spouses*

b. *Survivor*

c. *Joe Millionaire*

d. *Lost*

GAME 4 Q6 ANSWER a
Debuting in 2001, *The Amazing Race* had low Nielsen ratings for the first few seasons despite critical praise. Reportedly, calls from celebrity fans such as Sarah Jessica Parker prevented CBS President Leslie Moonves from cancelling the show before its ratings began to take off.

7. Who was Johnny Carson's regular guest host on *The Tonight Show* from 1983 to 1986?

a. David Brenner

b. Joan Rivers

c. Jay Leno

d. Garry Shandling

GAME 24 Q6 ANSWER d
Mervyn "Merv" Griffin's career started as a singer, bandleader, and actor before he became a well-known TV talk show host, entertainer, and creator of the game shows *Wheel of Fortune* and *Jeopardy!* With a total of thirty-two Daytime Emmy nominations and ten wins, Griffin was presented with the Daytime Emmy Lifetime Achievement Award in 2005.

7. What was the theme song for *The Jeffersons*?

a. "Nothing's Gonna Stop Me"

b. "Movin' On Up"

c. "We've Got Each Other"

d. "Higher and Higher"

GAME 44 Q6 ANSWER a
Starring William Katt as a somewhat inept superhero, *The Greatest American Hero* aired from 1981 to 1983 on ABC. Its theme song "Believe It or Not," written by Stephen Geyer and Mike Post, rose to #2 on the Billboard Hot 100 chart in 1981, and lived on long after the show's demise.

7. Which show's title is correctly written with two exclamation points?

a. *Gimme a Break!!*

b. *What's Happening!!*

c. *Here's Lucy!!*

d. *Sledge Hammer!!*

GAME 64 Q6 ANSWER a
As the sassiest and most cynical of the Partridge kids, Danny (Danny Bonaduce) spent most of his time on the show trying to make a fast buck for himself and the group. His greed is at its worst in the 1971 episode "Whatever Happened to Moby Dick?," in which he suggests that The Partridge Family cut a record with a whale.

6. Which *Simpsons* character is *not* voiced by Harry Shearer?

a. Troy McClure
b. Principal Skinner
c. Reverend Lovejoy
d. Montgomery Burns

Mocked by the show's writers for typifying the hypocrisy of organized religion, the Flanders family lives next door to the Simpsons. Ned's store is called the Leftorium because all store items are designed just for left-handed people. Ned Flanders is just one of the characters on the show voiced by actor Harry Shearer.

---

6. On *I Love Lucy,* whose footprints does Lucy steal from Hollywood Boulevard?

a. Humphrey Bogart's
b. Clark Gable's
c. Tab Hunter's
d. John Wayne's

Originally, William Frawley was to be the star of *My Three Sons*. But the network not only made a series of changes in the show's plot, but also snapped up Disney's top movie star Fred MacMurray as the lead. As a result, Frawly again had a supporting role, this time as grandfather Michael Francis "Bub" O'Casey.

---

6. Who was Colonel Potter's often-mentioned but unseen wife on *M*A*S*H*?

a. Lorraine
b. Louise
c. Mildred
d. Peg

Using the pseudonym Richard Hooker, surgeon H. Richard Hornberger wrote the book on which the series *M*A*S*H* was modeled. He based the fictitious experiences of the 4077th unit on those of the real-life 8055th Mobile Army Surgical Hospital—the unit in which he served during his stint in Korea.

---

6. The creators of *Married . . . with Children* named the Bundy family after a famous:

a. Football player
b. Political commentator
c. Wrestler
d. Serial killer

Although *The Donna Reed Show* (1958–1966) was in many ways an ordinary sitcom of its time, it was in some ways ahead of its time. For instance, housewife Donna Stone, played by Donna Reed, took an active part in solving her kids problems, and even more important, she frequently worked as a nurse.

GAME 4

8. Who is the host of the ABC series *Extreme Makeover: Home Edition*?

a. Paul DiMeo
b. Bob Vila
c. Kevin O'Connor
d. Ty Pennington

GAME 4 Q7 ANSWER b
Expedition: Robinson is one of the most successful and controversial television programs in Scandanavia. The last episode of Season Four was viewed by over 4 million people in Sweden, making it one of the most viewed programs in that country's TV history.

GAME 24

8. Which *Tonight Show* band-leader was known for his outlandish wardrobe?

a. Kevin Eubanks
b. Skitch Henderson
c. Doc Severinsen
d. Tommy Newsom

GAME 24 Q7 ANSWER b
Rivers was the show's permanent and only guest host during that time. Prior to 1983 (during the shows first twenty-one years), she had hosted the show 93 times, second only to Joey Bishop, who had been guest host 177 times. Other regularly scheduled guest hosts included Bob Newhart, David Brenner, Jerry Lewis, and John Davidson.

GAME 44

8. Who sang the theme song for *The Dukes of Hazzard*?

a. Randy Newman
b. Willie Nelson
c. Waylon Jennings
d. Roy Clark

GAME 44 Q7 ANSWER b
"Movin' On Up," *The Jeffersons* buoyant theme song, was composed by Jeff Barry and Ja'net Du Bois, and sung by Du Bois. It was certainly a fitting choice for the 1975–1985 show, which centered on a nouveau riche couple that moved from a working-class section of Queens to a luxury high-rise apartment on Manhattan's upper East side.

GAME 64

8. On *The Mary Tyler Moore Show*, who was *not* fired from the news team?

a. Mary Richards
b. Ted Baxter
c. Lou Grant
d. Murray Slaughter

GAME 64 Q7 ANSWER b
Based on the 1975 film *Cooley High,* this ABC sitcom debuted in August 1976. It turned Fred Berry (aka Rerun) into an overnight sensation, and gave him TV's corner market on suspenders until Robin Williams started wearing them on *Mork and Mindy* in 1978. Famed composer Henry Mancini wrote the show's bouncy theme song.

5. Which *Simpsons* character owns the Leftorium?

a. Mr. Burns

b. Ned Flanders

c. Apu

d. Barney

GAME 17 Q4 ANSWER c
Even though Tony Bennett was the first musical guest to do a cameo on *The Simpsons* when it debuted on FOX in 1991, Aerosmith was the first rock band to appear on the show that same year. The trend caught on and other bands made cameos, including U2, Red Hot Chili Peppers, The Ramones, Smashing Pumpkins, and Sonic Youth.

5. On what sitcom other than *I Love Lucy* was William Frawley also a regular?

a. *My Little Margie*

b. *My Three Sons*

c. *Bachelor Father*

d. *Our Miss Brooks*

GAME 37 Q4 ANSWER c
Before Lucille Désirée Ball took the role of Lucy McGillicuddy Ricardo, she was a fashion model and stage performer. She then became a contract player for RKO and appeared in many small movie roles. Ball was acting in a radio program called *My Favorite Husband* when CBS asked her to develop a TV show—and the rest is history.

5. What was the unit number of the army surgical hospital in *M*A*S*H*?

a. 101st

b. 4077th

c. 82nd

d. 3rd

GAME 57 Q4 ANSWER a
In *M*A*S*H's* finale, Klinger marries a Korean girl named Soon-Lee and—after trying to leave Korea for so long—decides to stay there to look for his bride's family. This was just one of the events that occurred in the February 28, 1983 episode, which became the most-watched episode in the history of US television.

5. Which TV mom presided over her family's affairs in the town of Hilldale?

a. Carol Brady

b. Shirley Partridge

c. Donna Stone

d. June Cleaver

GAME 77 Q4 ANSWER c
Running from 1998 to 2006, *That '70s Show* followed the life of teenager Eric Forman (Topher Grace) and his five teenage friends. The show was recognized for providing a retrospective of a decade packed with political events, social phenomena, and technological milestones.

9. Who is the creator of *The Apprentice*?

a. Mark Burnett
b. Simon Fuller
c. Donald Trump
d. Bertram Van Munster

GAME 4 Q8 ANSWER d
Pennington, a carpenter, formerly appeared on *Trading Spaces*. In *Extreme Makover: Home Edition*, he brings together a team of builders and designers that make over the homes of people in need of new hope. Families helped by the crew have included victims of Hurricane Katrina.

9. Who spent twelve years as the announcer for *The Tonight Show* with Jay Leno?

a. Rod Roddy
b. Edd Hall
c. Don Pardo
d. Alan Kalter

GAME 24 Q8 ANSWER c
The trumpet-playing Carl Hilding "Doc" Severinsen was the NBC Orchestra bandleader from 1967 to 1992. Well known for leading the *Tonight Show* band during Johnny Carson's reign, Severinsen was also famous for his fun, flashy clothes. In the 1940s and 1950s, he played with the Tommy Dorsey, Charlie Barnet, and Benny Goodman bands.

9. "As Long as We Got Each Other" was the theme song for which family sitcom?

a. *Family Ties*
b. *Growing Pains*
c. *The Cosby Show*
d. *Kate and Allie*

GAME 44 Q8 ANSWER c
The Dukes of Hazzard's theme song, "The Good Ol' Boys," was both written and performed by Waylon Jennings, who also provided the voice of the narrator for the 1979–1985 show. Before that, Jennings had narrated the 1975 film *Moonrunners*—the movie on which *The Dukes of Hazzard* was based.

9. Which celebrity did *not* make an appearance on *Diff'rent Strokes*?

a. Muhammad Ali
b. First Lady Nancy Reagan
c. Mr. T
d. Frank Sinatra

GAME 64 Q8 ANSWER b
When new management at the WJM-TV began firing people in an attempt to improve ratings, Ted Baxter, the bumbling, egotistical news anchor, was the only one who kept his job. "The Last Show," as this final episode was called, remains one of the most poignant good-bye moments in TV history. The episode won an Emmy in 1977.

4. Which rock group was the first to "appear" on *The Simpsons*?

a. Red Hot Chili Peppers
b. U2
c. Aerosmith
d. The Ramones

GAME 17 Q3 ANSWER c
In the 1992 episode "Colonel Homer," Homer becomes Lurleen's manager after hearing her sing at the Beer N' Brawl. Lurleen (voiced by Beverly D'Angelo) later tries to seduce Homer while singing "Bunk With Me Tonight." D'Angelo sang all of Lurleen's songs, just as she did when playing singer Patsy Cline in the 1980 film *Coal Miner's Daughter*.

4. What was Lucy Ricardo's maiden name?

a. O'Reilly
b. Richards
c. McGillicuddy
d. Hamilton

GAME 37 Q3 ANSWER b
In the show's finale, titled "The Ricardos Dedicate a Statue," Lucy destroys the statue of a minuteman an hour before its dedication, and then tries to stand in for it. Appearing for the first and only time on the show were Luci and Desi, Jr., standing in the crowd on hand for the dedication ceremonies.

4. Which character got married in the final episode of *M*A*S*H*?

a. Maxwell Klinger
b. Radar O'Reilly
c. Hawkeye Pierce
d. Hot Lips Houlihan

GAME 57 Q3 ANSWER c
The symbol shown on the door of Hawkeye Pierce's "Swamp" was never explained during the run of *M*A*S*H*. Some have said that it's an Indian symbol found in James Fenimore Cooper's *The Last of the Mohicans*. Others have said that it comes from the Somerset Maugham novel *The Razor's Edge*, and is intended to ward off the evil eye.

4. The majority of *That '70s Show* took place in the home of what family?

a. Bluth
b. Wilkerson
c. Forman
d. Barone

GAME 77 Q3 ANSWER c
Running from 1983 to 1980, *Mama's Family* was a spinoff of sketches that had been featured on *The Carol Burnett Show*. Loosely based on Burnett's childhood experiences, the series starred Vicki Lawrence as Thelma Harper, a sharp-tongued widow who begrudingly took in family members who had nowhere else to live.

GAME 4 — **10.** Trista Rehn was one of the stars of which reality TV show? a. *Star Search* b. *Joe Millionaire* c. *Big Brother* d. *The Bachelorette*	**GAME 4 Q9 ANSWER a** London-born Mark Burnett is known for pioneering the genre of reality television. His creations include not only *The Apprentice* but also *Survivor, The Restaurant, The Casino, Rock Star,* and *The Contender.* Burnett's 2005 autobiography *Jump In!: Even If You Don't Know How to Swim* details his career in the United States.
GAME 24 — **10.** Host Jack Paar walked off *The Tonight Show* in 1960 after NBC censored a joke using which words? a. Busty broad b. Water closet c. Big boobs d. Lady of the night	**GAME 24 Q9 ANSWER b** Edd Hall joined the show in 1992. After announcing the guests during the show's opening, he would introduce himself, saying, "And me, I'm Edd Hall." Starting out as an NBC page, Hall worked with *Saturday Night Live's* Not-Ready-for-Prime-Time Players. He is also known for his comedy writing, graphic designing, and voiceover work.
GAME 44 — **10.** Who wrote the controversial second theme song for the *Monk* series? a. Randy Newman b. Jeff Beal c. Carole King d. Paul Anka	**GAME 44 Q9 ANSWER b** This *Growing Pains* theme song—with music by John Dorff and lyrics by John Bettis—was sung by different people over the years. One version was performed by BJ Thomas and Jennifer Warnes; another, by BJ Thomas and Dusty Springfield; and a third version, by BJ Thomas alone.
GAME 64 — **10.** What 1990s TV dad had kids named Taylor, Molly, and Will? a. Robert Barone b. Steve Keaton c. Tim Taylor d. Wood Newton	**GAME 64 Q9 ANSWER d** Although he did a cameo on ABC's *Who's the Boss?* and appeared opposite Tom Selleck in an episode of the CBS show *Magnum, P.I.,* Ol' Blue Eyes never dropped by the Drummond residence. Both Mr. T and Muhammad Ali made appearances, and Nancy Reagan used the show to publicize her "Just Say No" anti-drug campaign.

Answers are in right-hand boxes on page 101.

3. Which *Simpsons* character becomes a country music star?

a. Ashley Grant

b. Jessica Lovejoy

c. Lurleen Lumpkin

d. Mindy Simmons

GAME 17 Q2 ANSWER d
Apu Nahasapeemapetilon (voiced by Hank Azaria) runs the Kwik-E-Mart and marries Manjula in an episode from the 1997–1998 season. Voiced by *SNL* alum Jan Hooks, Manjula goes on to have octuplets named Anoop, Gheet, Nabendu, Poonam, Priya, Sandeep, Sashi, and Uma. One of Apu's pet names for Manjula is "Chutney Butt."

3. Who made a cameo appearance on the last episode of the *I Love Lucy* series?

a. Bob Hope

b. The Arnaz children

c. John F. Kennedy

d. Lucille Ball's mother

GAME 37 Q2 ANSWER c
The two had met while performing in vaudeville and retired to manage Ethel's New York City brownstone. It is now widely known that William Frawley and Vivian Vance, the actors who played Fred and Ethel, disliked each other, possibly because Vance was heard to complain about being "married" to a man old enough to be her father.

3. What was called "The Swamp" on *M*A*S*H*?

a. Mess hall

b. Operating room

c. Hawkeye's tent

d. Latrine

GAME 57 Q2 ANSWER b
When McLean Stevenson left *M*A*S*H* at the end of Season Three, the writers decided that his character, Colonel Blake, would be discharged and sent home— and die in a crash on the way there. But to keep emotions real, the cast was kept in the dark about Blake's death until they shot the scene in which Radar announced the accident.

3. What was the lead character's name on the TV series *Mama's Family*?

a. Fran Crowley

b. Naomi Harper

c. Thelma Harper

d. Eunice Higgins

GAME 77 Q2 ANSWER d
Played by Joanna Kerns throughout *Growing Pains* 1985 to 1992 run, Maggie was a reporter who returned to work, leaving her psychiatrist husband (played by Alan Thicke) to care for the kids during the day. Since a lot of moms were returning to work during the eighties, the series struck a chord with many viewers.

11. Evan Marriott had a starring role in which reality show?

a. *The Surreal Life*

b. *The Bachelorette*

c. *Joe Millionaire*

d. *High School Reunion*

A veteran reality show participant, Rehn has appeared not only in *The Bachelorette* but also in *The Bachelor, Fear Factor*, and *Dancing with the Stars*. ABC paid Rehn $1 million for the right to televise her 2003 wedding to Ryan Sutter, the bachelor she chose to marry. The event drew over 26 million viewers.

---

11. Which *Tonight Show* guest told Jay Leno, "I did a bad thing. And there you have it"?

a. George Michael

b. Russell Crowe

c. Hugh Grant

d. Robert Blake

Water closet is the English term for bathroom. Before walking off the show, Paar said, "There must be a better way to make a living than this . . ." Upon his return a few weeks later, Paar began with, "As I was saying before I was interrupted . . . There must be better way to make a living than this. Well I've looked . . . and there isn't." He then apologized.

---

11. What was the theme song for *Friends*?

a. "Thank You for Being a Friend"

b. "My Friend"

c. "I'll Be There for You"

d. "Best Friends"

During the first season of *Monk*, the theme song was a jazzy instrumental written by Jeff Beal. Although the song won a 2003 Emmy Award, the second season brought a new theme song— "It's a Jungle Out There." Written and sung by Randy Newman, the replacement outraged many fans and critics, who had adored the original theme.

---

11. Who played Rick Schroeder's wealthy grandfather on *Silver Spoons*?

a. Alec Guinness

b. John Houseman

c. Charlton Heston

d. Rod Steiger

For his role as high school football coach Wood Newton in the CBS sitcom *Evening Shade*, Burt Reynolds won the 1991 Emmy for Lead Actor in a Comedy Series. The show also featured Marilu Henner of *Taxi* fame and Michael Jeter, who won a Best Supporting Actor Emmy for his role as the assistant coach and fragile math teacher Herman Stiles.

---

2. Who is Apu's wife on *The Simpsons*?

a. Indira

b. Benazir

c. Hasina

d. Manjula

2. Before becoming landlords, what did Fred and Ethel Mertz do for a living?

a. Played the stock market

b. Gave dance lessons

c. Performed in vaudeville

d. Ran a luncheonette

2. Which *M*A*S*H* character died when his plane was shot down?

a. Trapper John

b. Colonel Blake

c. Colonel Potter

d. Radar

2. In the series *Growing Pains*, what was Maggie Seaver's occupation?

a. Teacher

b. Realtor

c. Social worker

d. Journalist

GAME 17 Q1 ANSWER c
The least sentimental member of the Simpson family, Bart "bart"-ers away his soul to resident Springfield nerd Milhouse Van Houten following a church prank. By the end of this 1995 episode, however, Bart realizes his humanity and prays to God for the return of his soul. His sister Lisa, the most philosophical Simpson, buys it back for him.

GAME 37 Q1 ANSWER a
Cuban-born Desi Arnaz was a successful bandleader when he and Lucille Ball married, so it was natural for him to play a singer and bandleader on the show. One of the show's recurring themes was Lucy's desire to join her husband in show business—even though she apparently possessed no musical ability.

GAME 57 Q1 ANSWER d
A spinoff of *M*A*S*H*, the 1983–1985 show *AfterMASH* took place right after the end of the Korean War. The show presented the adventures of three characters from the original show: Father Francis Mulcahy, played by William Christopher; Max Klinger, played by Jamie Farr; and Colonel Sherman Potter, portrayed by Harry Morgan.

GAME 77 Q1 ANSWER b
Producer Irwin Allen based this 1965–1968 TV series on the comic book *Space Family Robinson*, as well as the novel *Swiss Family Robinson*. But the series name *Space Family Robinson* was ultimately discarded—possibly due to legal problems involving a writer who proposed a similar project with the exact same name.

12. The star of ABC's *Super-nanny* is more commonly called:

a. Nanny Roberts

b. Jo Frost

c. Mrs. Cartman

d. Cris Poli

Contestants thought that Marriott was a multimillionaire looking for a wife, but he was actually an average Joe—a construction worker. (The media discovered that he was also an underwear model.) Marriott chose Zora Andrich at the show's end, and the two split a $1 million check before parting ways.

12. Johnny Carson and which songwriter are credited with co-writing "Johnny's Theme" for *The Tonight Show*?

a. Barry Manilow

b. Paul Anka

c. Steve Allen

d. Burt Bacharach

Famous for his roles in such films as *Love Actually, Bridget Jones's Diary,* and *Four Weddings and a Funeral,* English actor High Grant was arrested in 1995 when caught with Hollywood hooker Divine Brown. He was fined and ordered to attend an AIDS awareness program. Shortly after, he and girlfriend, model Elizabeth Hurley, split.

12. What was the theme song for *The Partridge Family*?

a. "Sweet Harmony

b. "When We're Together"

c. "Love Is All Around"

d. "Come On, Get Happy"

Written for *Friends* by Michael Skloff and Allee Willis, "I'll Be There for You" was performed by the Rembrandts. Originally, the song was not produced as a single, but after the show's 1994 debut, radio stations played it anyway. When the single was finally released, the song rose to #17 on the Billboard Hot 100.

12. On *Diff'rent Strokes,* who was the school bully that bothered Arnold?

a. Gooch

b. Flats

c. Dudley

d. Wayne

Houseman played Edward Stratton II on this popular NBC sitcom. Although much of Houseman's early career was spent as a behind-the-scenes producer both alongside filmmaker Orson Welles and on his own, he found fame only after winning a Best Supporting Actor Oscar in 1973 for his role as the rigid Professor Kingsfield in *The Paper Chase.*

GAME 17	**1.** Which member of the Simpson family sells his/her soul for five dollars? a. Homer b. Lisa c. Bart d. Maggie	The answer to this question is on: **page 102, top frame, right side.**
GAME 37	**1.** On *I Love Lucy*, what was the name of the nightclub where Ricky worked? a. The Tropicana b. The Copacabana c. The Copa Lounge d. The Club Havana	The answer to this question is on: **page 102, second frame, right side.**
GAME 57	**1.** Which *M*A*S*H* character also appeared in *AfterMASH*? a. B.J. Hunnicut b. Hot Lips Houlihan c. Radar O'Reilly d. Father Mulcahy	The answer to this question is on: **page 102, third frame, right side.**
GAME 77	**1.** What series was originally to be titled *Space Family Robinson*? a. *Land of the Lost* b. *Lost in Space* c. *The Others* d. *Fantastic Journey*	The answer to this question is on: **page 102, bottom frame, right side.**

GAME 5

Prime-Time Soaps

*Turn to page 107
for the first question.*

GAME 4 Q12 ANSWER b
In each episode, British-born nanny Jo Frost helps a family whose children are out of control. Frost is known for her effective use of praise and positive encouragement, and her book *Supernanny: How to Get the Best From Your Children* spent seventeen weeks on the *New York Times* Best Sellers list.

GAME 25

MTV

*Turn to page 107
for the first question.*

GAME 24 Q12 ANSWER b
When commissioned by Carson and his company to write *The Tonight Show's* theme song, Anka suggested re-using an old tune of his called "It's Really Love." The catchy upbeat tune was perfect. A short drum solo was added before the music started, enabling Carson to become a part author of the "new" song —for copyright and royalty purposes.

GAME 45

British Imports

*Turn to page 107
for the first question.*

GAME 44 Q12 ANSWER d
Although *The Partridge Family's* theme song was "Come On, Get Happy," the group's biggest hit was 1970's "I Think I Love You." Featuring teen heartthrob David Cassidy, "I Think I Love You" began climbing the Billboard charts in September, and rose to #1 by the end of the year.

GAME 65

In the Classroom

*Turn to page 107
for the first question.*

GAME 64 Q12 ANSWER a
The Gooch bullied Arnold (Gary Coleman) during most of the series—he even gave Arnold a black eye in the first season. However, in a nice twist on stereotypes, Gooch finally got his comeuppance in a 1984 episode when a girl named Carmella Robinson (Martine Allard) beat him up. The Gooch was never actually seen on the show.

GAME 17

The Simpsons

Turn to page 104 for the first question.

GAME 16 Q12 ANSWER d
This show, which earned the top spot in 1956, had its origins in radio, first as *Take It or Leave It* on CBS in the '40s, then later on NBC, where it was renamed *The $64 Question* in 1950. By the time the TV version of the game debuted in 1955, the title changed yet again to *The $64,000 Question* and paved the way for future big-money game shows.

GAME 37

I Love Lucy

Turn to page 104 for the first question.

GAME 36 Q12 ANSWER b
Running from 1979 to 1987, the original *Dance Fever* was a musical variety show in which celebrities judged amateur dancers as they performed to the disco hits of the time. The show was revived in 2003 with Eric Nies as host and Jamie King, Carmen Electra, and MC Hammer as judges, but the new version ran for only one year.

GAME 57

M*A*S*H

Turn to page 104 for the first question.

GAME 56 Q12 ANSWER a
Although the show was broadcast from New York, Presley's September 9, 1956 appearance was aired from Hollywood (he was filming *Love Me Tender*). Sullivan was recovering from a near-fatal car accident, so Charles Laughton was the show's guest host. He introduced Presley's segment with, "And now away to Hollywood to meet Elvin [Elvis] Presley."

GAME 77

More Family Fun

Turn to page 104 for the first question.

GAME 76 Q12 ANSWER b
A 1974 TV movie written by Roddenberry with fellow *Star Trek* creator Gene L. Coon, *The Questor Tapes* was actually a pilot for a planned NBC television series. Although the film was ultimately embraced by critics, its production was plagued by run-ins between Roddenberry and network and studio executives, and the series was never made.

GAME 5

1. Which prime-time soap featured the wealthy Tates and the middle-class Campbells?

a. *Falcon Crest*

b. *Dallas*

c. *Soap*

d. *Knots Landing*

The answer to this question is on:

page 109, top frame, right side.

GAME 25

1. Which show never aired on MTV?

a. *The Week in Rock*

b. *Remote Control*

c. *Liquid Television*

d. *Politically Incorrect*

The answer to this question is on:

page 109, second frame, right side.

GAME 45

1. In *The Prisoner,* what was Patrick McGhoohan's character called?

a. Number 2

b. Number 3

c. Number 6

d. Number 10

The answer to this question is on:

page 109, third frame, right side.

GAME 65

1. Which brainy student on *Head of the Class* wore polyester pants and carried a slide rule?

a. Arvid

b. Simone

c. Alan

d. Dennis

The answer to this question is on:

page 109, bottom frame, right side.

12. What was the first game show to become the season's top-rated TV program?

a. *Beat the Clock*
b. *You Bet Your Life*
c. *The Price Is Right*
d. *The $64,000 Question*

GAME 16 Q11 ANSWER a
S.W.A.T.—spinoff of the popular ABC cop show *The Rookies*—debuted in February 1975. The show's theme song was performed by Rhythm Heritage and reached the top of the Billboard charts in 1976. Despite its popularity, however, the show was canceled in April 1976 due to complaints about its depiction of violence.

---

12. What was the name of the *Dance Fever* house dancers?

a. Groove Patrol
b. Motion
c. Emotion
d. Jam!

GAME 36 Q11 ANSWER c
Created and originally hosted by Don Cornelius, *Soul Train* premiered in 1970, and claims to be the "longest running first-run syndicated program in television history." The show primarily features R&B, soul, and hip hop artists, and always ends with a "dance line" that showcases individual dancers and, on occasion, new dance moves.

---

12. Who hosted *The Ed Sullivan Show* during Elvis Presley's first appearance?

a. Charles Laughton
b. Steve Allen
c. Jack Paar
d. Ed Sullivan

GAME 56 Q11 ANSWER b
Martin's girlfriend, a dancer on the show, helped him land the job by showing his work to head writer Mason Williams (who first paid Martin out of his own pocket). Other writers for the show who went on to become big names in comedy included Rob Reiner, David Letterman, Don "Father Guido Sarducci" Novello, and Bob "Super Dave Osborne" Einstein.

---

12. Who wrote the teleplay for the TV movie *The Questor Tapes*?

a. Arthur C. Clarke
b. Gene Roddenberry
c. Alan Dean Foster
d. Isaac Asimov

GAME 76 Q11 ANSWER c
Played by Marina Sirtis, the character of Deanna Troi appeared not only in *Star Trek: The Next Generation,* but also in *Star Trek: Voyager, Star Trek: Enterprise,* and several *Star Trek* films. An extra-sensory empath with a degree in psychology, Troi was well suited to be counselor on the *USS Enterprise-D* and the *USS Enterprise-E.*

Answers are in right-hand boxes on page 106.

GAME 5

2. Which series featured femme fatale Paige Matheson?

a. *Knots Landing*

b. *Dynasty*

c. *Hotel*

d. *Melrose Place*

GAME 25

2. Which comic was *not* affiliated with MTV's *Remote Control*?

a. Denis Leary

b. Adam Sandler

c. David Spade

d. Colin Quinn

GAME 45

2. Rowan Atkinson starred in which British TV comedy?

a. *Fawlty Towers*

b. *Absolutely Fabulous*

c. *Spitting Image*

d. *Blackadder*

GAME 65

2. What school did Denise Huxtable attend on *A Different World*?

a. Spellman College

b. Lincoln University

c. Fisk University

d. Hillman College

GAME 5 Q1 ANSWER c
Running from 1977 to 1981 on ABC, *Soap* was a prime-time comedy with a format similar to that of a soap opera. The cast included former soap opera actors Robert Mandan and Donnelly Rhodes, as well as regulars Katherine Helmond, Cathryn Damon, Richard Mulligan, Robert Urich, Robert Guillaume, and Billy Crystal.

GAME 25 Q1 ANSWER d
Hosted by Bill Maher, the half-hour political talk show premiered on Comedy Central in 1993 and was picked up by ABC in 1997. In 2002, shortly after Maher made a controversial statement following the 9/11 terror attacks that was interpreted as a criticism of American soldiers, ABC canceled the show.

GAME 45 Q1 ANSWER c
In the 1967 UK import *The Prisoner*, Patrick McGhoohan played a former secret agent who, after resigning his position, was kidnapped and held prisoner in a small isolated village. Throughout the series, the character—who was never identified by name, but known only as Number 6—tried to escape while defying attempts to break his will.

GAME 65 Q1 ANSWER a
In the 1986–1991 show *Head of the Class*, the ten kids who made up the Individualized Honors Program (IHP) at Manhattan's fictitious Monroe High School were all gifted students. Through their history teacher, Charlie Moore (Howard Hesseman), they learned that there was more to life than just pulling good grades.

11. Which TV theme song was the first to reach #1 on the Billboard charts?

a. *S.W.A.T.*

b. *Welcome Back, Kotter*

c. *Moonlighting*

d. *Dragnet*

GAME 16 Q10 ANSWER d

Debuting in April 1987 as FOX's second prime-time show (the first was *Married . . . With Children,* which started in October 1986), *The Tracey Ullman Show* won the Emmy for Outstanding Variety, Music or Comedy Program in 1989 and again in 1990. This show also first introduced *The Simpsons* to TV viewers as a recurring skit.

---

11. Who hosted *Soul Train* from its creation to 1993?

a. Bobby Sherman

b. Rapmaster Mel Melle

c. Don Cornelius

d. Jimmy Jazz

GAME 36 Q10 ANSWER a

Created by Flowers in the mid-1960s, Madame is an "outrageous old broad" based on movie stars such as Gloria Swanson. Dressed in fabulous evening-wear and diamonds, the puppet is known for her witty combacks and double entendres. Although Flowers died in 1988, Madame is still with us.

---

11. Steve Martin began his career as a writer for which variety show?

a. *Hee Haw*

b. *The Smothers Brothers Comedy Hour*

c. *The Tonight Show*

d. *Laugh-In*

GAME 56 Q10 ANSWER d

Bob Paul, the 1960 Olympic gold medalist in pairs figure skating, choreographed the show's skating segments. The Osmond siblings were the first brother-sister team (and the youngest cohosts) of a prime-time variety series. Producer Fred Silverman first decided to develop the show when he saw the two on *The Mike Douglas Show* in 1961.

---

11. Which sci-fi series featured counselor Deanna Troi?

a. *Deep Space Nine*

b. *Battlestar Galactica*

c. *Star Trek: The Next Generation*

d. *Space: 1999*

GAME 76 Q10 ANSWER d

From 1950 to 1955, viewers watched Frankie Thomas, Jr. play Tom Corbett, Space Cadet—a trainee attending the Space Academy in order to become a member of the Solar Guard. The *Tom Corbett* series has since been lauded for being more scientifically accurate than most media sci-fi of the time, in part due to science advisor Willy Ley.

GAME 5

3. Which soap ended a season with a wedding/gunfight combination called "The Moldavian Massacre"?

a. *Dallas*

b. *Falcon Crest*

c. *Dynasty*

d. *Knots Landing*

GAME 5 Q2 ANSWER a

When *Knots Landing* completed its 1979 to 1993 run on CBS, it had the distinction of being the second longest-running prime-time drama in TV history, the first being *Gunsmoke*. The character of Paige Matheson—who was on from 1986 to 1993—was played by Nicollette Sheridan, who later would become Edie Britt on *Desperate Housewives*.

GAME 25

3. Of the following, who was *not* a VJ when MTV was launched in 1981?

a. Martha Quinn

b. JJ Jackson

c. Mark Goodman

d. Daisy Fuentes

GAME 25 Q2 ANSWER c

Hosted by Ken Ober, the TV and pop music trivia game was set in the basement of his parents' house and cohosted by Colin Quinn. Denis Leary's first gig was on *Remote Control*, which aired from 1987 to 1990. While on the show, Adam Sandler developed a number of characters he would later play on *Saturday Night Live*.

GAME 45

3. What was Patsy Stone's job on the politically incorrect UK sitcom *Absolutely Fabulous*?

a. Hair stylist

b. Gossip columnist

c. Fashion editor

d. Talk show host

GAME 45 Q2 ANSWER d

The generic name used to encompass four series of one British historical sitcom, *Blackadder* followed the fortunes of Edmund Blackadder (Rowan Atkinson), a member of an English family dynasty, and his servant Baldrick (Tony Robinson). Each *Blackadder* series took place in a different period of history.

GAME 65

3. What subject did Max teach on *The Education of Max Bickford*?

a. English

b. History

c. Mathematics

d. Economics

GAME 65 Q2 ANSWER d

According to *A Different World's* premise, Cliff and Clair Huxtable (of *The Cosby Show*) attended Hillman, and their daughter Denise (Lisa Bonet) chose to follow in their footsteps. Bonet left the show after the first season, so for the remainder of the series' 1987–1993 run, a different lead character carried each week's story.

GAME 16

10. Which was the first FOX show to win an Emmy Award?

a. *The Simpsons*

b. *In Living Color*

c. *Married . . . with Children*

d. *The Tracey Ullman Show*

GAME 16 Q9 ANSWER c

Hudson played the handsome horse-breeder Daniel Reece in this final role of his career—he died in October 1985. Although known best for his leading roles in movies like *Pillow Talk* (1959) with Doris Day, Hudson also enjoyed TV success starring opposite Susan Saint James in the '70s CBS series *McMillan and Wife.*

GAME 36

10. What was the name of the puppet manipulated by Wayland Flowers on *Solid Gold*?

a. Madame

b. Pooky

c. Duchess

d. Weezer

GAME 36 Q9 ANSWER d

An actor, singer, dancer, and fashion model, Eric Nies initially gained fame on the first season of *The Real World* (1992). He then went on to host *The Grind,* which featured a live studio audience that danced to popular music. After leaving *The Grind* in 1995, Nies introduced a number of dance workout videos.

GAME 56

10. Which variety show was famous for its figure skating numbers?

a. *The Flip Wilson Show*

b. *The Mike Douglas Show*

c. *The Carol Burnett Show*

d. *Donny & Marie*

GAME 56 Q9 ANSWER c

LaRosa, who also appeared on Godfrey's *Talent Scouts,* was a popular young singer during the 1950s with a fast-growing fan base. Supposedly, a dispute over a missed dance lesson caused the unexpected firing, but many felt it was because LaRosa's fan mail became greater than Godfrey's. The act led to Godfrey's own fall from grace with the public.

GAME 76

10. What is the name of the "space cadet" for whom a 1950s TV series was named?

a. Flash Gordon

b. Tom Mix

c. Lyle Swann

d. Tom Corbett

GAME 76 Q9 ANSWER a

Debuting in 2004 on the USA Network, *The 4400* chronicles the story of 4,400 people who were abducted by humans in the Earth's future, and given special powers—such as telekinesis, telepathy, and precognition. The purpose of these "gifts" is to prevent coming events that will impact the future of mankind.

GAME 5

4. Who is the narrator of *Desperate Housewives*?

a. Retired schoolteacher
b. Dead woman
c. Beauty shop owner
d. Guardian angel

GAME 5 Q3 ANSWER c
One of *Dynasty's* many cliffhangers, "The Moldavian Massacre" occurred when character Amanda Carrington (Catherine Oxenberg) married Prince Michael of Moldavia (Michael Praed), and Moldavian revolutionaires gunned down everyone in the palace chapel. The disappointing resolution to this cliffhanger quickly resulted in falling ratings.

GAME 25

4. Which high school did MTV's Beavis and Butt-Head attend?

a. Calvin Coolidge High
b. Morse High
c. Highland High
d. Serra High

GAME 25 Q3 ANSWER d
Quinn, Jackson, and Goodman, along with Nina Blackwood and Alan Hunter were the original MTV VJs. Daisy Fuentes, who had been reporting weather for a local NY affiliate of the Latin network Univision, joined MTV in the late 1980s. She was the first VJ to crossover from the Spanish-language MTV Internacional to the original MTV.

GAME 45

4. What did *Fawlty Towers'* manager Basil Fawlty actually manage?

a. An office building
b. A country hotel
c. A high-rise apartment
d. A posh spa

GAME 45 Q3 ANSWER c
Portrayed by Joanna Lumley, *Absolutely Fabulous's* Patsy Stone was a substance-abusing, fashion- and fad-obsessed Londoner who valued fame, style, and drugs over all else. Other main characters on the show included Edwina Monsoon, played by Jennifer Saunders, and Saffron Monsoon, portrayed by Julia Sawalha.

GAME 65

4. What was the name of the school on *Room 222*?

a. Emily Dickinson
b. John Greenleaf Whittier
c. Walt Whitman
d. Amy Lowell

GAME 65 Q3 ANSWER b
From 2001 to 2002, Richard Dreyfuss, the star of *Mr. Holland's Opus* (1995), had another teaching job, this time at a women's college. Between Professor Andrea Haskell (Marcia Gay Harden), Max's former student and brief sexual fling, and daughter Nell (Katee Sackhoff), an eighteen-year-old with attitude, Max learned humility.

9. On which prime-time soap did Rock Hudson appear from 1984 to 1985?

a. *Falcon Crest*

b. *Remington Steele*

c. *Dynasty*

d. *Knots Landing*

GAME 16 Q8 ANSWER b
In the second episode of the series, Jerry said Elaine's middle name as he teased her about a new boyfriend. It was, in fact, the first time Julia Louis-Dreyfus appeared on the show as Elaine. Speaking of middle names, George Costanza's middle name was Louis.

9. Which participant of *The Real World* later became the host of MTV's *The Grind*?

a. Heather B.

b. Rebecca Blasband

c. Norman Korpi

d. Eric Nies

GAME 36 Q8 ANSWER c
Created by Simon Fuller and Nigel Lythgoe of *American Idol, So You Think You Can Dance* premiered in 2005. Like *Idol*, the show holds nationwide auditions and chooses a mix of contestants, ranging from winners of international championships to unknown street performers. Contestants then compete using different dance styles and partners.

9. Whom did Arthur Godfrey fire from *Arthur Godfrey and His Friends* on the air?

a. Lenny Bruce

b. Pat Boone

c. Julius LaRosa

d. The McGuire Sisters

GAME 56 Q8 ANSWER b
Art Linkletter's Emmy-winning *House Party* was a half-hour late-morning favorite from 1952 to 1969. The show featured special guests, musical groups, and audience participation in an effort to win prizes. The show ended with the host interviewing young children, which resulted in his best-selling 1957 book *Kids Say the Darndest Things*.

9. Who abducted "The 4400" in the TV show of that name?

a. Humans from the future

b. Insects

c. Ancient Mayans

d. Aliens

GAME 76 Q8 ANSWER c
Based on the 1950 book by Ray Bradbury, *The Martian Chronicles* TV series described the colonization of Mars by humans who had fled a troubled Earth. Rock Hudson starred as Colonel Wilder, the main linking character in Ray Bradbury's epic. Other cast members included Darren McGavin, Bernadette Peters, Roddy McDowall, and Barry Morse.

GAME 5

5. Which *Melrose Place* character cheated on his wife Jane with her sister Sydney?

a. Matt Fielding
b. Jake Hanson
c. Keith Gray
d. Michael Mancini

GAME 5 Q4 ANSWER b
In 2004, *Desperate Housewives* opened with the suicide of Mary Alice Young (Brenda Strong), who narrated the show from beyond the grave. The first season unraveled the mystery of Mary Alice's suicide and explored the lives of her friends. *Everwood* fans know that before *Desperate Housewives,* Strong played another deceased wife—Julia Brown.

GAME 25

5. Who replaced Jenny McCarthy on MTV's *Singled Out*?

a. Carmen Electra
b. Cindy Crawford
c. Molly Sims
d. Amber Valletta

GAME 25 Q4 ANSWER c
The school is named after the real Highland High School in Albuquerque, New Mexico, where series creator, Mike Judge, lived. The famous fictitious duo was also inspired by real-life students. Teachers on the MTV Highland High include the gentle hippie, Mr. David Van Driessen, and his polar opposite, ex-Marine Mr. Bradley Buzzcut.

GAME 45

5. Who was a stock character on *The Benny Hill Show*?

a. Professor Marvel
b. Boss Tweed
c. Major Gowan
d. Luigi Vercotti

GAME 45 Q4 ANSWER b
Set in a fictional hotel called Fawlty Towers, the show—which starred John Cleese as Basil Fawlty—was inspired by the Monty Python team's stay in a bad hotel in Torquay, England. Although only twelve episodes were produced, the series was included in the British Film Institute's 2000 list of great British television programs.

GAME 65

5. Who was *not* a Sweathog on *Welcome Back, Kotter*?

a. Richard Stabone
b. Vinnie Barbarino
c. Juan Epstein
d. Arnold Horshack

GAME 65 Q4 ANSWER c
Based upon both the politics of the time and teenage concerns, the 1969–1974 series *Room 222* won a 1969 Emmy for Outstanding New Series. While boasting its own great cast, it also included appearances from future stars such as Cindy Williams, Teri Garr, Jamie Farr, Rob Reiner, Richard Dreyfuss, Chuck Norris, Kurt Russell, and Mark Hamill.

GAME 16

8. On *Seinfeld,* what is Elaine Benes's middle name?

a. Joanne

b. Marie

c. Ariel

d. Jeannie

GAME 16 Q7 ANSWER b

This 1994 made-for-TV movie about an American family accused of spying was based on Allen's 1966 play. A feature film was made from the play in 1969 starring Jackie Gleason, but Woody Allen never felt it did justice to his work. Prior to 1994, Allen's only other TV show was 1971's unaired *Men of Crisis: The Harvey Wallinger Story.*

GAME 36

8. What is the FOX dancing reality show with a format similar to *American Idol*?

a. *Take a Step*

b. *You Have the Moves*

c. *So You Think You Can Dance*

d. *American Dancer*

GAME 36 Q7 ANSWER b

Debbie Allen was not only lead choreographer for both the film and TV show *Fame,* but also played teacher Lydia Grant in both the big screen and small screen versions, winning two Emmy Awards and one Golden Globe Award. Allen is the sister of actress Phylicia Rashad, who played Clair Huxtable on *The Bill Cosby Show.*

GAME 56

8. Whose show featured a segment called "Kids Say the Darndest Things"?

a. Jackie Gleason

b. Art Linkletter

c. Andy Williams

d. Dinah Shore

GAME 56 Q7 ANSWER a

The variety-comedy series was hosted by the legendary crooner, whose spontaneity (due to lack of rehearsing) added to the show's comedic value. If he flubbed a line or forgot a lyric during the show's taping, the mistake (and his recovery from it) was left in. Show regulars included Dom DeLuise, Charles Nelson Reilly, and Rodney Dangerfield.

GAME 76

8. Which veteran actor starred in the 1980 TV adaptation of *The Martian Chronicles*?

a. Gregory Peck

b. Jimmy Stewart

c. Rock Hudson

d. Dean Martin

GAME 76 Q7 ANSWER b

Running from 1974 to 1977, *Land of the Lost* revolved around the Marshall family, which, while on a rafting trip, fell through a time portal into a strange world inhabited by dinosaurs and Sleestak—a race of lizard-like humanoids. Episode plots focused mostly on the family's efforts to return to their own world.

GAME 16 / GAME 36 / GAME 56 / GAME 76

6. On which prime-time soap did Lana Turner, Kim Novak, Cliff Robertson, and Anne Archer all have starring roles?

a. *Dynasty*

b. *Falcon Crest*

c. *Dallas*

d. *Knots Landing*

GAME 5 Q5 ANSWER d
When *Melrose Place* debuted in 1992, Dr. Michael Mancini, played by Thomas Calabro, and his fashion designer wife Jane, played by Josie Bissett, were the *stable* couple in the apartment block that served as the focus of the series. But Michael's infidelity soon led to a broken marriage and further affairs.

6. What icon sits atop the MTV Video Music Award statue?

a. Astronaut

b. Video camera

c. Crossed drumsticks

d. Microphone

GAME 25 Q5 ANSWER a
Former Playboy Model Jenny McCarthy cohosted the show, which ran from 1995 to 1998, with Chris Hardwick. When McCarthy left, she was replaced by Carmen Electra, another Playboy model. Electra went on to become a well-known TV personality, model, and actress.

6. Who hosted the award-winning *Masterpiece Theatre* from 1971 to 1992?

a. Ralph Bellamy

b. Sir John Mills

c. Alistair Cooke

d. Alec Guinness

GAME 45 Q5 ANSWER a
The Benny Hill Show featured British comic Benny Hill—as well as show regulars, such as Henry McGee, Bob Todd, and Rita Webb—in numerous short sketches. Hill himself was versatile and portrayed many different characters, both male and female. His hallmarks were double entendre and slapstick comedy.

6. On *The Paper Chase*, what field of law did Professor Charles Kingsfield teach?

a. Contract law

b. Torts

c. International law

d. Criminal law

GAME 65 Q5 ANSWER a
The central Sweathogs on ABC's 1975–1979 sitcom *Welcome Back, Kotter* included Vinnie Barbarino (future star John Travolta), Juan Epstein (Robert Hegyes), Arnold Horshack (Ron Palillo), and Freddie "Boom Boom" Washington (Lawrence Hilton-Jacobs). Comedian Gabriel Kaplan played teacher (and former Sweathog) Gabe Kotter.

7. Who made a rare TV appearance in the ABC movie *Don't Drink the Water*?

a. Marlon Brando
b. Woody Allen
c. Jack Nicholson
d. Warren Beatty

GAME 16 Q6 ANSWER a
The first name of Mr. Big (played by Chris Noth) is revealed in the series finale when he finally commits to Carrie (Sarah Jessica Parker). By series' end, Miranda (Cynthia Nixon) ends up with bartender Steve, Charlotte (Kristin Davis) converts to Judaism and marries lawyer Harry, and Samantha (Kim Cattrall) finds love with actor Jerry "Smith" Jerrod.

---

7. Whose elaborately choreographed dances gave TV's *Fame* its flair?

a. Twyla Tharp
b. Debbie Allen
c. Phylicia Rashad
d. Paula Abdul

GAME 36 Q6 ANSWER d
Running from 1965 to 1966, *Hullabaloo* was NBC's big-budget answer to ABC's *Shindig!* Each week, a different host presided—Sammy Davis, Jr., Paul Anka, Petula Clark, and the like. The host would introduce acts such as Sonny and Cher, the Supremes, and Herman's Hermits, and the Hullabaloo Dancers would perform.

---

7. What was the theme song of *The Dean Martin Show* (1965–1974)?

a. "Everybody Loves Somebody"
b. "Sittin' on Top of the World"
c. "Return to Me"
d. "Memories Are Made of This"

GAME 56 Q6 ANSWER d
Hosted by former big-band singer Mike Douglas, the Emmy-winning show, which ran from 1961 to 1981, featured light banter with guests, musical performances, and a different cohost each week—John and Yoko's stint was in 1972. The show also featured the first TV appearance of 2-year-old Tiger Woods, who showed off his swing for Bob Hope.

---

7. What sci-fi show took place in a world inhabited by Sleestak, dinosaurs, and humans?

a. *The Forbidden Planet*
b. *Land of the Lost*
c. *Logan's Run*
d. *Lost in Space*

GAME 76 Q6 ANSWER a
The X-Files' Cigarette Smoking Man (William B. Davis) and Well-Manicured Man (John Neville) were both members of the Syndicate—an organization determined to discredit Fox Mulder (David Duchovny) and Dana Scully (Gillian Anderson), and keep the public from knowing that extraterrestrials planned to repopulate the Earth.

---

7. What kept Pam Barnes Ewing from marrying millionaire Mark Graison on *Dallas*?

a. He killed himself

b. He loved Bobby more

c. He was her half brother

d. He believed J.R.'s lies

GAME 5 Q6 ANSWER b

In addition to the stars who were part of the *Falcon Crest* cast, the series often featured Hollywood royalty in guest roles. During the 1987 to 1988 season alone, Leslie Caron, Eddie Albert, Eve Arden, and Ursula Andress all made appearances on the CBS show. Other seasons featured Lana Turner, Celeste Holm, and Gina Lollobrigida.

7. Which show was a spinoff of *Beavis and Butt-Head*?

a. *Celebrity Deathmatch*

b. *Clone High*

c. *Daria*

d. *Downtown*

GAME 25 Q6 ANSWER a

An astronaut on the moon—one of MTV's earliest representations—tops the seven-pound, twelve-inch statue. Because of this, the statues are commonly known as "Moon Men." The first Video Music Awards were presented in 1984. Madonna has won twenty-one, the most to date.

7. Before Diana Rigg became an *Avenger*, who played opposite Patrick Macnee on the series?

a. Honor Blackman

b. Joanna Lumley

c. Linda Thorson

d. Shirley Bassey

GAME 45 Q6 ANSWER c

A journalist and broadcaster, Alistair Cooke was born in England but became a nationalized American citizen, living most of his adult life in New York City. Although he is best known for hosting *Masterpiece Theatre*, he once said he was proudest of creating *Alistair Cooke's America*—a thirteen-part TV series about United States history.

7. Which character did Mario Lopez play on NBC's *Saved by the Bell*?

a. "Screech" Powers

b. Richard Belding

c. Zack Morris

d. A.C. Slater

GAME 65 Q6 ANSWER a

Based on John Jay Osborn's 1970 novel of the same name, *The Paper Chase* featured John Houseman as Professor Charles W. Kingsfield, Jr.—a role Houseman also played in the 1973 movie. The critically acclaimed series ran from 1978 to 1979, after which its reruns aired on PBS. Then in 1983, Showtime brought back the series for three seasons.

GAME 16

6. On *Sex and the City*, what was Mr. Big's real name?

a. John

b. Steve

c. Harry

d. Smith

GAME 16 Q5 ANSWER c

The CBS sitcom *Kate & Allie* featured Susan Saint James ("Kate") and Jane Curtin ("Allie") as divorced best friends who lived together with their kids in a New York City brownstone. During the show's fifth season, when Kate became bored as a travel agent and Allie couldn't find a good job, they began the catering business.

GAME 36

6. What was NBC's answer to the popular music variety show *Shindig!*?

a. *Soul Train*

b. *Shiveree*

c. *Groovin'*

d. *Hullabaloo*

GAME 36 Q5 ANSWER a

ABC's *Shindig!* variety show aired from 1964 to 1966, showcasing popular performers of the day, from The Everly Brothers to Roy Orbison, Glen Campbell, The Supremes, Sonny and Cher, and The Beach Boys. Accompanying the musicians of the week was a group of dancers called the Shindiggers.

GAME 56

6. On which show did John and Yoko have a week-long stint as cohosts?

a. *The Merv Griffin Show*

b. *The Steve Allen Show*

c. *The Flip Wilson Show*

d. *The Mike Douglas Show*

GAME 56 Q5 ANSWER c

In this recurring sketch, Sonny played the dim-witted owner of a pizza parlor with Cher as Rosa, the sexy waitress. Gilda Radner played the fiery (but hard-of-hearing) Emily Litella on *Saturday Night Live*; Mrs. Wiggins was a Carol Burnett creation; and Loretta Castorini was Cher's character in *Moonstruck*—for which she won a Best Actress Oscar.

GAME 76

6. What sci-fi series included the Cigarette Smoking Man and Well-Manicured Man?

a. *The X-Files*

b. *Tracker*

c. *3rd Rock from the Sun*

d. *Roswell*

GAME 76 Q5 ANSWER d

Running from 1993 to 1998, *Babylon 5* focused on a space station that was a center of political intrigue and conflict. Conceived as a novel—with a beginning, a middle, and an end—the program was actually described as a "novel for television," and was known for its reliance on planned story arcs.

8. Who played the title role in *Mary Hartman, Mary Hartman*?

a. Mary Kay Place
b. Renee Taylor
c. Michele Lee
d. Louise Lasser

GAME 5 Q7 ANSWER a
Played by Victoria Principal, Pam had a rough time on *Dallas*. In Season Eight, for instance, Pam and ex-husband Bobby Ewing (Patrick Duffy) decided to remarry. Unfortunately for them both, Bobby was hit by a car when trying to save Pam from being hit, and was rushed to the hospital, where he died.

8. Johnny Knoxville helped turn which MTV show into a hit?

a. *Cribs*
b. *Punk'd*
c. *Jackass*
d. *Pimp My Ride*

GAME 25 Q7 ANSWER c
Daria, the duo's nerdy, droll, and sarcastic high school classmate (whom they often called "Diarrhea") went on to star in her own animated comedy. In it, Daria (voiced by Tracy Grandstaff) moves to Lawndale, where she continues her adventures in alienation while trying to get through high school with as little human contact as possible.

8. Who was the unseen son of Hyacinth and Richard on the BBC's *Keeping Up Appearances*?

a. Michael
b. Bruce
c. Onslow
d. Sheridan

GAME 45 Q7 ANSWER a
Although Honor Blackman's Cathy Gale preceded Rigg's character, Emma Peel, the classic *Avengers* episodes are generally considered to be those featuring Macnee and Rigg. The brilliant Mrs. Peel was a formidable fencer and was skilled in martial arts. Just as important, she looked quite fabulous in the Emmapeeler catsuit.

8. Who played Principal Steven Harper in *Boston Public*?

a. Nicky Katt
b. Michael Rapaport
c. Chi McBride
d. Anthony Heald

GAME 65 Q7 ANSWER d
This 1989–1993 teen show focused on Zack Morris and his friends at Bayside High School in Palisades, California. The show was popular enough to spawn two spinoffs—*Saved by the Bell: The College Years*, which followed several of the show's characters in college, and *Saved by the Bell: The New Class*.

GAME 16

5. Which TV duo started a catering business?

a. Laverne and Shirley

b. Mary and Rhoda

c. Kate and Allie

d. Janet and Chrissie

GAME 16 Q4 ANSWER a

When Suzanne Somers demanded a higher salary to play the part of "dumb blonde" Chrissie Snow, the show's producers slowly wrote the character out of the show and brought in Jenilee Harrison as Chrissie's cousin Cindy. Cindy never really caught on with viewers, though, and she was replaced in 1981 by Priscilla Barnes as Terri.

GAME 36

5. *Shindig!* once dedicated an entire episode to which of the following legends?

a. Elvis Presley

b. Fats Domino

c. Hank Williams

d. Sam Cooke

GAME 36 Q4 ANSWER b

Formerly a singer with the group 98 Degrees, Drew Lachey—along with partner Cheryl Burke, a professional dancer based in New York—was crowned champion, beating out such celebrity contestants as actor George Hamilton, actress Tatum O'Neal, and NFL player Jerry Rice.

GAME 56

5. Which character did Cher play on *The Sonny and Cher Comedy Hour*?

a. Emily Litella

b. Mrs. Wiggins

c. Rosa the Waitress

d. Loretta Castorini

GAME 56 Q4 ANSWER d

It was a common belief that Elvis's "indecent" hip gyrations caused this decision by Sullivan. But according to one of the camera directors, it was due to a rumor that just before his entrance, Presley was going to hang a sock inside his pants near the top of his leg. When no such device was used, Sullivan called Elvis "A real decent, fine boy."

GAME 76

5. Where was the *Babylon 5* space station located?

a. Centauri Prime

b. Alpha Quadrant

c. Neutral Zone

d. Euphrates Sector

GAME 76 Q4 ANSWER c

Created by Gene Roddenberry of *Star Trek* fame, *Earth: Final Conflict* was not produced until 1997—six years after Roddenberry's death. The show, which ran until 2002, initially involved a race of aliens called the Taelons, who willingly shared their advanced technology with humans. Unfortunately, the Taelons had a hidden agenda.

GAME 5

9. What was the occupation of fun-loving Gary Shepherd on *Thirtysomething*?

a. Advertising executive
b. Professor
c. Photographer
d. Magazine reporter

GAME 5 Q8 ANSWER d
A prime-time soap opera parody, *Mary Hartman, Mary Hartman* aired from 1976 to 1978. The series concerned Mary Hartman, played by Louise Lasser; her husband (Greg Mullavey); her mother (Dody Goodman), her best friend (Mary Kay Place), and other quirky and bizarre characters living in the fictional town of Fernwood, Ohio.

GAME 25

9. MTV's *Road Rules* always ended with what kind of reward?"

a. Handsome
b. Crazy
c. Hearty
d. Rapid

GAME 25 Q8 ANSWER c
The idea for the show, with its outrageous, often dangerous stunts, came from Knoxville, who, as the basis for a magazine article, had himself shot with pepper spray, a taser gun, and a .38 (while wearing a vest), so he could write about it. Shortly after videos of these and other stunts were aired, MTV jumped at the chance to air *Jackass*.

GAME 45

9. What nightclub did Sharon Watts run in *EastEnders*?

a. The Cobra Club
b. Angie's Den
c. e20
d. The Market Cellar

GAME 45 Q8 ANSWER d
Keeping Up Appearances—which was voted one of Britain's Best Sitcoms in a 2004 BBC poll—revolved around the struggles of social climber Hyacinth Bucket, played by Patricia Routledge. A dedicated social climber, Hyacinth pronounced her surname *Bouquet*—although long-suffering husband Richard had always said *Bucket* before their marriage.

GAME 65

9. Which *Sex and the City* star got her start on the cult favorite *Square Pegs*?

a. Kristin Davis
b. Kim Cattrall
c. Cynthia Nixon
d. Sarah Jessica Parker

GAME 65 Q8 ANSWER c
Set at Winslow High School, the show *Boston Public* (2000–2004) provided a quirky look at the world of education. A tough principal with a heart of gold, McBride's Steven Harper was one of the most important characters of the series, and often struggled with the problems of both the school's teachers and its students.

4. On *Three's Company*, who was Chrissie Snow's cousin?

a. Cindy
b. Terri
c. Vicky
d. Farrah

GAME 16 Q3 ANSWER b
Roseanne, which followed the antics of the working-class Connor family, took place in fictional Lanford, Illinois. On *Family Ties*, the Keatons lived in Columbus, Ohio, while The Drew Carey Show took place in Cleveland. The extraterrestrial "family" of *3rd Rock* resided in the fictional Ohio town of Rutherford.

4. Which celebrity won the second season of TV's *Dancing with the Stars* contest?

a. Jerry Rice
b. Drew Lachey
c. George Hamilton
d. Master P

GAME 36 Q3 ANSWER a
This variety show, which was set up like a large party, ran from 1950 to 1960. Essentially an ad for the Arthur Murray dance studios, each program would show hosts Arthur and Kathryn Murray teaching celebrity guests how to perform a particular dance. The show would always end with the couple dancing a Johann Strauss waltz.

4. On Elvis's last *Ed Sullivan Show* appearance in 1957, he had to:

a. Sing only gospel songs
b. Button up his shirt
c. Carry an American flag
d. Be filmed from the waist up

GAME 56 Q3 ANSWER d
Bubbles floated in the air as the former big-band leader led the show's orchestra and its "light-as-champagne-bubbles" music. The program catered to an over-fifty audience, featuring singers, dancers, and musicians. Occasionally couples from the audience danced to the music. The singing Lennon Sisters, classmates of Welk's son, were show regulars.

4. Who was the protagonist of the series *Earth: Final Conflict*?

a. Matthew Sikes
b. John Sheridan
c. William Boone
d. Quinn Mallory

GAME 76 Q3 ANSWER b
Considered TV's first sci-fi space adventure, *Captain Video* debuted in 1949 with actor Richard Coogan in the title role. Al Hodge took over as Captain from 1951 until the show's end in 1955. Set in the year 2254, the live program followed Captain Video as he battled aliens. Among the show's villains were actors Ernest Borgnine and Arnold Stang.

10. Which prime-time soap originally concerned characters who were fraternal twins?

a. *Beverly Hills, 90210*
b. *Dallas*
c. *Melrose Place*
d. *Peyton Place*

Fans were outraged when Gary, played by Peter Horton, was killed in a traffic accident. The death of an important and popular character was rare during *Thirtysomething's* 1987–1991 run, but it eventually became a regular part of TV, as viewers of *Law & Order, Buffy the Vampire Slayer,* and *Lost* can testify.

---

10. What was the first music video shown on MTV?

a. "You Better Run"
b. "She Won't Dance"
c. "Video Killed the Radio Star"
d. "You Better You Bet"

Sister show of *The Real World* (MTV's first reality show), *Road Rules* followed five or six young adults, who were stripped of their own money, put into an RV, and set on a road trip. Guided only by clues, they traveled to various locations and had to complete a mission at each. Upon finishing all of the missions, they were rewarded "handsomely."

---

10. Which character was *not* an extra on the UK series *Extras*?

a. Andy
b. Maggie
c. Greg
d. Darren

EastEnders' Angie's Den was named after Sharon Watts' mother, Angie Watts. Before the club was owned by Sharon, it was named The Cobra Club, The Market Cellar, and e20. When Sharon sold it to Johnny Allen, it was renamed Scarlet after his deceased eldest daughter.

---

10. *The Greatest American Hero* was a teacher known as "Mr. H." What did the "H" stand for?

a. Harrington
b. Houlihan
c. Hinkley
d. Harper

Best friends Lauren Hutchinson (Amy Linker) and Patty Greene (Sarah Jessica Parker) desperately wanted to fit in at Weemawee High School. Unfortunately, their time at the school was limited to the show's 1982–1983 run, because while *Square Pegs* was praised for its realistic portrayal of teenage life, it was canceled after a year.

---

3. Which sitcom did *not* take place in Ohio?

a. *3rd Rock from the Sun*

b. *Roseanne*

c. *The Drew Carey Show*

d. *Family Ties*

GAME 16 Q2 ANSWER d
In addition to playing NYPD detective Anthony Dellaventura in this short-lived CBS series, Danny Aiello was the show's executive producer. Although Aiello played Sal in Spike Lee's film *Do the Right Thing* (1989) and Frank in the comedy *29th Street* (1991), he is perhaps best remembered as Johnny Cammareri in *Moonstruck* (1988).

3. On which show did the host teach dance steps and encourage viewers to join his dance school?

a. *The Arthur Murray Party*

b. *Your Show of Shows*

c. *The George Gobel Show*

d. *Arthur Godfrey & Friends*

GAME 36 Q2 ANSWER b
Originally one of the Mouseketeers, Bobby Burgess first appeared on *The Lawrence Welk Show* in 1961 after winning a dance contest with friend and dancing partner Barbara Boylan. Burgess remained on the show until 1982, first paired with Boylan, and later with other partners, including Cissy King.

3. Of the following, what is *not* affiliated with *The Lawrence Welk Show* (1955–1982)?

a. Champagne bubbles

b. Dancing couples

c. The Lennon Sisters

d. Comedy skits

GAME 56 Q2 ANSWER b
Considered country music's best variety show, *Hee Haw* started as a 1969 summer replacement for *The Smothers Brothers Comedy Hour*. Hosted by Buck Owens and Roy Clark, it featured lots of country, bluegrass, and gospel music, and plenty of down-home humor. In 1971, CBS dropped *Hee Haw,* which continued in syndication another twenty years.

3. Who played the Captain in the 1950s series *Captain Video and His Video Rangers*?

a. Richard Webb

b. Al Hodge

c. Ernest Borgnine

d. Don Hastings

GAME 76 Q2 ANSWER a
With Lorne Greene playing Adama, the original *Battlestar Gallactica* series lasted only from 1978 to 1979. It had a strong fan base, though, and in 1980, the story was continued in the short-lived *Galactica 1980*—again starring Lorne Greene. Then in 2003, *Battlestar Galactica* was "re-imagined," this time with Edward James Olmos at the helm.

GAME 5

11. Who played Rodney Harrington on the 1960s soap *Peyton Place*?

a. Christopher Connelly
b. Robert Redford
c. Ryan O'Neal
d. James Douglas

GAME 5 Q10 ANSWER a

When *Beverly Hills, 90210* debuted in 1990, it concerned twins Brenda and Brandon Walsh (Shannen Doherty and Jason Priestly), who had just moved with their parents from Minneapolis to Beverly Hills. The show eventually made household names of not only Doherty and Priestly, but also cast members Tori Spelling and Luke Perry.

GAME 25

11. Which heavily aired MTV music video features the line "I want my MTV!"?

a. "Losing My Religion"
b. "Take on Me"
c. "Money for Nothing"
d. "With or Without You"

GAME 25 Q10 ANSWER c

When MTV was launched on August 1, 1981, the first music video it broadcast was "Video Killed the Radio Star" by England's electric-pop group The Buggles. The second video aired was Pat Benatar's "You Better Run," followed by "She Won't Dance" by Rod Stewart. The Who's "You Better You Bet" was fourth.

GAME 45

11. Who was the only American member of the *Monty Python* group?

a. Eric Idle
b. John Cleese
c. Terry Gilliam
d. Michael Palin

GAME 45 Q10 ANSWER d

Andy Millman (Ricky Gervais), Maggie Jacobs (Ashley Jensen), and Greg (Shaun Pye) were all struggling extras on *Extras*. Darren Lamb (Stephen Merchant), though, was a truly awful agent who was incapable of breaking an act or negotiating a contract favorable to his client, but excelled at deducting his 12.5-percent commission.

GAME 65

11. Who were Felicity's two loves on the show of the same name?

a. Sean and Troy
b. Ben and Noel
c. Rick and David
d. Scott and Mike

GAME 65 Q10 ANSWER c

The Greatest American Hero's title character was originally called Ralph Hinkley, but after John Hinckley's attempted assassination of Ronald Reagan in 1981, the name was changed to Hanley for one episode, and the character was usually called "Mr. H." Outraged fans caused the show to reinstate the original name, but it was rarely used.

2. What was the title character's first name on the detective series _Dellaventura_?

a. Frank

b. Johnny

c. Sal

d. Anthony

GAME 16 Q1 ANSWER a
FOX network's _Beverly Hills, 90210_ was a huge hit for producer Aaron Spelling. In 1992, Spelling's partner Darren Star created the _90210_ spinoff _Melrose Place,_ which starred Courtney Thorne-Smith opposite Andrew Shue. Thorne-Smith also appeared on FOX's _Ally McBeal_ and as Jim Belushi's wife on ABC's _According to Jim._

2. Which dancer performed on _The Lawrence Welk Show_ for over two decades?

a. Barbara Boylan

b. Bobby Burgess

c. Cissy King

d. Arthur Duncan

GAME 36 Q1 ANSWER c
Premiering in 1952 as simply _Bandstand,_ the show was first hosted by Bob Horn. Dick Clark took over in 1956 and a year later, the program's name was changed to _American Bandstand._ Over the years, many changes took place, and in 1989, _American Bandstand_—now hosted by comedian David Hirsh—finally ended.

2. From which setting were corny jokes delivered on _Hee Haw_?

a. Barnyard

b. Cornfield

c. General store

d. Front porch

GAME 56 Q1 ANSWER a
Hosted by entertainment columnist Ed Sullivan, the Sunday night program ran from 1948 to 1971 (the name was changed in 1955). The show aired brief acts of every type from slapstick comedy and juggling to dancing and operatic singing. Through it, legends such as Elvis Presley and The Beatles were introduced into American homes.

2. Which TV sci-fi vessel was commanded by the heroic leader Adama?

a. The Battlestar Galactica

b. The USS Enterprise

c. Moonbase Alpha

d. The USS Seaview

GAME 76 Q1 ANSWER d
Based on a 1988 movie of the same name, _Alien Nation_ ran for just one season, from 1989 to 1990. It starred Gary Graham as Matthew Sikes, a Los Angeles policeman who is (reluctantly) obliged to work with alien George Francisco, played by Eric Pierpoint. Although the show was popular, FOX Network's financial problems led to its cancellation.

12. Which *L.A. Law* character plunged to her death after stepping into an empty elevator shaft?

a. Abby Perkins

b. Grace Van Owen

c. Ann Kelsey

d. Roz Shays

GAME 5 Q11 ANSWER c
As Rodney Harrington, Ryan O'Neal was the love interest of *Peyton Place's* Allison MacKenzie (Mia Farrow)—as well as the show's bad girl Betty Anderson (Barbara Parkins). But when Farrow left the series in 1966 to focus on a career in movies and her marriage to Frank Sinatra, the character of Betty had Rodney all to herself.

12. Who was the original host of MTV's *Total Request Live*?

a. Rick James

b. Jimmy Kimmel

c. Jon Stewart

d. Carson Daly

GAME 25 Q11 ANSWER c
This Dire Straits song, first released on its *Brothers in Arms* album, was an international hit. In addition to its controversial lyrics, the song was known for its computer-animated music video and its guest vocalist, Sting, who began and ended the song with, "I want my MTV!" It was the first music video aired on MTV Europe in 1987.

12. Which actor did *not* appear in the miniseries *Brideshead Revisited*?

a. Anthony Hopkins

b. Anthony Andrews

c. Laurence Olivier

d. Jeremy Irons

GAME 45 Q11 ANSWER c
Terry Gilliam—who has this distinction—began his career as an animator and strip cartoonist, and participated in *Monty Python's Flying Circus* from its formation. Later, he became a motion picture director, working on such films as *Time Bandits, Brazil,* and *Twelve Monkeys.*

12. Who played Mr. Feeny on the show *Boy Meets World*?

a. William Daniels

b. John Stamos

c. David Hasselhoff

d. Bob Saget

GAME 65 Q11 ANSWER b
The trouble began when high school senior Felicity Porter (Keri Russell) followed the boy of her dreams, Ben Covington (Scott Speedman), to the University of New York. There she met resident advisor Noel Crane (Scott Foley), only to create a love triangle that moved the plot along from 1998 to 2002, when *Felicity* was canceled.

GAME 16

1. Which actress did *not* appear on *Beverly Hills, 90210*?

a. Courtney Thorne-Smith

b. Shannen Doherty

c. Tori Spelling

d. Lindsay Price

The answer to this question is on:

page 128, top frame, right side.

GAME 36

1. Who hosted *American Bandstand* for over twenty years?

a. Dick Cavett

b. Chubby Checker

c. Dick Clark

d. Lloyd Thaxton

The answer to this question is on:

page 128, second frame, right side.

GAME 56

1. What was *The Ed Sullivan Show* first known as?

a. *Toast of the Town*

b. *Omnibus*

c. *Your Show of Shows*

d. *The Sunday Cavalcade*

The answer to this question is on:

page 128, third frame, right side.

GAME 76

1. Who played Detective Matthew Sikes on *Alien Nation*?

a. Jerry O'Connell

b. Colm Meaney

c. Jerry Doyle

d. Gary Graham

The answer to this question is on:

page 128, bottom frame, right side.

GAME 6

American Idol

*Turn to page 133
for the first question.*

Turn to page 133
for the first question.

GAME 5 Q12 ANSWER d

In the 1991 *L.A. Law* episode titled "Good to the Last Drop," ruthless litigator Rosalind Shays, played by Diana Muldaur, fell to her death down an elevator shaft. Many critics and fans claimed that the show "jumped the shark" with this episode, but the series, which had debuted in 1986, continued until 1994.

GAME 26

Seinfeld

*Turn to page 133
for the first question.*

GAME 25 Q12 ANSWER d

In 1997, Daly first appeared on MTV as a VJ, and in the fall of 1998, he became the first host of *Total Request Live* (*TRL*)—the network's Top-10 video countdown show. In 2002, Daly made his debut as a late-night NBC talk show host on *Last Call with Carson Daly*. By 2003, he had stepped down from TRL to concentrate full time on *Last Call*.

GAME 46

Cop Shows

*Turn to page 133
for the first question.*

GAME 45 Q12 ANSWER a

Adapted from Evelyn Waugh's novel of the same name, *Brideshead Revisted* concerned college student Charles Ryder (Jeremy Irons), who befriends fellow student Lord Sebastian Flyte (Anthony Andrews). Ryder gets caught up in Flyte's world and visits his palatial home, Brideshead Castle. Laurence Olivier played Lord Marchmain, Flyte's father.

GAME 66

TV Theme Songs II

*Turn to page 133
for the first question.*

GAME 65 Q12 ANSWER a

Boy Meets World ran on ABC from 1993 to 2000, long enough to see lead character Cory Matthews (Ben Savage) grow and mature from boy to married man. Daniels, who also supplied the voice for the car KITT on *Knight Rider*, played Cory's next-door neighbor, high school principal, and mentor.

131

GAME 16
GRAB BAG

Turn to page 130
for the first question.

GAME 15 Q12 ANSWER c
In early 1976, *SNL* was still called *NBC's Saturday Night* to avoid confusion with ABC's short-lived show *Saturday Night Live with Howard Cosell*. It won Emmys for Best Comedy-Variety Show, along with awards for Best Supporting Actor (Chevy Chase), Best Director, and Best Writing (eleven writers).

GAME 36
Get Up and Dance!

Turn to page 130
for the first question.

GAME 35 Q12 ANSWER c
Airing from August 2003 to November 2003, *Playmakers* dealt with such topics as homosexuality, drug abuse, and domestic abuse. When the NFL criticized *Playmakers* for its portrayal of professional players, ESPN—a sister network of ABC, which broadcast *Monday Night Football*—canceled the show.

GAME 56
Variety Shows

Turn to page 130
for the first question.

GAME 55 Q12 ANSWER c
Bill Bixby was Dr. David Banner ("Bruce" in the Marvel Comics version), whose experiment with gamma rays went terribly wrong. Afterward, anger or stress caused him to morph into the enormous green creature, played by 6'5" bodybuilder Lou Ferrigno. The 6'2" Arnold Schwarzenegger was considered for the role, but reportedly wasn't tall enough.

GAME 76
Sci-Fi II

Turn to page 130
for the first question.

GAME 75 Q12 ANSWER a
Quiz Kids made its TV debut in 1940, continued on the radio for several years, and reappeared on TV from 1949 to 1956. Host Joe Kelly posed the questions, and a panel of five kids chosen for their high IQs provided the answers. Among the child panelists was James D. Watson, who would later win the Nobel Prize for discovering the DNA molecule.

GAME 6

1. What foreign series gave birth to *American Idol*?

a. *Pop Idol*

b. *Rock Idol*

c. *Canadian Idol*

d. *Australian Idol*

The answer to this question is on:

page 135, top frame, right side.

GAME 26

1. Which of the following *Seinfeld* staples is the *only* one affiliated with the pilot episode?

a. Elaine

b. Director Tom Cherones

c. Jerry's standup routine

d. Monk's Café

The answer to this question is on:

page 135, second frame, right side.

GAME 46

1. Who starred as veteran detective Mike Stone in *The Streets of San Francisco*?

a. Karl Malden

b. Jack Lord

c. Jack Klugman

d. Craig Stevens

The answer to this question is on:

page 135, third frame, right side.

GAME 66

1. Ray Charles' classic "Georgia on My Mind" was the theme song for which TV series?

a. *Designing Women*

b. *Falcon Crest*

c. *The Dukes of Hazzard*

d. *Growing Pains*

The answer to this question is on:

page 135, bottom frame, right side.

12. How many Emmys did *SNL* earn for its first season?

a. None
b. Three
c. Four
d. Eight

GAME 15 Q11 ANSWER d

As the rather effeminate stripper known only as "Mango," *SNL* star Chris Kattan excited the desires of guest hosts like Garth Brooks, Ellen DeGeneres, and even Christopher Walken (he sang a song about Mango that was a note-for-note parody of the 1980 Kenny Rogers hit "Lady"). Chris Kattan was on *SNL* from 1998 to 2003.

12. What was the name of the fictional pro football team on ESPN's *Playmakers*?

a. Gladiators
b. Titans
c. Cougars
d. Assassins

GAME 35 Q11 ANSWER c

The world's oldest and longest-running sports program, *Hockey Night in Canada* broadcasts Canada's National Hockey League games, airing regular season NHL games every Saturday night on the English network of the CBC. Its theme song "The Hockey Theme," written by Dolores Claman in 1968, has been called Canada's second national anthem.

12. What caused Dr. David Banner to morph into *The Incredible Hulk*?

a. Passion
b. A full moon
c. Anger
d. Fire

GAME 55 Q11 ANSWER c

Duffy played Mark Harris, a survivor from the lost continent of Atlantis in this short-lived series (1977–1978). Harris's ability to breathe underwater and withstand depth pressure allowed him to fight evil while exploring the ocean depths. The show's cancellation enabled Duffy to play Bobby Ewing on the long-running prime-time soap opera *Dallas*.

12. What '50s game show tested the general knowledge of gifted children?

a. *Quiz Kids*
b. *From the Mouth of Babes*
c. *Brainiacs*
d. *Child's Play*

GAME 75 Q11 ANSWER c

Fran Allison hosted *Kukla, Fran and Ollie*, and was usually the only human to appear beside Kukla, who looked like a clown (but wasn't); Ollie, a one-toothed dragon; and a variety of other puppets. The popular show ran from 1948 to 1957, and although it was originally created for children, it ultimately had more adult than child viewers.

GAME 6

2. Which *American Idol* winner recorded the debut album *Some Hearts*?

a. Ruben Studdard
b. Fantasia Barrino
c. Kelly Clarkson
d. Carrie Underwood

GAME 6 Q1 ANSWER a

The format of the UK's *Pop Idol* was created in 1998 by music impresario Simon Fuller, who originally envisioned it as being web based. The show, which spun off dozens of sucessful programs, made use of high-priced viewer interactivity, with viewers voting by phone, through the "red button" on digital TV sets, and on the official website.

GAME 26

2. In the *JFK* parody on *Seinfeld*, who was the second spitter on the gravelly road?

a. Keith Hernandez
b. Crazy Joe Davola
c. Roger McDowell
d. Lenny Dykstra

GAME 26 Q1 ANSWER c

The pilot episode, directed by Art Wolff, was first broadcast in July 1989. In it, Jerry and George eat at Pete's Luncheonette instead of Monk's Café. Elaine's character hadn't been written yet. And Kramer, who actually knocked before entering Jerry's apartment (to borrow some meat), was called Kessler (in this episode only).

GAME 46

2. In which cop show did the characters Wojo and Fish appear?

a. *Starsky And Hutch*
b. *Hill Street Blues*
c. *Kojak*
d. *Barney Miller*

GAME 46 Q1 ANSWER a

Malden's costar was a young Michael Douglas as his partner Steve Keller. The ABC crime series ran from 1972 to 1977, and was filmed entirely on location in San Francisco. In 1975, Douglas won an Oscar as producer of the film *One Flew Over the Cuckoo's Nest*. He later won a Best Actor Oscar for the 1987 movie *Wall Street*.

GAME 66

2. Which group recorded the theme song for *Malcolm in the Middle*?

a. They Might Be Giants
b. Sugar Ray
c. Mighty Mighty Bosstones
d. Smash Mouth

GAME 66 Q1 ANSWER a

In the first five seasons of this popular CBS sitcom, bandleader Doc Severinsen of NBC's *The Tonight Show* fame created an instrumental version of the song for the series. However, the series' sixth season featured Ray Charles performing a new version of the song with the show's leading cast standing around him at his piano.

---

11. Which "Chris" played the recurring role of Mango on *SNL*?

a. Chris Rock

b. Chris Farley

c. Chris Parnell

d. Chris Kattan

George Carlin started things off right for *SNL* when he hosted the first show on October 11, 1975. He returned to host again in 1984. Since then, Carlin has played a number of roles in various TV shows and feature films, while continuing to perform stand-up comedy specials for the cable network HBO.

---

11. When did *Hockey Night in Canada* make its television premiere?

a. 1973

b. 1957

c. 1952

d. 1946

During the 1994 interview, Rome repeatedly called Everett "Chris"—after female tennis player Chris Evert—alluding to Everett's reputation of shying away from hits. Everett warned Rome against doing it again, and when Rome repeated the insult, the quarterback charged him, overturning a table and knocking Rome down.

---

11. What superhero series starred a pre-*Dallas* Patrick Duffy?

a. *The Man from U.N.C.L.E.*

b. *The Man from Glad*

c. *The Man from Atlantis*

d. *The Man from Smallville*

John Wesley Shipp starred as the DC Comics superhero with superhuman speed in this short-lived CBS series (1990–1991). Hamill, who played the Trickster, later reprised his role as the colorful supervillain on the animated series *Justice League Unlimited*. The role also led to his success as The Joker in *Batman: The Animated Series*.

---

11. On *Kukla, Fran and Ollie*, what was Ollie?

a. A frog

b. An alligator

c. A dragon

d. A dinosaur

An Australian band specializing in children's entertainment, The Wiggles includes Anthony Field, Greg Page, Murray Cook, and Jeff Fatt. The group became a huge hit in Australia in the early 1990s, and became popular in the US in the 2000s, with the US TV show *The Wiggles* premiering in 2002.

---

3. *American Idol* winner Kelly Clarkson is from:

a. Texas
b. Ohio
c. Maine
d. Idaho

GAME 6 Q2 ANSWER d
Oklahoma-born Carrie Marie Underwood won Season Four of *American Idol,* with Simon Cowell stating that she had the "it" factor. He must have been right, because Underwood's album *Some Hearts* hit #1 on the Billboard Top Country Albums soon after its release in November 2005, and has since been certified Triple Platinum.

3. What did Kramer say he would name his child if he ever had one?

a. Seven
b. Bosco
c. Cosmo
d. Isosceles

GAME 26 Q2 ANSWER c
Kramer and Newman pass Keith Hernandez in the parking lot after a disappointing Mets loss. When Newman calls him "pretty boy," Hernandez allegedly spits at Kramer. The spit ricochets and hits Newman. In the Magic Loogie sequence, Jerry parallels the *JFK* "laws of physics" to clear Hernandez—and implicate teammate Roger McDowell.

3. What was the name of Lacey's husband on *Cagney and Lacey*?

a. Harry
b. Harvey
c. Marvin
d. Barry

GAME 46 Q2 ANSWER d
The series' pilot aired on ABC in 1974 as *The Life and Times of Captain Barney Miller.* The only characters in the series who were also featured in the pilot were Hal Linden as Captain Barney Miller and Abe Vigoda as Detective Phillip Fish. In 1977, Abe Vigoda starred in a spinoff series called *Fish,* which lasted only one season.

3. How many versions of *The Mary Tyler Moore Show* theme song were used for the series?

a. Four
b. Three
c. Two
d. One

GAME 66 Q2 ANSWER a
"Boss of Me" is the name of the theme song from this clever FOX comedy that made teen actor Frankie Muniz into a star. In 2002, They Might Be Giants won a Grammy for it. A long-time alternative music favorite, They Might Be Giants also recorded all the music in every episode of the show's first two seasons.

GAME 15

10. Who was the very first guest host on *SNL*?

a. Rob Reiner
b. Lily Tomlin
c. George Carlin
d. Steve Martin

GAME 15 Q9 ANSWER c
Ball did not appear with ex-husband Arnaz when he hosted *SNL* in February 1976, but he sent Lucy his love on the air at the end of the show. Norman Lear, producer of such classic '70s TV shows as *All in the Family* and *The Jeffersons*, hosted the show in September 1976. Milton Berle hosted in April 1979.

GAME 35

10. Which former NFL passer attacked ESPN host Jim Rome during an on-air confrontation?

a. Bernie Kosar
b. Jim Everett
c. Boomer Esiason
d. Jim Kelly

GAME 35 Q9 ANSWER a
From 1987 to 2005, *Primetime* aired every Sunday night during the NFL football season, with Berman and Jackson recapping Sunday afternoon's NFL games through highlights, statistics, and commentary. The show was designed to provide greater depth of analysis than that offered by shows which present only scoring highlights.

GAME 55

10. On which series did Mark Hamill play a villain named Trickster?

a. *Spider-man*
b. *The Flash*
c. *Enterprise*
d. *V*

GAME 55 Q9 ANSWER b
He was also "faster than a speeding bullet" and "able to leap tall buildings in a single bound." Actor George Reeve played the mild-mannered reporter, and performed most of the athletic-challenging stunts (he swung through windows, jumped from great heights, and worked on wires to create flying scenes). The classic series ran from 1952 to 1958.

GAME 75

10. What country gave us The Wiggles?

a. USA
b. Australia
c. Canada
d. New Zealand

GAME 75 Q9 ANSWER a
Running from 1984 to 1993, *Kids Incorporated* revolved around a group of children and teenagers who had their own rock group—Kids Incorporated. Playing Robin, Jennifer Love Hewitt was a member of the cast from 1989 to 1991. Four years later, she won a role on the successful TV drama *Party of Five*.

4. Of whom did Ryan Seacrest say, "He actually tries to get under your skin"?

a. Ruben Studdard
b. Randy Jackson
c. Simon Cowell
d. Clay Aiken

GAME 6 Q3 ANSWER a
Kelly Brianne Clarkson was born on April 24, 1982 in Fort Worth, Texas, and grew up in Burleson, Texas. Her life was changed when a middle school teacher overheard Clarkson singing in a hallway, and persuaded her to audition for the school choir. She appeared in several high school musicals as well.

4. Which Hollywood movie-makers cowrote *Seinfeld's* "The Virgin" episode?

a. Abrahams & Zucker
b. The Coen Brothers
c. The Hughes Brothers
d. The Farrelly Brothers

GAME 26 Q3 ANSWER d
Seven is the name George planned to give his future child. Unfortunately, his fiancé, Susan, mentioned it to her cousin, who then (according to an irate George) "stole" the name for her baby. Bosco is George's pin code for the ATM machine. Cosmo, of course, is Kramer's first name.

4. "In a moment, a result of that trial" was a common line on which cop show?

a. *The Blue Knight*
b. *Police Story*
c. *The F.B.I.*
d. *Dragnet*

GAME 46 Q3 ANSWER b
This series ran from 1982 to 1988 and teamed up two very different women as NYC police detectives—the single, career-driven Christine Cagney (Sharon Gless) and the married working mother Mary Beth Lacey (Tyne Daly). For their roles, Daly won Best Actress Emmys in 1983, 1984, 1985, and 1988, while Gless earned them in 1986 and 1987.

4. Which TV theme song was *not* written by Oscar-winning composer John Williams?

a. *Land of the Giants*
b. *Lost in Space*
c. *The Man From U.N.C.L.E.*
d. *Amazing Stories*

GAME 66 Q3 ANSWER c
The show's theme song, "Love Is All Around," was written and sung by singer/songwriter Sonny Curtis. In the show's first season (1970–1971), the song's opening lyric asked, "How will you make it on your own?" By the second season, the lyric had been changed to "Who can turn the world on with her smile?"

9. Which of the following TV legends never hosted *SNL*?

a. Desi Arnaz
b. Norman Lear
c. Lucille Ball
d. Milton Berle

GAME 15 Q8 ANSWER c
Carvey based the character on a composite of women from his hometown church in San Carlos, California. There was quite a stir in 1987 when actor Sean Penn, married to Madonna at the time, appeared on the show. The Church Lady character took Madonna to task for blasphemy. Penn responded by punching Church Lady in the face!

---

9. What former NFL player was Chris Berman's partner on ESPN's *NFL Primetime* for nearly two decades?

a. Tom Jackson
b. Deacon Jones
c. Ahmad Rashad
d. Joe Theismann

GAME 35 Q8 ANSWER d
Set against the backdrop of the fictional World Championship of Poker, this 2005 miniseries starred Michael Madsen as legendary gambler Don "The Matador" Everest. The title of the show referred to being "on tilt"—poker jargon for allowing stress to interfere with poker-playing judgment.

---

9. On *The Adventures of Superman*, the "man of steel" is more powerful than a:

a. Jet engine
b. Locomotive
c. Steamship
d. Tornado

GAME 55 Q8 ANSWER d
Daughter of the Gotham City police commissioner, Barbara Gordon was a librarian by day. Her crime-fighting career began after she stopped a kidnapping attempt on Bruce Wayne (Adam West). As Batgirl, actress Yvonne Joyce Craig was credited for paving the way for other TV heroines in the years that followed.

---

9. On which children's show did Jennifer Love Hewitt made her first TV appearance?

a. *Kids Incorporated*
b. *Sesame Street*
c. *Romper Room*
d. *Mickey Mouse Club*

GAME 75 Q8 ANSWER a
From 1952 to 1956, Frances Rappaport Horwich hosted *Miss Frances' Ding Dong School*—a series that was hugely popular with preschoolers. In addition to being known for her uncompromising principles, Miss Frances has been credited with being the first children's show host to speak directly to her viewers as if they were in the room with her.

---

5. For what arena band was Randy Jackson a temporary bassist?

a. Cheap Trick
b. Talking Heads
c. The B-52's
d. Journey

GAME 69 Q4 ANSWER c
Cowell has become infamous for his blunt, controversial, and just plain rude criticism of *American Idol* contestants. In fact, on August 27, 2006, Cowell was nearly booed off the stage at the Emmy Awards, indicating the disrespect earned by his behavior.

5. What's the name of the Bubble Boy, who appeared in Season Four of *Seinfeld*?

a. Harold
b. Donald
c. Ronald
d. Robert

GAME 26 Q4 ANSWER d
Hailing from Providence, Rhode Island, Bobby and Peter Farrelly scored their first writing credit with this 1992 Seinfeld episode. Their first film, the 1994 commercial hit *Dumb and Dumber,* was followed by a string of box-office successes, including *Kingpin, Outside Providence, There's Something About Mary,* and *Shallow Hal.*

5. What was the nickname of Angie Dickinson's character on *Police Woman?*

a. Cookie
b. Pepper
c. Honey
d. Foxy

GAME 46 Q4 ANSWER d
Dragnet started out as a radio program on NBC in 1949. Because of his fondness for old-time radio, actor/producer Jack Webb (aka Joe Friday) kept the radio version of the show going until 1957. Webb's first *Dragnet* TV series ran from 1952 to 1959, followed by a second series from 1967 to 1970.

5. Quincy Jones composed the theme song for which popular TV show?

a. *Sanford and Son*
b. *The Jeffersons*
c. *Good Times*
d. *In Living Color*

GAME 66 Q4 ANSWER c
Most people who know Williams' rousing theme songs from movies like *Star Wars* and *Raiders of the Lost Ark* don't realize that he got his start in the 1960s writing TV music for producer Irwin Allen. But that's what he did—as did the Oscar-winning film composer Jerry Goldsmith, who wrote the theme for *The Man From U.N.C.L.E.*

GAME 15

8. Which *SNL* character was played by Dana Carvey?

a. Stewart Smalley

b. Goat Boy

c. Church Lady

d. Mango

GAME 15 Q7 ANSWER a
Although she later went on to produce several films for Woody Allen, Doumanian's tenure with *SNL* lasted only one season. NBC executive Dick Ebersol then produced the show from 1981 to 1985, at which point Lorne Michaels returned. One good thing that Doumanian brought to *SNL* was Eddie Murphy.

GAME 35

8. Who played the lead role of Don Everest on ESPN's poker drama series *Tilt*?

a. Bart "Lowball" Rogers

b. Eddie Towne

c. Clark Marcellin

d. Michael Madsen

GAME 35 Q7 ANSWER a
ABC's *Sports Night* concerned a fictional sports news show and the people who worked there. Huffman played producer Dana Whitaker while Robert Guillaume played managing editor Isaac Jaffe; Peter Krause, anchor Casey McCall; Josh Charles, anchor Dan Rydell; and Sabrina Lloyd, senior associate producer Natalie Hurley.

GAME 55

8. Who was Batgirls' father on TV's *Batman*?

a. The Joker

b. Alfred the Butler

c. Batman

d. Commissioner Gordon

GAME 55 Q7 ANSWER b
When Clark's (Tom Welling) best childhood friend Pete (Sam Jones, III) discovers the spacecraft that had been in the Kent's storm cellar, Clark tells him about his powers. Pete starts feeling inferior to Clark and becomes jealous of his new friendships with Chloe and Lex. At the end of the third season, Pete's character was written out of the series.

GAME 75

8. Which children's show featured "Miss Frances"?

a. *Ding Dong School*

b. *Sesame Street*

c. *Mr. Rogers*

d. *Wonderama*

GAME 75 Q7 ANSWER c
Shari Lewis learned ventriloquism as a child, and in 1953, began hosting a local children's show in New York. Lewis graduated to network TV in 1960 as host and puppeteer of *The Shari Lewis Show*. Of all Lewis's puppets, it is probably Lamb Chop—a feisty little sheep—who is best remembered by those who grew up watching the show.

6. What *American Idol* contestant was charged with a misdemeanor after a food fight?

a. Bo Bice

b. Corey Clark

c. Scott Savol

d. Justin Guarini

GAME 6 Q5 ANSWER d
Although best known as an *American Idol* judge, Randall Matthew Jackson began playing professionally when he was seventeen years old. In addition to his time with Journey, Jackson has played with Billy Joel, Billy Cobham, Clarence "Gatemouth" Brown, Blue Oyster Cult, and Bob Dylan.

6. What does *Seinfeld's* George do immediately after Susan's funeral?

a. Goes to Monk's Café

b. Steals back the marble rye

c. Asks out Marisa Tomei

d. Double dips a chip

GAME 26 Q5 ANSWER b
The Bubble Boy's father asks Jerry to visit "my son Donald." During a game of Trivial Pursuit, the sick boy, who turns out to be rude and nasty, gets into a fight with George over a typo on the game card—"Moors," the correct answer, appeared as "Moops." (Supposedly, it was an actual error that appeared in a home version of *Jeopardy!*)

6. In which city did *Homicide: Life on the Street* take place?

a. *Philadelphia*

b. *St. Louis*

c. *Baltimore*

d. *Chicago*

GAME 46 Q5 ANSWER b
The pilot for this show aired in 1973 as an episode on the NBC anthology series *Police Story*. In the pilot, Dickinson's character's name is Lisa Beaumont, but her name was changed to Sergeant "Pepper" Anderson for the series. During the series, which ran from 1974 to 1978, Sergeant Anderson's real name was given only once as Leanne.

6. Which of these ABC shows used a Beatles song as its theme?

a. *Roseanne*

b. *Grace Under Fire*

c. *Thirtysomething*

d. *The Wonder Years*

GAME 66 Q5 ANSWER a
Jones also wrote the themes for Bill Cosby's first sitcom *The Bill Cosby Show* in 1969 and the Raymond Burr court drama *Ironside* in 1967. The year 1968 saw Jones receive an Oscar nomination for the film score of *In Cold Blood*. In the 1990s, Jones was a producer of Will Smith's *The Fresh Prince of Bel-Air*.

GAME 15

7. When Lorne Michaels left SNL in 1979, who took over as producer?

a. Jean Doumanian
b. Michael O'Donoghue
c. Dick Ebersol
d. Jon Landis

GAME 15 Q6 ANSWER b
A master mimic on *SNL*, Murphy also portrayed Stevie Wonder opposite Joe Piscopo's Frank Sinatra, as well as soul singer James Brown in a classic skit called "Celebrity Hot Tub Party." Although he hasn't portrayed the late Rick James on *SNL*, Eddie Murphy did record a hit song with him in 1985 called "Party All the Time."

GAME 35

7. Who starred in the 1998–2000 series *Sports Night*?

a. Felicity Huffman
b. Teri Hatcher
c. Marcia Cross
d. Eva Longoria

GAME 35 Q6 ANSWER c
The hoops drama ran on CBS from 1978 to 1981, starring Ken Howard as a white ex-NBA basketball player who is hired to coach a mostly black and Hispanic urban high school team. *The White Shadow* has been credited as being the first prime-time TV drama with a predominantly black cast.

GAME 55

7. In *Smallville*, who was the first of Clark's friends to discover his powers?

a. Whitney Fordman
b. Pete Ross
c. Chloe Sullivan
d. Lana Lang

GAME 55 Q6 ANSWER c
Winger appeared in only three episodes as Drusilla, the Amazon teenage sister of Wonder Woman. Audiences first took notice of Winger as John Travolta's wife in *Urban Cowboy*. Shortly after, she became the voice of ET. Winger has received Best Actress Oscar nominations for *An Officer and a Gentleman*, *Terms of Endearment*, and *Shadowlands*.

GAME 75

7. Which series featured the puppets Hush Puppy, Charlie Horse, and Lamb Chop?

a. *Andy's Gang*
b. *Howdy Doody*
c. *The Shari Lewis Show*
d. *Sesame Street*

GAME 75 Q6 ANSWER d
Nickelodeon's *The Angry Beavers* concerned the two beaver brothers, who left their parents' home to become bachelors in the forest. The show debuted in 1997 and ended in 2001 amid controversy generated by a final episode that violated Nickelodeon rules, and therefore, was never aired.

7. The first guest judge on *American Idol 4* was the vocalist for what pop/rock group?

a. Restless Heart

b. Kool & The Gang

c. Spandau Ballet

d. Sugar Ray

Before the food fight incident, which also involved record company manager Laura Kathleen Troy, Clark made waves by claiming he had had an affair with judge Paula Abdul. Despite Abdul's alleged coaching of Clark, he was removed from the show for failing to disclose his criminal arrest history.

---

7. Who is the first to lose in the famous *Seinfeld* "Contest" episode?

a. Jerry

b. George

c. Elaine

d. Kramer

This Season Seven finale begins with George trying to think of a way out of his engagement to Susan. Later in the episode, Susan dies from licking the poison glue on her wedding invitations. With his newfound freedom, George decides to try once again to go out with Marisa Tomei. Many fans of the show felt the episode was in poor taste.

---

7. What series debuted Leslie Nielsen's *Naked Gun* character, Frank Drebin?

a. *Adam-12*

b. *Night Court*

c. *Police Squad!*

d. *Precinct 87*

Baltimore native and notable screenwriter/actor/director Barry Levinson was executive producer of this '90s NBC series, which focused on the homicide unit of the Baltimore Police Department. Baltimore was also the setting for a series of films written and directed by Levinson—Oscar-nominated *Diner, Tin Men, Avalon,* and *Liberty Heights.*

---

7. On which TV series did the main characters perform the theme song?

a. *All in the Family*

b. *Good Times*

c. *Growing Pains*

d. *Roseanne*

Telling the story of 1960s kid Kevin Arnold (Fred Savage), this nostalgic ABC Baby Boomer sitcom featured Joe Cocker's famous 1968 cover version of "With a Little Help From My Friends" from *Sgt. Pepper's Lonely Hearts Club Band.* The show's episodes also featured Beatles songs like "Blackbird" and "Your Mother Should Know."

6. Of the following, who was *not* portrayed by Eddie Murphy on *SNL*?

a. Muhammad Ali
b. Rick James
c. Michael Jackson
d. Jesse Jackson

Novello played Father Sarducci on *SNL* from 1977 to 1980, and from 1985 to 1986. The character caused him some trouble, though; in 1981, while dressed as Father Sarducci, Novello was arrested at the Vatican for "impersonating a priest" (charges were later dropped). In 1990, Novello had a small role in *The Godfather, Part III*.

---

6. What was the coach's name in *The White Shadow*?

a. Tim Cavanaugh
b. Phil Jeffers
c. Ken Reeves
d. Jim Willis

Kerrigan had been attacked by cohorts of figure skating rival Tonya Harding, who clubbed the skater in the knee. Kerrigan nonetheless competed, winning a silver medal while the gold went to Oksana Baiul and Harding ended up in eighth place. The broadcast of the show was the sixth highest-rated program in US television history.

---

6. Who played Wonder Woman's younger sister?

a. Holly Hunter
b. Farrah Fawcett
c. Debra Winger
d. Phoebe Cates

When Xena (Lucy Lawless) was a villain-ous warlord (before she was reformed), she had her army torch Callisto's village, killing her family. A child at the time, the traumatized Callisto (Hudson Leick) be-came obsessed with getting revenge on Xena. The series, a historical fantasy that aired from 1995 to 2000, was filmed in New Zealand.

---

6. *The Angry _____* focused on brothers Norbert and Daggett.

a. Tigers
b. Lynxes
c. Wolverines
d. Beavers

Playing a character called "Easy Read-er," Morgan Freeman appeared on *The Electric Company* from 1971 through 1976—years before he began his work in films. He later said that he remained on the children's show "three years too long," and should have begun "serious work" in films much sooner.

8. What rap singer was a guest judge on the Cleveland audition stop of *American Idol 4*?

a. LL Cool J

b. Tone Loc

c. Eminem

d. Puff Daddy

GAME 6 Q7 ANSWER d
Besides being frontman for Sugar Ray, the charismatic and personable Mark McGrath has appeared on a variety of television programs, from award shows to series like *Las Vegas, North Shore,* and *Law & Order: SVU*. Then in 2004, he began hosting *Extra,* an Entertainment Television news program

---

8. Which of the following names was *not* used by Kramer?

a. Art Vandelay

b. Dr. Martin van Nostrand

c. H.E. Pennypacker

d. Assman

GAME 26 Q7 ANSWER d
When George's mother catches him doing "you know," he swears he'll stop. This prompts a contest between the four friends to see who can go the longest without doing "you know." Kramer spies a naked girl in the window across from Jerry's apartment. He leaves Jerry's, returns in a few minutes, and slams down his money exclaiming, "I'm out!"

---

8. In which cop drama did William Shatner star?

a. *Renegade*

b. *T.J. Hooker*

c. *Starsky & Hutch*

d. *Cop Rock*

GAME 46 Q7 ANSWER c
Following the success of their 1980 movie *Airplane!,* producers Jim Abrahams and brothers David and Jerry Zucker created this cop spoof series for NBC in 1982. Despite critical acclaim, it was canceled after only six episodes. In 1988, Nielsen's clueless Detective Drebin finally became a big hit in the first of three *Naked Gun* movies.

---

8. Which 1980s sitcom featured Billy Joel's hit "My Life" as its theme song?

a. *Perfect Strangers*

b. *Bosom Buddies*

c. *Working Stiffs*

d. *Buffalo Bill*

GAME 66 Q7 ANSWER a
As the Bunkers, Jean Stapleton and Carroll O'Connor sang "Those Were the Days" during the opening credits to this classic sitcom. The show's closing instrumental theme, "Remembering You," was co-written by O'Connor. Another show that had the main characters sing its theme song was *Green Acres,* starring Eddie Albert and Eva Gabor.

GAME 15

5. Who is the actor behind the *SNL* character Father Guido Sarducci?

a. Chris Elliott

b. Rich Hall

c. Don Novello

d. Tim Meadows

GAME 15 Q4 ANSWER c

Before appearing from 1990 to 1992 on his brother Keenan Ivory Wayans' hit show *In Living Color*, Damon Wayans was on *SNL* during the 1985–1986 season. He was fired from the show in 1986 after a creative disagreement with producer Lorne Michaels. Despite this incident, Wayans was invited back to host the show in 1995.

GAME 35

5. In the 1994 Lillehammer Olympics, which figure skater stole the media show due to a knee injury?

a. Oksana Baiul

b. Nancy Kerrigan

c. Katarina Witt

d. Kristi Yamaguchi

GAME 35 Q4 ANSWER a

At the age of fifty-five, male champion Bobby Riggs challenged twenty-nine-year-old female champion Billie Jean King to a tennis match, saying that he would win because he was male, and therefore had superior strength. On September 20, 1973, the players got prime-time coverage as King beat Riggs in three straight sets.

GAME 55

5. On *Xena: Warrior Princess*, what did Xena do to Callisto to make her an enemy?

a. Killed her husband

b. Married her brother

c. Burned her village

d. Stole her birthright

GAME 55 Q4 ANSWER b

Burgess Meredith played the evil Penguin, whose real name was Oswald Chesterfield Cobblepot. Most actors enjoyed appearing on the show because they were able to overact. Other popular evildoers were The Joker (Cesar Romero), King Tut (Victor Buono), and Egghead (Vincent Price). ABC aired two episodes a week for most of its run (1966–1968).

GAME 75

5. Which Academy Award nominee was a regular on *The Electric Company*?

a. Morgan Freeman

b. Thomas Haden Church

c. Alan Alda

d. Clive Owen

GAME 75 Q4 ANSWER b

Produced by Jay Ward and Bill Scott, who also produced *The Rocky and Bullwinkle Show*, *George of the Jungle* ran from 1967 to 1970 on ABC. Designed as a parody of Tarzan, the show featured a dim-witted yet kind "ape man" who—when he wasn't swinging face-first into trees—was often called upon to save his jungle friends.

GAME 6

9. Which *American Idol* winner admitted to being illiterate?

a. Carrie Underwood

b. Fantasia Barrino

c. Ruben Studdard

d. Kelly Clarkson

GAME 6 Q8 ANSWER a

Born James Todd Smith III, LL Cool J ("Ladies Love Cool James") is known for both romantic ballads like "I Need Love" and hardcore rap such as "Mama Said Knock You Out." When his 1984 release "I Need a Beat" became the first hit record for Def Jam Recordings, the artist dropped out of school to record *Radio*.

GAME 26

9. On *Seinfeld*, Susan loses her job at NBC because George:

a. Kisses her at a meeting

b. Sabotages her ideas

c. Is late for a meeeting

d. Tries to negotiate her contract

GAME 26 Q8 ANSWER a

Once, as H.E. Pennypacker, Kramer faked interest in buying an apartment so he could use the bathroom. As Dr. van Nostrand, he tried to erase some negative comments from Elaine's medical chart. And after he received license plates that were issued to him in error, he was sometimes referred to as Assman. (Art Vandelay was George's alter ego.)

GAME 46

9. What campy ABC classic had the tagline "One Black, One White, One Blonde?"

a. *The Rookies*

b. *I Spy*

c. *Starsky & Hutch*

d. *The Mod Squad*

GAME 46 Q8 ANSWER b

When NBC canceled *Star Trek* in 1969, Shatner's career took a nosedive—he found himself acting in low-budget klinkers like the 1977 horror movie *Kingdom of the Spiders*. By 1982, however, the *Star Trek* movies made him a star again and producer Aaron Spelling invited him to play Sergeant Thomas Jefferson "TJ" Hooker on ABC.

GAME 66

9. "Suicide Is Painless" was the theme song for what popular TV show?

a. *Three's Company*

b. *M*A*S*H*

c. *Bewitched*

d. *Fawlty Towers*

GAME 66 Q8 ANSWER b

Starring Peter Scolari and a pre-Oscar Tom Hanks, this popular sitcom featured a version of "My Life" that was sung by the cast. The show debuted on ABC in 1980 and was canceled in 1982. In 1984, after Hanks had achieved movie-star fame in the Ron Howard movie *Splash*, NBC began airing reruns of the show.

---

4. Which brothers have not *both* made appearances on *SNL*?

a. John & Jim Belushi

b. Bill & Brian-Doyle Murray

c. Damon & Marlon Wayans

d. Dan & Peter Aykroyd

GAME 15 Q3 ANSWER d
In a parody of the 1975 slavery film *Mandingo*, Simpson and Bill Murray made history by locking lips in TV's first interracial kiss between two men. When introducing the kiss as an "*SNL* Moment" on NBC's 15th Anniversary show in 1990, Simpson joked that the black man on that show was, in fact, fellow football star Walter Payton.

4. Which male tennis player competed in the 1973 primetime "battle of the sexes" match?

a. Bobby Riggs

b. Vitas Gerulaitis

c. Pancho Gonzales

d. John Newcombe

GAME 35 Q3 ANSWER d
Since the late 1970s, the "agony of defeat" has been illustrated by Vinko Bogataj's crash of March 21, 1970. Due to bad course conditions, Bogataj had tried to stop his ski jump, but instead, the Slovenian skier lost his balance, rocketed out of control, and crashed through a fence. Amazingly, his injuries were only minor.

4. Which villain did Burgess Meredith play on TV's *Batman*?

a. The Joker

b. The Penguin

c. King Tut

d. Egghead

GAME 55 Q3 ANSWER a
Teacher Ralph Hinkley (William Katt) is visited by aliens, who give him the red suit. Although wearing the suit gives him super powers to fight crime, clumsy Ralph loses the instruction manual and must figure out how to use the suit on his own. Robert Culp and Connie Sellecca also starred in this ABC drama-comedy, which aired from 1981 to 1983.

4. Which of these characters is *not* an animal?

a. Marmaduke

b. George of the Jungle

c. Gentle Ben

d. Quick Draw McGraw

GAME 75 Q3 ANSWER b
The brainchild of Bob Keeshan—the original Clarabell on *Howdy Doody*—*Captain Kangaroo* debuted in 1955 and ran on CBS for almost thirty years before going into syndicated reruns. The show had a loose structure, built around life in the "Treasure House." Besides creating the show, Keeshan also played the title character.

10. According to his debut album's title, *American Idol* star Bo Bice is *The Real* ____.

a. Winner
b. McCoy
c. Thing
d. Deal

Fantasia Barrino admitted to being functionally illiterate in her 2005 memoir *Life Is Not a Fairy Tale*, the *New York Times* Best Seller that was dictated by Barrino to a freelance writer. The R&B singer said that because of her problem, she had signed record deals and contracts that she was unable to read and, therefore, understand.

10. Where did Kramer work before *Seinfeld* began?

a. Macy's, as a store Santa
b. Schnitzer's Deli
c. Poppie's Pizza Parlor
d. H&H Bagels

George and Jerry were at the meeting to pitch the sitcom *Jerry* to the NBC execs when George gave her a kiss. Although George was a less-than-perfect fiancé, Susan *really* hated Kramer for many reasons—he threw up on her after drinking bad milk, he burned down her father's cabin, and after she became a lesbian, he stole her girlfriend.

10. Which NY police detective wore a cowboy hat and a sheepskin jacket?

a. Cannon
b. Kojak
c. McCloud
d. Baretta

The Mod Squad debuted on ABC in 1968. At a time when race relations, women's liberation, and the generation gap were tearing at the fabric of American society, this show incorporated elements of hip counterculture into the mainstream. The show was nominated for an Emmy in 1970, and stayed on the air until August 1973.

10. "Without Us" was the theme song for which 1980s NBC sitcom?

a. *Alf*
b. *Gimme a Break!*
c. *Cheers*
d. *Family Ties*

This song was first written for Robert Altman's 1969 movie *MASH* by noted composer John Mandel and Altman's fourteen-year-old son Mike, who wrote the lyrics. Meant to convey the madness of war (especially the Vietnam War), the lyrics were deemed too political for TV and an instrumental version was used instead.

GAME 15

3. Which *SNL* host kissed Bill Murray on the lips?

a. Robert Klein

b. Milton Berle

c. Anthony Perkins

d. OJ Simpson

GAME 15 Q2 ANSWER b

This smarmy Aykroyd character appeared on the show in March 1979 when Margot Kidder was the guest host. In 1999, the Fred Garvin idea was further developed by *SNL* actor Rob Schneider into his wildly popular *Deuce Bigalow: Male Gigolo* movies.

GAME 35

3. Since the late 1970s, what shot has shown the "agony of defeat" in the opening of *Wide World of Sports*?

a. Motorcyclist

b. Figure skater

c. Football player

d. Ski jumper

GAME 35 Q2 ANSWER a

When *Monday Night Football* premiered on ABC in 1970, the first broadcasting team included controversial newscaster Howard Cosell, veteran football play-by-play man Keith Jackson, and former Dallas Cowboy quarterback Don Meredith. ABC had wanted Frank Gifford as the third member of the trio, but Gifford was under contract to CBS.

GAME 55

3. What gave Ralph of *The Greatest American Hero* his super powers?

a. Red suit

b. Red boots

c. Red belt

d. Red cape

GAME 55 Q2 ANSWER c

The gifted artist, played by Santiago Cabrera, is a junkie who is the creator of the comic book *9th Wonders.* When the NBC show premiered in fall of 2006, it attracted 14.3 million viewers overall—the highest rating for any NBC drama premiere since *Crossing Jordan* in September of 2001.

GAME 75

3. What kids show, hosted by Robert James Keeshan, started its long run in 1955?

a. *Mickey Mouse Club*

b. *Captain Kangaroo*

c. *Mr. Wizard*

d. *Wonderama*

GAME 75 Q2 ANSWER a

Based on the children's books written and illustrated by Marc Brown, *Arthur* premiered in 1996. An eight-year-old anthropomorphic aardvark, Arthur lives in the fictitious town of Elwood City, attends Elwood Elementary School, and deals with problems common to all children of that age.

---

11. What feature film satirizes the *American Idol* tv show?

a. *American Idiot*

b. *American Beauty*

c. *American Pimp*

d. *American Dreamz*

GAME 6 Q10 ANSWER c
Bice was runner-up to Carrie Underwood in the 2005 *Idol* competition. His solo debut album *The Real Thing,* released in December 2005, opened at #4, making Bice one of the few American Idol non-winners to enjoy success. His nickname Bo is actually short for "Humphrey Bogart"—his grandmother's name for him when he was a child.

11. When George worked at Kruger Industries, what nickname did he want?

a. Art

b. Buck Naked

c. T-Bone

d. Biff

GAME 26 Q10 ANSWER d
Kramer was perpetually unemployed after going on strike from H&H Bagels. Throughout the series, he pursued a number of jobs and foolish money-making schemes, which were mostly his own ideas. A cologne that smelled like the beach, a make-your-own-pizza business, and "The Real Peterman Reality Bus Tour" were just a few.

11. Which detective was known for saying, "Book 'em, Danno, Murder One"?

a. Steve McGarrett

b. Frank Cannon

c. Barney Miller

d. Robert Ironside

GAME 46 Q10 ANSWER c
Dennis Weaver played Deputy US Marshal Sam McCloud, a New Mexico marshal on loan to New York. From 1970 to 1977, NBC presented episodes of *McCloud* along with *McMillan and Wife* and *Columbo* as part of its weekly *NBC Mystery Movie* series. As McCloud, Weaver was nominated for Best Actor Emmys in 1974 and 1975.

11. How many different theme songs were used for *The Drew Carey Show*?

a. One

b. Three

c. Five

d. Seven

GAME 66 Q10 ANSWER d
The theme was sung by Johnny Mathis and Deniece Williams. Speaking of the show's music, the song "At This Moment" became a #1 hit in 1986 when heard in the episode in which Alex P. Keaton (Michael J. Fox) falls in love with Ellen Reed (Tracy Pollan).

GAME 15

2. Which *SNL* cast member played Fred Garvin: Male Prostitute?

a. Chevy Chase
b. Dan Aykroyd
c. Eddie Murphy
d. Rob Schneider

GAME 15 Q1 ANSWER c
Bill Murray replaced Chevy Chase, who left *SNL* in 1976 after only one season with the show. Chase went on to star opposite Goldie Hawn in the 1978 feature film *Foul Play*. When he returned as guest host of *SNL* during the 1977–1978 season, it caused considerable tension, especially between Chase and Bill Murray.

GAME 35

2. Who was a member of *Monday Night Football's* first broadcasting team?

a. Don Meredith
b. Alex Karras
c. Frank Gifford
d. John Brodie

GAME 35 Q1 ANSWER c
Airing from 1989 to 1997, *Coach* starred Craig T. Nelson as Hayden Fox, coach of the Screaming Eagles, a Minnesota college football team. Jerry Van Dyke played befuddled assistant coach Luther Van Dam, and Shelley Fabares of *Donna Reed Show* fame was the head coach's wife, Christine Armstrong Fox.

GAME 55

2. What is Isaac Mendez's super power on *Heroes*?

a. Hears people's thoughts
b. Flies
c. Paints the future
d. Manipulates time

GAME 55 Q1 ANSWER a
Actress and former Miss World USA, Lynda Carter played the *DC Comics*-based superhero. She wore a belt that gave her tremendous strength, bracelets that could stop bullets, and a tiara that doubled as a weapon. Anyone entwined in Wonder Woman's golden lasso was magically forced to tell the truth. The series ran from 1976 to 1979.

GAME 75

2. *Arthur* features a little boy who is an:

a. Aardvark
b. Anteater
c. Antelope
d. Alligator

GAME 75 Q1 ANSWER d
Barney, a purple dinosaur, was created in 1987 by Sheryl Leach, who got the idea while looking for a fun and educational show for her son. Leach began by gathering a team to produce home videos—videos that were only modestly successful. Then in 1992, PBS started producing the *Barney & Friends* series, which met with great success.

12. Which *American Idol* star received dating advice from Dr. Phil in a 2006 CBS TV special?

a. Paula Abdul

b. Simon Cowell

c. Randy Jackson

d. Ryan Seacrest

In the 2006 film *American Dreamz*, Hugh Grant plays celebrity Martin Tweed, who hosts a top-rated TV talent show that gives average Americans their chance at stardom. The plot thickens when the White House Chief of Staff (Willem Dafoe) pushes the President (Dennis Quaid) into becoming a guest judge on the popular program.

12. Why was George fired from Pendant Publishing?

a. He never read anything

b. He slept under his desk

c. He had sex in the office

d. He altered the boss's photo

George told his coworkers that he wanted to be nicknamed T-Bone, but another employee got the name instead. Irate, George began flailing his arms like a monkey, so he was given the name KoKo. To get a new name, he hired a cleaning woman at work named CoCo. He was then re-nicknamed Gammy. Buck Naked was his "porn star" name choice.

12. Which of these cop shows was the first to appear on network TV?

a. *Naked City*

b. *Dragnet*

c. *Highway Patrol*

d. *Car 54, Where Are You?*

Appearing on CBS from 1968 to 1980, *Hawaii Five-O* starred Jack Lord as Steve McGarrett and James MacArthur as Danny "Danno" Williams. Nearly every episode of the show was filmed on location in Hawaii. The CBS series *Magnum, P.I.*, which premiered in 1980 and starred Tom Selleck, used several leftover sets from *Hawaii Five-O*.

12. Which of these TV theme songs uses the show title as its only lyric?

a. *Mary Hartman, Mary Hartman*

b. *Batman*

c. *Taxi*

d. *Rhoda*

ABC's *The Drew Carey Show* aired from 1995 to 2004. In the first season, the theme song was "Moon Over Parma" as sung by Drew Carey himself. By the second season, the show went with an old Top Ten hit from 1966 by The Vogues called "Five O'Clock World." The third season introduced a cover of the '70s rocker "Cleveland Rocks."

GAME 15	**1.** Of the following, who was *not* in the original *SNL* cast? **a.** John Belushi **b.** Dan Aykroyd **c.** Bill Murray **d.** Jane Curtin	The answer to this question is on: **page 154,** **top frame,** **right side.**
GAME 35	**1.** Who played assistant coach Luther Van Dam on the TV show *Coach*? **a.** Vincent Gardenia **b.** Tom Poston **c.** Jerry Van Dyke **d.** Harry Morgan	The answer to this question is on: **page 154,** **second frame,** **right side.**
GAME 55	**1.** How did Diana Prince transform herself into Wonder Woman? **a.** Spun in a circle **b.** Drank from a magic cup **c.** Slid down a pole **d.** Rubbed a silver ball	The answer to this question is on: **page 154,** **third frame,** **right side.**
GAME 75	**1.** "I Love You, You Love Me" is the theme song to which children's program? **a.** *Zoom* **b.** *Sesame Street* **c.** *Electric Company* **d.** *Barney & Friends*	The answer to this question is on: **page 154,** **bottom frame,** **right side.**

GAME 7

Monsters, Demons, and the Supernatural

*Turn to page 159
for the first question.*

Turn to page 159
for the first question.

In a special entitled "Love Smart" after Dr. Phil's best-selling book of the same name, Dr. Phil schooled Abdul on the rules of dating and gave her a pool of bachelors from which to choose. He then observed her behavior and, on *The Early Show,* discussed the "experiment" with Abdul and co-anchor Julie Chen.

GAME 27

Beverly Hills, 90210

*Turn to page 159
for the first question.*

Turn to page 159
for the first question.

When Elaine got George the job as a reader at Pendant, he began having sex with the cleaning woman there. He also gave Elaine a "slightly flawed" cashmere sweater as a thank you. Elaine saw the flaw and gave the sweater back to George. To keep the cleaning lady quiet, George gave it to her, but she also spotted the flaw. George was fired.

GAME 47

Westerns

*Turn to page 159
for the first question.*

Turn to page 159
for the first question.

This show starred a young Broderick Crawford in the role of Chief Dan Matthews. *Highway Patrol* aired from October 1955 to September 1959. It was syndicated nationwide by Ziv Television Programs, which produced dozens of popular television shows throughout the '50s, including *Sea Hunt* starring Lloyd Bridges.

GAME 67

Animation Favorites

*Turn to page 159
for the first question.*

Turn to page 159
for the first question.

The theme song *Mary Hartman, Mary Hartman* featured an orchestra and a woman's voice simply calling out the title character's name twice. The lyrics to the *Batman* theme included the word "Batman" and a bunch of "Na Nas;" and the one lyric in the *Rhoda* theme song was "La." The theme song for *Taxi* had no lyrics.

GAME 15

Saturday Night Live

Turn to page 156
for the first question.

GAME 14 Q12 ANSWER a
The 1987 CBS movie focused on Barrows, who ran a high-class escort service in New York City during the early 1980s. Daughter of radio ventriloquist Edgar Bergen, Candice Bergen earned five Emmy's for her comedic talents as the title character on *Murphy Brown*, which aired on CBS from 1988 to 1998.

GAME 35

Sports Shows

Turn to page 156
for the first question.

GAME 34 Q12 ANSWER c
Savannah Kinkirk is the name of Lucy Camden and Kevin Kinkirk's baby on the family drama *7th Heaven*. Since Savannah is the daughter of a minister Mom and a policeman Dad, it's pretty certain that she wouldn't act like those *Sex and the City* girls. By the way, the character missing from the listing is Miranda Hobbes.

GAME 55

Superheroes, Superheroines, & Villains

Turn to page 156
for the first question.

GAME 54 Q12 ANSWER a
After the first six years of the series, Richie (Ron Howard) and Ralph Malph (Donny Most) left the show. Their characters joined the Army and were immediately sent to Greenland. Howard became a successful director, whose works have included such films as *Splash, Cocoon, Apollo 13, A Beautiful Mind, Cinderella Man,* and *The DaVinci Code*.

GAME 75

Kid Stuff

Turn to page 156
for the first question.

GAME 74 Q12 ANSWER b
In this episode, George convinces Jerry that they should pretend to be the "O'Brien" who has a limo waiting for him at the airport. George passes himself off as O'Brien, while Jerry takes the name Dylan Murphy. O'Brien, however, is a famous (although never-before-seen) neo-Nazi leader and the limo is met by an angry mob of protestors.

GAME 7

1. On *The Munsters*, what was Grandpa's coffin on wheels called?

a. The Vamp-Mobile
b. The Monster-Coupe
c. Drag-u-la
d. Black Mariah

The answer to this question is on:

page 161, top frame, right side.

GAME 27

1. Who shared a beach apartment with Donna and Kelly on *Beverly Hills, 90210*?

a. Brandon Walsh
b. Steve Sanders
c. David Silver
d. Dylan McKay

The answer to this question is on:

page 161, second frame, right side.

GAME 47

1. Who was TV's first cowboy hero?

a. Hopalong Cassidy
b. Roy Rogers
c. Gene Autry
d. The Lone Ranger

The answer to this question is on:

page 161, third frame, right side.

GAME 67

1. Which series holds the record as the longest-running prime-time cartoon show?

a. *Scooby-Doo*
b. *The Flintstones*
c. *The Jetsons*
d. *The Simpsons*

The answer to this question is on:

page 161, bottom frame, right side.

GAME 14

12. Who played Sydney Biddle Barrows in *The Mayflower Madam*?

a. Candice Bergen
b. Jane Seymour
c. Jacqueline Bisset
d. Joan Collins

GAME 14 Q11 ANSWER a
This 1978 *ABC Afternoon Special* starring Arquette was based on the true story of Gabriel Grayson, who grew up in Philadelphia as the hearing son of deaf parents (Grayson made a brief cameo in the film). For the part, Arquette learned sign language, so she could really communicate with the deaf actors who played her parents.

GAME 34

12. Which female character was *not* part of the *Sex and the City* universe?

a. Samantha Jones
b. Carrie Bradshaw
c. Savannah Kinkirk
d. Charlotte York

GAME 34 Q11 ANSWER d
Francine Lawrence was her real name, but her surfing friends called her Gidget—short for "girl midget." Eighteen-year-old Sally Field, fresh from a Columbia acting workshop, beat out seventy-five other teenage girls for the role, which she played from 1965 to 1966, before moving on to *The Flying Nun*.

GAME 54

12. On *Happy Days*, which branch of the service did Richie join?

a. Army
b. Air Force
c. Navy
d. Marines

GAME 54 Q11 ANSWER a
Legendary home-run king Hank Aaron made a guest appearance as himself in a seventh-season episode of the show. When Mr. Cunningham decided to make a commercial to boost business, Aaron showed up unexpectedly during the dress rehearsal. Aaron is best known for breaking Babe Ruth's career home-run record of 714 with a total of 755 runs.

GAME 74

12. Pretending it's meant for them, George and Jerry get into whose limo at the airport?

a. A New York Yankee's
b. A neo-Nazi leader's
c. George Steinbrenner's
d. Jon Voight's

GAME 74 Q11 ANSWER c
In this final-season episode called "The Puerto Rican Day," the Seinfeld gang gets caught in the city traffic because of the Puerto Rican Day Parade. The show sparked a controversy among members of the Puerto Rican community, who were offended by the burning of their flag. As a result, this episode was kept from syndication until 2002.

GAME 7

2. In the *Star Trek* episode "The Devil in the Dark," what creature terrorizes a mining colony?

a. Horta
b. Flying Parasites
c. Tribbles
d. Salt Vampires

GAME 7 Q1 ANSWER c
Built by George Barris, Drag-u-la—which appeared in an episode entitled "Hot Rod Herman"—had a fiberglass body that was molded from an actual coffin resting on a dragster-type tube frame. Power was supplied by a Ford Mustang engine. Other features included a purple velvet interior, organ pipe exhausts, and an air scoop.

GAME 27

2. Which character did Hilary Swank play on *Beverly Hills, 90210*?

a. Emily Valentine
b. Carly Reynolds
c. Susan Keats
d. Clare Arnold

GAME 27 Q1 ANSWER c
During the group's college years at Cal U, David (Brian Austin Green) moved in with Donna (Tori Spelling) and Kelly (Jennie Garth) because he couldn't get on-campus housing. David was Kelly's stepbrother and Donna's on-again-off-again boyfriend. After *90210*, Green dropped his middle name and pursued an unsuccessful career as a rap artist.

GAME 47

2. Which Carradine family member played Wild Bill Hickok on HBO's *Deadwood*?

a. John
b. Keith
c. David
d. Robert

GAME 47 Q1 ANSWER a
Hopalong Cassidy first aired on NBC in June 1949. Actor William "Hoppy" Boyd, who made more than sixty Hopalong Cassidy films in the '30s and '40s, owned the TV rights to his movies. A keen businessman, Boyd made nearly a million dollars when NBC paid him to use portions of the films in the first episodes of the TV series.

GAME 67

2. Most versions of the *Bugs Bunny Show* began with a musical number starring Bugs and:

a. Porky Pig
b. Daffy Duck
c. Elmer Fudd
d. Sylvester the Cat

GAME 67 Q1 ANSWER d
Created by Matt Groening as a parody of the "Middle American" lifestyle, *The Simpsons* began in 1987 as animated shorts on *The Tracy Ullman Show*, and debuted as a full-fledged series in 1989 on the FOX Network. So successful was the new show that Ullman filed a lawsuit, demanding a share of the profits. She lost.

11. One of whose first starring roles was in the TV movie _Mom and Dad Can't Hear Me_?

a. Rosanna Arquette
b. Pam Dawber
c. Nancy McKeon
d. Dana Plato

Known to most TV viewers as _Gidget_ or _The Flying Nun,_ Sally Field won a well-earned Emmy for her intense portrayal of Sybil Dorsett—a woman with multiple-personality disorder. In 2001, she won a second Emmy for her supporting role on _ER_ as the bipolar mother of Dr. Abby Lockhart (Maura Tierney).

---

11. Francine Lawrence was the name of the teen featured in which series?

a. _The Donna Reed Show_
b. _Father Knows Best_
c. _Bachelor Father_
d. _Gidget_

In 1982, Helgenberger made her TV debut on _Ryan's Hope,_ where she stayed for four years. Her next major role was that of K.C. Koloski, the hooker with the heart of gold, on ABC's _China Beach_ (1988–1991). But she may be best known for her portrayal of Catherine Willows on _CSI: Crime Scene Investigation_—a role that began in 2000.

---

11. Which baseball great appeared in a _Happy Days_ episode?

a. Hank Aaron
b. Mickey Mantle
c. Carlton Fisk
d. Reggie Jackson

Richie's girlfriend Laurie Beth (Lynda Goodfriend) first appeared on the show in 1977. Interestingly, the series, which focused on Potsie and Richie during the first season, was almost canceled. But viewer interest in the Fonzie character was so strong that the writers changed their focus . . . and the show ran another ten years.

---

11. What national flag did Kramer accidentally burn on _Seinfeld_?

a. Israeli
b. American
c. Puerto Rican
d. Korean

George joins a reading group in the 1994 episode "The Couch" and is assigned this Truman Capote novella; but instead of reading the book, he decides to rent the movie. The movie, however, has already been taken out at the local video store. George tracks down the family that has it, and "annoys" them into letting him watch the movie with them.

---

3. Who played "The Demon with a Glass Hand" in *The Outer Limits*?

a. Edward Asner
b. John Considine
c. Robert Redford
d. Robert Culp

Like so many monsters, the Horta was misunderstood in this March 1967 episode. The Horta began killing the miners on planet Janus VI only when they unwittingly started breaking into her egg chamber and destroying her eggs. When Kirk and Spock learn this, they broker a peace.

3. *Beverly Hills, 90210* **twins Brandon and Brenda moved to California from which state?**

a. Wyoming
b. Minnesota
c. Alaska
d. Indiana

Swank's role as single mother Carly Reynolds lasted only one season (1997–1998). Being cut from the show allowed her to audition for the part of transgendered Nebraskan teen Brandon Teena in *Boys Don't Cry* (1999). The role, based on the true story of Nebraskan woman Teena Brandon, earned Swank her first Oscar—Best Actress in a Leading Role.

3. Which of these shows remains TV's longest-running Western?

a. *Bonanza*
b. *The Virginian*
c. *Gunsmoke*
d. *Wagon Train*

Keith isn't the only Carradine who appeared in Westerns. His father, John, played the cowboy villain in the 1939 classic John Ford film *Stagecoach*. In 1980, Keith appeared with brothers David and Robert in the Western *The Long Riders*. Keith also starred in the 1975 film *Nashville*, and wrote its Oscar-winning song "I'm Easy."

3. Who was *not* **a member of the Jetson family?**

a. Jill
b. Elroy
c. Judy
d. George

While Porky, Elmer, and all the other Bugs Bunny characters appeared in the opening sequence, it was Daffy Duck and Bugs himself who sang the Mack David and Jerry Livingston tune, "The Bugs Bunny Overture (This Is It!)." Then, after commercial breaks, the show would focus on Bugs standing between two lights.

10. What was the occupation of the title character in the 1976 TV movie *Sybil*?

a. Doctor
b. Substitute teacher
c. Salesgirl
d. Student

GAME 14 Q9 ANSWER b
Working with seven other producers, George Clooney arranged with CBS to have this 2000 remake of the 1964 film done as a live TV performance and shot in black-and-white. Clooney chose to shoot in black-and-white again when he directed his Oscar-nominated film *Good Night, and Good Luck,* starring David Strathairn as Edward R. Murrow.

---

10. Who played hooker K.C. Koloski on *China Beach*?

a. Dana Delaney
b. Marg Helgenberger
c. Nan Woods
d. Megan Gallagher

GAME 34 Q9 ANSWER a
Running from 1984 to 1989, the show starred Susan Saint James as Kate McArdle and Jane Curtain as Allie Lowell, friends who decided to share a Greenwich Village apartment after their marriages broke up. Kate's daughter was Emma, played by Ari Meyers, and Allie's kids were Chip (Frederick Koehler) and Jennie (Allison Smith).

---

10. Which character was *not* on *Happy Days* during the first season?

a. Lori Beth
b. Ralph
c. Joanie
d. Potsie

GAME 54 Q9 ANSWER d
When Arnold (Pat Morita) asks Fonzie (Henry Winkler) to be best man at his arranged marriage to Momo Okamoto (Nobu McCarthy), Fonzie doesn't seem excited. He then tells his friends about the curse—he'd been best man two times before, and both weddings were disasters. In spite of his fears, Fonzie dons a kimono and serves as Arnold's best man.

---

10. On *Seinfeld,* when George joins a reading group, which book is he assigned?

a. *The Grapes of Wrath*
b. *Gone With the Wind*
c. *Breakfast at Tiffany's*
d. *To Kill a Mockingbird*

GAME 74 Q9 ANSWER c
Jean-Paul (Jeremiah Birkett) had previously overslept during his Olympic event. Jerry, himself a high school runner, wanted to help Jean-Paul wake up on time for the marathon. Unfortunately, while Jean-Paul slept on Jerry's couch, Kramer's hot tub blew out the building's electrical power so the alarm clock never rang—and Jean-Paul overslept.

4. What body organ was *X-Files* killer Eugene Tooms fond of eating?

a. Liver

b. Heart

c. Brain

d. Kidney

GAME 7 Q3 ANSWER d
In this October 1964 episode, Culp plays a man without a memory, whose right hand, covered by a transparent material, is a speaking computer. The character seeks to discover who he is and why he is being pursued by humanoid aliens called the Kyben. Like many *Outer Limits* episodes, this one ends with a twist.

---

4. Which *Melrose Place* character also appeared on *Beverly Hills, 90210*?

a. Michael Mancini

b. Billy Campbell

c. Jake Hanson

d. Matt Fielding

GAME 27 Q3 ANSWER b
Born and raised in Minneapolis, Minnesota, the Walsh twins, played by Jason Priestly and Shannen Doherty, moved to Beverly Hills when their dad got a job promotion. The show catapulted the two unknowns to stardom. It also made household names of many other members of its cast, including Jennie Garth, Tori Spelling, and Luke Perry.

---

4. What is the title character's first name on *Dr. Quinn, Medicine Woman*?

a. Michaela

b. Edwina

c. Frederica

d. Roberta

GAME 47 Q3 ANSWER c
With 233 half-hour episodes and 400 hour episodes filmed, *Gunsmoke* ran on CBS for twenty years—from 1955 to 1975. Second to *Gunsmoke* was *Bonanza* with a fourteen-year run. *The Virginian* aired nine years, while *Wagon Train* ran eight. *Gunsmoke* featured a young Burt Reynolds who played blacksmith Quint Asper.

---

4. What animal did Wilma use as a vacuum cleaner on *The Flintstones*?

a. Anteater

b. Whooping crane

c. Baby elephant

d. Flamingo

GAME 67 Q3 ANSWER a
Anyone who can sing the *Jetsons* jingle knows that George was the dad, Jane was his wife, and their kids were Judy and Elroy. The Jetson household also included Astro the Dog, who sounded a lot like Scooby-Doo (Don Messick did both voices); and Rosie the Robot Maid, who appeared in only two episodes of the original '60s show.

GAME 14

9. Which actor was *not* cast in George Clooney's TV version of *Fail Safe*?

a. Richard Dreyfuss

b. David Strathairn

c. Hank Azaria

d. Don Cheadle

GAME 14 Q8 ANSWER c
Best known for playing tomboy Vada Sultenfuss in the 1991 feature film *My Girl*, actress Anna Chlumsky starred as Missy Chandler in this TV movie based on the true story of Melissa Weaver, a young girl who died of cancer. Missy's wish is to meet President Clinton before she dies—and by film's end, the girl's wish is granted.

GAME 34

9. What was the name of Kate's daughter on CBS's *Kate and Allie*?

a. Emma

b. Jennie

c. Tofana

d. Susan

GAME 34 Q8 ANSWER d
The first woman detective to be a central character in an American network show, Honey West was played by Anne Francis in a series that first aired in 1965—and was canceled in 1966. But viewers remember Honey's skill in karate and judo, her form-fitting cat suits, and her pet ocelot, Bruce.

GAME 54

9. According to Fonzie, what wedding event is his "Fonzarelli Curse"?

a. Dancing with the bride

b. Catching the garter

c. Kissing a bridesmaid

d. Serving as best man

GAME 54 Q8 ANSWER b
Joanie (Erin Moran) was called "Shortcake" by the Fonz (Henry Winkler); "Blue Eyes" by boyfriend Chachi Arcola (Scott Baio); and "Joans" by best friend Jenny Piccalo (Cathy Silver). Jenny's character, though spoken of often in the series, did not appear until 1980. Her father, played by real-life father, Phil Silvers, appeared in one episode.

GAME 74

9. On *Seinfeld*, what was the name of the Olympic runner who overslept for the NYC Marathon?

a. Jean-Luc

b. Jean Valjean

c. Jean-Paul

d. Jean-Pierre

GAME 74 Q8 ANSWER b
This 1980 hit song was first heard in an eighth-season episode called "The Bizarro Jerry" in which Kramer starts working in an office for no pay. The song was heard again in a later episode called "The Butter Shave" in which George pretends to have a physical disability so he can have use of a roomy handicapped bathroom.

---

5. In early episodes of *Angel*, what was the name of the demon who aided the title character?

a. Whistler

b. Doyle

c. Spike

d. Harmony

GAME 7 Q4 ANSWER a
In the show's September 1993 episode "Squeeze," Mulder and Scully meet Tooms—a genetic mutant who can fit his body through small spaces and who, in order to hibernate for thirty years, has to consume five human livers. The mutant proved so popular that he was brought back for the April 1994 episode "Tooms."

5. What was the name of the diner where the *90210* kids hung out?

a. Joe's Place

b. Rodeo Club

c. Peach Pit

d. The Max

GAME 27 Q4 ANSWER c
Actor Grant Show portrayed *Melrose Place's* hunky carpenter Jake Hanson. The character also appeared in two *90210* episodes as Dylan's older friend, who was hired to build a canopy for a wedding and who was briefly pursued by Kelly (Jennie Garth). Show's acting career began as a regular on the soap opera *Ryan's Hope*.

5. Who played Rowdy Yates on *Rawhide*?

a. Burt Reynolds

b. Clint Eastwood

c. Charles Bronson

d. Guy Madison

GAME 47 Q4 ANSWER a
This popular show explored the Old West through a female perspective. Its heroine, Dr. Michaela Quinn (played by one-time Bond girl Jane Seymour), proves her skills as a woman doctor in Colorado during the late 1800s. The show ran on CBS from 1993 to 1998, and was followed by two CBS movies in 1999 and 2001.

5. What does Hank Hill, the redneck dad on *King of the Hill*, sell?

a. Farm equipment

b. Used cars

c. Hunting gear

d. Propane gas

GAME 67 Q4 ANSWER c
The Flintstone family had all of life's "modern" conveniences; they were simply powered by animals. A hungry buzzard was the garbage disposal; a bird sat inside the instant camera, carving images on a stone tablet; a giant pterodactyl served as an airplane; and elevators were pulled up and down by brontosaurs.

8. In which 1997 CBS movie did President Bill Clinton appear?

a. *The Westing Game*

b. *Mandela & De Klerk*

c. *A Child's Wish*

d. *Weapons of Mass Distraction*

GAME 14 Q7 ANSWER b

Written by TV screenwriting legend Richard Matheson, this early Spielberg-directed flick focuses on a character named David Mann (Dennis Weaver) who is pursued by an evil tanker truck on a desert highway. To magnify the terror, the menacing driver of the truck is never seen. *Duel* was an ABC "Movie of the Week."

8. What exotic pet kept *Honey West* company?

a. A cobra

b. A wolf

c. A tarantula

d. An ocelot

GAME 34 Q7 ANSWER a

This spinoff of *Man From U.N.C.L.E.* aired on NBC for only one season (1966–1967). The show starred Stefanie Powers as agent April Dancer and Noel Harrison (Rex's son) as partner Mark Slate, with Leo G. Carroll as their superior, Alexander Waverly. April Dancer's name was suggested by Ian Fleming, the creator of James Bond.

8. What was *not* one of Joanie's nicknames on *Happy Days*?

a. Shortcake

b. Freckles

c. Blue Eyes

d. Joans

GAME 54 Q7 ANSWER a

Basketball-dribbling Chuck disappeared in the show's second season—and never reappeared. Creator Garry Marshall felt Fonzie was the only "older brother" Richie needed. In Marshall's autobiography, he said that whenever he was asked what happened to Chuck, he'd say, "He got a 12-year basketball scholarship to the University of Outer Mongolia."

8. Which Sheena Easton hit song is featured in two *Seinfeld* episodes?

a. "For Your Eyes Only"

b. "Morning Train (9 to 5)"

c. "Sugar Walls"

d. "Strut"

GAME 74 Q7 ANSWER d

Although this title is from the 1970 Edwin Starr song "War," Elaine passed Jerry's story along and offended Yuri Testikov, a Russian writer to whom she had been assigned as editor. This episode also found George pretending to be a marine biologist. As luck would have it, while walking along the beach, he is called upon to save a beached whale.

6. Jennifer Love Hewitt plays what character on *The Ghost Whisperer*?

a. Melinda Gordon
b. Sarah Reeves
c. Julie James
d. Brooke Figler

GAME 7 Q5 ANSWER b
Born to a human mother and a Brachen demon father in Dublin, Ireland, Allen Francis Doyle didn't realize his demonic abilities until he was twenty-one years old. One of his key abilities is to have pain-causing visions—often vague, usually of people in peril—supplied by The Powers That Be.

---

6. Which *90210* character was the adopted son of a TV star?

a. Steve Sanders
b. Dylan McKay
c. David Silver
d. Jesse Vasquez

GAME 27 Q5 ANSWER c
At the start of the show's ten-year run, the Peach Pit was the local diner owned by Nat Buccigio (Joe E. Tata). Brandon (Jason Priestly) worked there, serving up burgers, fries, and the best peach pie in town. During the show's fourth season, Steve Sanders (Ian Ziering) turned the Peach Pit into the After Dark—a dance club.

---

6. What does the title refer to in the miniseries *Lonesome Dove*?

a. A town
b. A ranch
c. An Apache Indian
d. A song

GAME 47 Q5 ANSWER b
Eastwood got his first big break with the part of Yates on this CBS series. Thinking ahead, Clint used summer breaks from the show to go to Europe and star in a trilogy of violent but popular "Spaghetti Western" movies from director Sergio Leone. By 1967, his "Man With No Name" character in these movies made him a world-famous star.

---

6. In the *Peabody's Improbable History* segment of *The Rocky and Bullwinkle Show*, Sherman was a pet:

a. Dog
b. Boy
c. Squirrel
d. Rabbit

GAME 67 Q5 ANSWER d
Hank Hill, an assistant manager at Strickland Propane, is the proud salesman of "propane and propane accessories." A well-meaning man, he is confused by modern trends, and seeks refuge in the joys of such tasks as car repair and yard work, the latter of which he sometimes does for his neighbors, as well for himself.

GAME 14

7. Which 1971 TV thriller starred Dennis Weaver?

a. *The Immortal*

b. *Duel*

c. *Night Stalker*

d. *When Michael Calls*

GAME 34

7. Who played *The Girl From U.N.C.L.E.*?

a. Stefanie Powers

b. Jill St. John

c. Diana Rigg

d. Linda Evans

GAME 54

7. On *Happy Days*, who was Richie's Cunningham's older brother?

a. Chuck

b. Charlie

c. Carl

d. Chas

GAME 74

7. On *Seinfeld*, Jerry told Elaine that the original title for *War and Peace* was:

a. *Non-negotiable Demands*

b. *Fight and Time Out*

c. *Tiff and Truce*

d. *War—What Is It Good For?*

GAME 14 Q6 ANSWER d
Based on the 1976 Bob Woodward/Carl Bernstein book of the same name, this film starred character actor Lane Smith as President Nixon and Theodore Bikel as Henry Kissinger. It was nominated for four Emmys and garnered a Golden Globe nod for Lane Smith. After suffering from a major stroke, President Nixon died on April 22, 1994.

GAME 34 Q6 ANSWER b
The name *Harry's Angels* was discarded presumably to avoid confusion with the ABC show *Harry-O*, starring David Jannsen. The final title must have been a good choice because the show ran from 1976 to 1981, eventually inspiring feature films, video games, and even a British comic strip.

GAME 54 Q6 ANSWER b
Fonzie (Henry Winkler) thought the *Rebel Without a Cause* star epitomized the definition of "cool." According to Winkler, some of his character's movements and the way he spoke were based on his *Lords of Flatbush* costar Sylvester Stallone. As for "The Lone Ranger," Fonzie carried a picture of him in his wallet!

GAME 74 Q6 ANSWER c
Larry David, co-creator of *Seinfeld*, provided more than a dozen voiceover appearances on the show during its ten-year run. He also made a bizarre on-screen cameo in a 1994 episode as a caped man who was talking to Frank Costanza (Jerry Stiller) on a city street. The character was later identified as Frank's lawyer.

7. When The Gentlemen come to *Buffy the Vampire Slayer's* town, what do they steal?

a. Ancient amulets

b. Voices

c. Corpses

d. Clothing

GAME 7 Q6 ANSWER a
Created by producer and screenwriter John Gray, *The Ghost Whisperer,* which first aired on CBS in 2005, concerns a young woman who is able to communicate with the dead. It is said that the series' stories are partly based on the work of Mary Ann Wintkowski, an Ohio spirit communicator.

7. Which character did *not* appear in the first season of *Beverly Hills, 90210*?

a. Keith

b. Andrea Zuckerman

c. Nat Buccigio

d. Clare Arnold

GAME 27 Q6 ANSWER a
Steve Sander's mom, Samantha (Christine Belford), appeared early in the series as a former star of the fictional TV sitcom *Hartley House.* Actor Ian Ziering, probably best known for his *90210* role as Steve Sanders, began his acting career doing commercials when he was a child.

7. Which Western series helped launch actor Steve McQueen to fame?

a. *Rawhide*

b. *The Big Valley*

c. *Wanted: Dead or Alive*

d. *Maverick*

GAME 47 Q6 ANSWER a
This 1989 CBS miniseries, based on Larry McMurtry's novel, tells the story of former Texas Ranger Gus McCrae (Robert Duvall) and his adventures while organizing a cattle drive to Montana. The eight-hour miniseries won seven Emmys and two Golden Globes, one for Best Miniseries and one for Best Actor in a Miniseries, which went to Duvall.

7. Which of these *South Park* boys has a baby brother named Ike?

a. Kenny

b. Stan

c. Kyle

d. Cartman

GAME 67 Q6 ANSWER b
In a twist on the standard "boy and his dog" theme, Peabody was a brilliant dog who adopted a boy named Sherman to keep him company. The two used Peabody's WABAC (pronounced "way-back") machine to travel back in time and witness various events. Generally, they found that the history books had it all wrong.

GAME 14

6. What was the focus of the 1989 ABC movie *The Final Days*?

a. Christ's last days
b. Kennedy assassination
c. End of World War II
d. Nixon's fall from grace

GAME 14 Q5 ANSWER c
There were actually *three* TV movies made about the Amy Fisher/Joey Buttafuoco affair in 1992. First came NBC's *Amy Fisher: My Story,* which starred Noelle Parker. Next came Alyssa Milano in *Casualties of Love: The "Long Island Lolita" Story* on CBS, while Drew Barrymore starred in ABC's *The Amy Fisher Story.*

GAME 34

6. *Charlie's Angels* was at one time titled _____ *Angels.*

a. Frankie's
b. Harry's
c. Sammy's
d. Eddie's

GAME 34 Q5 ANSWER c
In this 1966–1971 sitcom, Marlo Thomas—daughter of Danny Thomas—played aspiring actress Ann Marie. Although only occasionally employed, Ann had a spacious apartment in New York City, as well as an extensive wardrobe. Ted Bessell played her boyfriend, while Lew Parker and Rosemary DeCamp were her concerned parents.

GAME 54

6. On *Happy Days*, whose poster did Fonzie hang in his apartment?

a. Al Capone
b. James Dean
c. Sylvester Stallone
d. The Lone Ranger

GAME 54 Q5 ANSWER a
After Richie and his buddies graduated from Jefferson High School, they attended the University of Wisconsin. Later, Richie and Ralph joined the service; Potsie worked at Cunningham's hardware; and Fonzie became co-owner of Arnold's, manager of Bronco's Auto Repairs, and a shop teacher at Jefferson High.

GAME 74

6. On *Seinfeld*, who provided the voice of Yankees owner George Steinbrenner?

a. Michael Richards
b. Jason Alexander
c. Larry David
d. Jerry Stiller

GAME 74 Q5 ANSWER b
Appearing in the eighth-season episode "The Pothole" as Jerry's girlfriend Jenna, Kristin Davis sends Jerry into a neurotic tailspin after she unknowingly brushes her teeth with a toothbrush that Jerry accidentally knocked into his toilet bowl. Davis was also the only *Sex and the City* star to appear on NBC's *Friends.*

8. On *The Addams Family*, what was the name of Wednesday's headless doll?

a. Cleopatra

b. Anne Boleyn

c. Lizzie Borden

d. Marie Antoinette

GAME 7 Q7 ANSWER b

As a result of this theft, the townspeople are unable to speak—and the episode "Hush" contains very little dialogue. Instead, the actors communicate the storyline through action, facial expression, and even drawings, helped enormously by composer Christophe Beck's soundtrack. This unique episode won *Buffy* its first Emmy nomination.

---

8. Which *Beverly Hills, 90210* regular was also on *Little House on the Prairie*?

a. Shannen Doherty

b. Ian Ziering

c. Luke Perry

d. Tori Spelling

GAME 27 Q7 ANSWER d

Clare (Kathleen Robertson) joined the series in 1994 and became friends with the group at California University. What was initially a five-episode role blossomed into two full seasons for the character. After *90210,* Robertson's career focused primarily on movies. She appeared in such films as *I Am Sam* (2001) and *Hollywoodland* (2006).

---

8. On *Bonanza*, which Cartwright had the nickname "Hoss?"

a. Adam

b. Eric

c. Joseph

d. Benjamin

GAME 47 Q7 ANSWER c

This series was a spinoff of another Western TV series called *Trackdown* starring Robert Culp. Debuting in 1959 on CBS, *Wanted: Dead or Alive* featured the intense acting of Steve McQueen as haunted bounty hunter Josh Randall. By the time the series was canceled in 1961, McQueen was a star.

---

8. Which 1960's sitcom appeared in animated form in the 1970s?

a. *The Beverly Hillbillies*

b. *Bewitched*

c. *Green Acres*

d. *The Addams Family*

GAME 67 Q7 ANSWER c

South Park began in 1992, when university students Trey Parker and Matt Stone created a short film with characters like those on the future series. TV executives were impressed, and eventually *South Park* was born. Although the show has been called offensive, the creators describe themselves as "equal opportunity offenders."

GAME 14

5. Who did both Alyssa Milano and Drew Barrymore portray in TV movies?

a. Monica Lewinsky
b. Donna Rice
c. Amy Fisher
d. Heidi Fleiss

GAME 14 Q4 ANSWER a
It was estimated that nearly half the US adult population viewed *The Day After* when it aired on November 20, 1983. The powerful movie, starring Jason Robards, JoBeth Williams, and Steve Guttenberg, centered on a group of people in a small Kansas town during the weeks leading up to and following a nuclear strike on the United States.

GAME 34

5. What was the name of *That Girl*?

a. Jennifer Hart
b. Samantha Stephens
c. Ann Marie
d. Rose Marie

GAME 34 Q4 ANSWER d
From 1968 to 1971, Carroll played widowed nurse Julia in the show of the same name. Although it's now viewed as being groundbreaking, during *Julia's* run, the black community criticized the show for failing to be sufficiently angry and political. Nevertheless, the role won Carroll the 1968 Golden Globe for Best Actress.

GAME 54

5. On *Happy Days*, what high school does Richie attend?

a. Jefferson
b. McKinley
c. Madison
d. Whitman

GAME 54 Q4 ANSWER b
Seasoned stage, screen, and TV actor Tom Bosley played the hardware store owner and patriarch of the Cunningham family. He was typically referred to as "Mr. C" by the show's characters, with the exception of Ralph (Donny Most), who called him "Howie." In 2004, Howard Cunningham ranked #9 on *TV Guide's* list of "50 Greatest TV Dads of All Time."

GAME 74

5. Which *Sex and the City* star appeared in a *Seinfeld* episode?

a. Kim Cattrall
b. Kristin Davis
c. Sarah Jessica Parker
d. Cynthia Nixon

GAME 74 Q4 ANSWER c
Since the Chef Boyardee company wouldn't allow use of the Beefaroni name, Kramer fed Rusty a product called Beef-A-Reeno (fit for a king and queen-o), which he had purchased in bulk at a warehouse club. When Kramer then took George's future in-laws on a carriage ride, Rusty developed digestive problems, resulting in a malodorous ride from hell.

GAME 7

9. In what state was the daytime soap *Dark Shadows* set?

a. Massachusetts

b. Nevada

c. Maine

d. Louisiana

GAME 7 Q8 ANSWER d

Wednesday, like the other *Addams Family* characters, was originally a creation of American cartoonist Charles Addams, who was known for his black humor and macabre characters. His Addams Family—rich, eccentric, and ghoulish—was designed to be a grotesque version of the ideal American nuclear family.

GAME 27

9. Who was the West Beverly High School principal on *Beverly Hills, 90210*?

a. Mr. Feeny

b. Mrs. Teasley

c. Miss Bliss

d. Dr. Kim

GAME 27 Q8 ANSWER a

After actor/producer Michael Landon saw the ten-year-old Memphis, Tennessee native in an episode of *Father Murphy*, he cast her a year later on *Little House on the Prairie* as Jenny Wilder. Along with her combative personality, Doherty is best known for her roles as Brenda Walsh on *90210* and Prue Halliwell on *Charmed*.

GAME 47

9. Eric Fleming starred in which hit Western series?

a. *Cheyenne*

b. *Rawhide*

c. *Wagon Train*

d. *Sugarfoot*

GAME 47 Q8 ANSWER b

Eric, the second of three sons to Ben Cartwright (Lorne Greene), was played by Dan Blocker and provided much of the show's comic relief. The first series to shoot all of its episodes in color, *Bonanza* ran on NBC from 1959 to 1973. It made a star of Michael Landon, who played Little Joe, the youngest of the Cartwright brothers.

GAME 67

9. Who provided the voice of Nigel Thornberry on the family cartoon *The Wild Thornberrys*?

a. Tim Curry

b. James Earl Jones

c. Elton John

d. Colin Firth

GAME 67 Q8 ANSWER d

Hanna-Barbera first used the Addams Family characters on *Scooby-Doo*. They were so well received that they were spun off into their own show, which ran from 1973 to 1975. Jackie Coogan and Ted Cassidy, who had played Uncle Fester and Lurch on the 1964–1966 TV show, provided voices for the same characters in the animated version.

GAME 14

4. *The Day After* was a controversial 1983 ABC film about:

a. Nuclear holocaust

b. Vietnam

c. Watergate

d. Chernobyl

GAME 14 Q3 ANSWER b
Based on the true story of Michigan wife and mother Francine Hughes, this powerful TV movie was the highest-rated program that season. Fawcett received an Emmy nomination for her work on this film, proving she was more than just one of *Charlie's Angels*. The movie costarred Paul LeMat as her abusive husband.

GAME 34

4. Who was the first black actress to star in her own series playing a nonstereotypical role?

a. Dorothy Dandridge

b. Pearl Bailey

c. Isabel Sanford

d. Diahann Carroll

GAME 34 Q3 ANSWER a
A spinoff of Norman Lear's *All in the Family,* the show cast Arthur as Maude Findlay, a liberal-minded middle-aged married woman living in Westchester County, New York. *Maude,* which ran from 1972 to 1978, also featured Rue McClanahan, who would go on to play "Golden Girl" Blanche Devereaux.

GAME 54

4. On *Happy Days,* what type of store did Mr. Cunningham own?

a. Grocery

b. Hardware

c. Book

d. Sporting Goods

GAME 54 Q3 ANSWER c
A newly recorded version of the original 1954 song by Bill Haley & His Comets served as the opening theme for the show's first two seasons. The closing song, "Happy Days," written by Norman Gimbel and Charles Fox, eventually replaced "Rock Around the Clock" as the show's opening theme. "Happy Days" was released as a single in 1976 and hit #5.

GAME 74

4. On *Seinfeld,* what did Kramer feed Rusty the horse before taking Susan's parents on a carriage ride?

a. Beef stew

b. Beefaroni

c. Beef-A-Reeno

d. SPAM

GAME 74 Q3 ANSWER b
In the 1992 episode "The Opera," Davola threatens to put the "kibosh" on Jerry after alleging that Jerry sabotaged his deal with NBC. He was also angry with Elaine, who had visited him at his bizarre apartment and sprayed Binaca in his face to escape. By the end of the episode, Davola is dressed as the cuckolded clown Pagliacci.

GAME 7

10. In Season Five of *Mystery Science Theater 3000,* who replaced host Joel Hodgson?

a. Mike Nelson
b. Joel Robinson
c. Bill Corbett
d. Tom Servo

GAME 7 Q9 ANSWER c
Set in Collinsport, Maine, *Dark Shadows* revolved around the rich and powerful Collins family, which owned a fishing fleet and cannery. At first, nothing supernatural occurred on the series. Then Willie Loomis opened a coffin, unleashing the 172-year-old vampire Barnabas Collins.

GAME 27

10. How did the *Beverly Hills, 90210* gang refer to Brenda and Brandon's home?

a. Casa Walsh
b. Walsh Central
c. Home Sweet Walsh
d. Walshville

GAME 27 Q9 ANSWER b
Denise Dowse played the role of Principal Yvonne Teasley on the show. Dowse has had a full acting career, appearing in numerous movies and TV shows since 1989. In the 2005 Samuel L. Jackson film *Coach Carter,* she was once again cast as a principal—Richmond High School's Principal Garrison.

GAME 47

10. On which Western was Dr. Miguelito Quixote Loveless the villain?

a. *Colt 45*
b. *Stoney Burke*
c. *Johnny Ringo*
d. *The Wild Wild West*

GAME 47 Q9 ANSWER b
One of TV's best Westerns, *Rawhide* ran on CBS from 1959 to 1966. Fleming starred as trail boss Gil Favor, and the show featured guest performances from well-known actors, such as Barbara Stanwyck and Buddy Ebsen. Tragically, Eric Fleming drowned on October 2, 1966 in South America, while making the film *High Jungle* for MGM.

GAME 67

10. Which *Rugrats* characters are related?

a. Phil and Dil
b. Angelica and Tommy
c. Chuckie and Lil
d. Tommy and Susie

GAME 67 Q9 ANSWER a
Running from 1997 to 2004, *The Wild Thornberrys* followed the adventures of a fictional wildlife-documentary-making family. Tim Curry—in one of his rare good-guy roles—played Nigel Thornberry, the father of the family and the narrator of their documentaries; while Jodi Carlisle played Marianne, Thornberry mom and camerawoman.

---

3. In which 1984 NBC movie did Farrah Fawcett kill her abusive husband?

a. *Small Sacrifices*

b. *The Burning Bed*

c. *Murder in Texas*

d. *Extremities*

GAME 14 Q2 ANSWER d
For his frightful portrayal of the Nazi leader in *The Bunker,* Hopkins earned an Emmy. *Hitler: The Last Ten Days* was a 1973 feature film starring Sir Alec Guinness in the title role, while the 2003 movie *Hitler: The Rise of Evil* starred Robert Carlyle. *The Great Dictator* was Charlie Chaplin's 1940 satire of Hitler.

3. Before Bea Arthur became a "Golden Girl," in what show did she star?

a. *Maude*

b. *Phyllis*

c. *Rhoda*

d. *The Bea Arthur Show*

GAME 34 Q2 ANSWER c
When *Designing Women* debuted in 1986, outspoken liberal Julia Sugarbaker (Dixie Carter) and self-centered former beauty queen Suzanne Sugarbaker (Delta Burke) ran Sugarbaker Designs. But the show dealt less with the sisters' work than it did with various social issues, and often involved a righteous monologue delivered by Julia.

3. Which famous '50's tune was the original *Happy Days* theme song?

a. "School Days"

b. "That'll be the Day"

c. "Rock Around the Clock"

d. "At the Hop"

GAME 54 Q2 ANSWER c
Mrs. Cunningham (Marion Ross) always called him "Arthur." Fonzie's full name was Arthur Herbert Fonzarelli. Instead of the name Fonzarelli, show creator Garry Marshall had wanted to use his own last name, Maschiarelli, for the character, who would then be nicknamed "Mash." But ABC feared it would remind viewers of rival network show *M*A*S*H.*

3. On *Seinfeld,* which opera are Jerry and Elaine in line for when they run into "Crazy" Joe Davola?

a. *Madame Butterfly*

b. *Pagliacci*

c. *La Traviata*

d. *Tosca*

GAME 74 Q2 ANSWER b
In a fifth-season episode, Elaine's seemingly "perfect" new boyfriend fell from grace when he failed to put an exclamation point at the end of his note about her friend's new baby. A later episode found Elaine miffed again when former boss Mr. Lippman used an exclamation point in the name of his new shop "Top of the Muffin to You!"

11. "Monsters are Due on Maple Street" was an episode of what TV series?

a. *Chiller Theater*

b. *Night Gallery*

c. *The Time Tunnel*

d. *The Twilight Zone*

GAME 7 Q10 ANSWER a
The premise of this series is that a man (Nelson) is trapped aboard a satellite, and forced by evil captors to watch the worst movies ever made—often science fiction movies involving monsters. Nelson is joined by robot friends who watch the film along with him, making fun of the plot, acting, and special effects.

11. Who did Dylan McKay marry on *Beverly Hills, 90210*?

a. Gina Kincaid

b. Janet Sosna

c. Toni Marchette

d. Emily Valentine

GAME 27 Q10 ANSWER a
Throughout the series, Casa Walsh served as the group's neighborhood haven—a place of comfort and solace, as well as the center of action. It "hosted" a number of outrageous parties, a group intervention focused on getting Dylan McKay to check into rehab, and a surprise Thanksgiving appearance by NFL quarterback Steve Young.

11. "Wagons Ho!" was the signature phrase of which '50s Western hero?

a. Ben Cartwright

b. Josh Randall

c. Rowdy Yates

d. Seth Adams

GAME 47 Q10 ANSWER d
Running from 1965 to 1969, this unique Western was set in the late 1800s and featured actors Robert Conrad and Ross Martin as Secret Service Agents James West and Artemus Gordon. The brilliant but insane Dr. Loveless, played memorably by dwarf-sized actor Michael Dunn, remained the most popular recurring villain of the series.

11. What was one of Peter Griffin's professions on the animated series *Family Guy*?

a. Fisherman

b. Librarian

c. Painter

d. School teacher

GAME 67 Q10 ANSWER b
Tommy and Angelica Pickles are cousins, and Dil is Tommy's younger brother. While Dil and Tommy are so young that they can communicate only with other little kids, three-year-old Angelica can understand and communicate with both the younger kids and the adults—a position that she often uses to manipulate those around her.

2. Which 1981 cable-TV movie featured Anthony Hopkins as Adolf Hitler?

a. *Hitler: The Rise of Evil*

b. *Hitler: The Last Ten Days*

c. *The Great Dictator*

d. *The Bunker*

GAME 14 Q1 ANSWER c

Taking two-and-a-half years to make, this TV movie tells the story of how the Bakkers and their evangelical ministry PTL (Praise the Lord) were destroyed by lust and greed. The film featured intense performances from a pre-Oscar Kevin Spacey as Jim Bakker and Emmy nominee Bernadette Peters as the unforgettable Tammy Faye Bakker.

---

2. What was the occupation of the Sugarbaker sisters on *Designing Women*?

a. Travel agents

b. Newscasters

c. Interior decorators

d. Costume designers

GAME 34 Q1 ANSWER a

In the first episode of the show, entitled "Love Is All Around" and broadcast in 1970, Mary Richards (Mary Tyler Moore) moves to Minneapolis, Minnesota after breaking off a relationship with her boyfriend. She soon finds a job on a TV news program, as well as a gaggle of coworkers, friends, and neighbors.

---

2. On *Happy Days*, who was the only person allowed to call Fonzie by his real name?

a. Mr. Cunningham

b. Father Delvecchio

c. Mrs. Cunningham

d. Leather Tuscadero

GAME 54 Q1 ANSWER b

Producers felt the Midwest locale would appeal to a broad audience. Also, one of the show's producers, Tom Miller, grew up in Milwaukee. Creator Garry Marshall felt that if they ever needed to do a location shoot, having a producer that knew the city would be advantageous. He also felt the cost involved wouldn't be exorbitant.

---

2. Elaine once ended a relationship on *Seinfeld* because her boyfriend didn't use:

a. Deodorant

b. An exclamation point

c. Ketchup on his fries

d. The subway

GAME 74 Q1 ANSWER a

Candy-bar heiress Sue Ellen Mishke (Brenda Strong) was a former schoolmate and constant source of angst for Elaine. In "The Betrayal," Elaine received a last-minute invitation to Sue Ellen's wedding (basically an "uninvitation"). This angered Elaine so much that she traveled all the way to India just to show up!

---

12. In the series *Forever Knight*, Nick the vampire worked as a:

a. Radio talk show host

b. Homicide detective

c. Librarian

d. Newspaper reporter

When odd things begin happening on Maple Street—power fails, telephones don't work, and a car starts by itself—the residents become frightened, suspicious, and ultimately violent. Although aliens start the trouble, the real monsters in this 1960 episode are the paranoid neighbors who turn on one another in a time of duress.

---

12. On *Beverly Hills, 90210*, how did Brandon and Brenda know Valerie Malone?

a. Classmates

b. Childhood friends

c. Cousins

d. Pen pals

Toni (Rebecca Gayheart) was the daughter of Tony Marchette (Stanley Kammel), who allegedly killed Dylan's dad. While plotting to get revenge, Dylan falls in love with Toni. On the couple's wedding night, Toni's father plans to kill Dylan, but accidentally kills his own daughter instead. That's when Dylan left the show as a cast regular.

---

12. Who was the title character in the Old West series *The Rifleman*?

a. Micah Torrance

b. Cheyenne Bodie

c. Lucas McCain

d. Jason McCord

Ward Bond played this rugged wagon master on NBC's *Wagon Train*, which premiered in 1957. When Bond died in November 1960, his character was replaced by a new wagon master named Christopher Hale (John McIntire). In 1962, *Wagon Train* switched networks from NBC to ABC, where it aired until 1965.

---

12. What dog breed was Ren in the 1990s cartoon *The Ren & Stimpy Show*?

a. Beagle

b. Pug

c. Cocker spaniel

d. Chihuahua

A toy factory worker, towel boy, brewery shipping clerk, and center for the New England Patriots are a few more of the many jobs held by Peter. *Family Guy* is one of a handful of shows that was canceled and later revived on the same network due to the strength of its fan support. After ending the show in 2002, FOX brought it back in 2005.

GAME 14

1. Who was the subject of the 1990 NBC movie *Fall from Grace*?

a. Jimmy Swaggart
b. Pete Rose
c. Jim & Tammy Faye Bakker
d. Donald & Ivana Trump

The answer to this question is on:

**page 180,
top frame,
right side.**

GAME 34

1. What city was the setting for *The Mary Tyler Moore Show*?

a. Minneapolis
b. Indianapolis
c. St. Louis
d. Pittsburgh

The answer to this question is on:

**page 180,
second frame,
right side.**

GAME 54

1. In what city did *Happy Days* take place?

a. Philadelphia
b. Milwaukee
c. Detroit
d. Minneapolis

The answer to this question is on:

**page 180,
third frame,
right side.**

GAME 74

1. On *Seinfeld*, whose wedding does Elaine travel to India to attend?

a. *Sue Ellen Mischke*
b. *Marla "the Virgin"*
c. *Susan Ross*
d. *Toby "the Heckler"*

The answer to this question is on:

**page 180,
bottom frame,
right side.**

GAME 8
TV of the 1950s

Turn to page 185
for the first question.

GAME 7 Q12 ANSWER b
Running from 1992 to 1996, the series centered on Nick Knight, an 800-year-old vampire seeking to repay society for his sins by working as a detective in present-day Toronto. *Forever Knight* began as a 1989 CBS movie starring Rick Springfield, but in the series, Springfield was replaced by Canadian actor Geraint Wyn Davies.

GAME 28
Make 'em Laugh

Turn to page 185
for the first question.

GAME 27 Q12 ANSWER b
Valerie (Tiffani-Amber Thiessen) was originally from Minnesota, where her parents were friends with Jim and Cindy. She moved in with the Walsh's after her father died. Early in Thiessen's career, she was well known as the perky cheerleader on *Saved by the Bell*. Before she was cast as Valerie Malone, Alicia Silverstone had turned down the part.

GAME 48
GRAB BAG

Turn to page 185
for the first question.

GAME 47 Q12 ANSWER c
Nearly a decade before finding TV fame as rugged cowboy Lucas McCain, actor Chuck Connors was a pro basketball player with the Boston Celtics and then a baseball player for the Brooklyn Dodgers. After starring in ABC's *The Rifleman* from 1958 to 1963, Connors starred in *Branded* on NBC from 1965 to 1966.

GAME 68
More British TV

Turn to page 185
for the first question.

GAME 67 Q12 ANSWER d
The Ren & Stimpy Show ran from 1991 to 1996, featuring a neurotic "asthma-hound" chihuahua named Ren, and a fat red cat named Stimpy. The show was controversial due to its grotesque imagery. At one point, creator John Kricfalusi was fired, and several episodes of the show were deemed unairable.

GAME 14

Made-for-TV Movies

Turn to page 182 for the first question.

GAME 13 Q12 ANSWER a
Following a stint on *NYPD Blue* as Officer Janice Licalsi, actress Amy Brenneman went on to create, produce, and star in *Judging Amy* for CBS. The show was based on Brenneman's mother, Frederica, a court judge in Connecticut. In the series, Amy Gray's headstrong mother, Maxine, was played by multiple Emmy-winner Tyne Daly.

GAME 34

Lovable Ladies

Turn to page 182 for the first question.

GAME 33 Q12 ANSWER d
Starring Haley Mills as teacher Carrie Bliss, *Good Morning, Miss Bliss* was intended to focus on the life of an inspiring teacher. The show was canceled after thirteen episodes but was spun off into *Saved by the Bell*. Afterwards, episodes of the first show were aired as episodes of the spinoff series.

GAME 54

Happy Days

Turn to page 182 for the first question.

GAME 53 Q12 ANSWER d
Veteran actor Tom Bosley starred as the Cabot Cove Sheriff during the first four years of *Murder, She Wrote* (1984–1996). When he left the series, his absence was explained by having Sheriff Tupper retire and move to Kentucky to live near his family. Bosley is probably best known as Howard Cunningham (Richie's dad) on *Happy Days*.

GAME 74

Seinfeld . . . Again!

Turn to page 182 for the first question.

GAME 73 Q12 ANSWER c
Cousin of NFL quarterback Chad Pennington, Tygert "Ty" Pennington began his TV career on TLC's *Trading Spaces*. His playful nature and master carpentry skills caught the eye of ABC executives, who chose him to lead a design team that transforms the homes of deserving families on *Extreme Makeover: Home Edition*.

GAME 8

1. What was the name of the lead character's horse in the 1950s TV show *The Cisco Kid*?

a. El Dorado

b. Diablo

c. Loco

d. Tornado

The answer to this question is on:
page 187, top frame, right side.

GAME 28

1. Which *Laugh-In* regular played a switchboard operator named Ernestine?

a. Judy Carne

b. JoAnne Worley

c. Ruth Buzzi

d. Lili Tomlin

The answer to this question is on:
page 187, second frame, right side.

GAME 48

1. On *Will & Grace*, what does Will do for a living?

a. Accountant

b. Lawyer

c. Clothing designer

d. Model

The answer to this question is on:
page 187, third frame, right side.

GAME 68

1. Which American sitcom was based on the British show *Man About the House*?

a. *Who's the Boss?*

b. *Full House*

c. *Three's Company*

d. *My Three Sons*

The answer to this question is on:
page 187, bottom frame, right side.

185

GAME 13

12. What did Amy Gray decide to do in the series finale of *Judging Amy*?

a. Become a US senator

b. Become a detective

c. Become a social worker

d. Become a housewife

GAME 33

12. *Good Morning, Miss Bliss* inspired which spinoff show?

a. *Dawson's Creek*

b. *Welcome Back, Kotter*

c. *Teachers*

d. *Saved by the Bell*

GAME 53

12. Sheriff Amos Tupper was a frequent aide of which TV detective?

a. Dan Tanna

b. Tony Baretta

c. Theo Kojak

d. Jessica Fletcher

GAME 73

12. Who got his big break as a featured carpenter on The Learning Channel's *Trading Spaces*?

a. Evan Farmer

b. Steve Irwin

c. Ty Pennington

d. Jeff Corwin

GAME 8

2. Who starred in the late 1950s police drama *M Squad*?

a. Lee Marvin

b. Steve McQueen

c. James Coburn

d. Eli Wallach

GAME 8 Q1 ANSWER b

Based on a character created by O. Henry in his 1907 short story "The Caballero's Way," *The Cisco Kid* ran from 1950 to 1956. The title character was played by Duncan Renaldo, who rode Diablo, while his comedic sidekick Pancho Gonzales was played by Leo Carillo, who rode Loco.

GAME 28

2. On *Saturday Night Live*, who gave us food for thought with his *Deep Thoughts*?

a. Al Franken

b. Robert Smigel

c. Jack Handey

d. Jerry Zucker

GAME 28 Q1 ANSWER d

Lily Tomlin gained national prominence as a comedian on *Laugh-In*. Her characters—the irascible Ernestine, who snorted when she laughed; and the impish child named Edith Ann, who sat on a gigantic chair and told the audience all the trouble she had caused that day—were hilarious. Tomlin re-enacted the characters on *Saturday Night Live*.

GAME 48

2. What was Doogie Howser's first name?

a. Edgar

b. Daniel

c. Douglas

d. Darrin

GAME 48 Q1 ANSWER b

Although Canadian-born Eric McCormack had appeared in a number of films and TV shows, including the series *Lonesome Dove,* it was his role as gay lawyer Will Truman that brought him widespread recognition. During the show's eight-season run, McCormack earned four Emmy nominations for Outstanding Lead Actor in a Comedy Series, with a win in 2001.

GAME 68

2. Which Beatle appeared twice on the BBC comedy show *Not Only . . . But Also*?

a. John Lennon

b. Ringo Starr

c. George Harrison

d. Paul McCartney

GAME 68 Q1 ANSWER c

Man About the House ran on BBC-TV from 1973 to 1976, and ABC introduced *Three's Company* in the US in 1977. Just as the British show produced two spinoffs (*George and Mildred* and *Robin's Nest*), *Three's Company* also produced two spinoffs (*The Ropers* and *Three's a Crowd*) with similar plotlines.

GAME 13

11. On which show did Adam Brody have a recurring role before starring on *The OC*?

a. *Charmed*
b. *Beverly Hills, 90210*
c. *Party of Five*
d. *Gilmore Girls*

GAME 13 Q10 ANSWER b
Heather Graham's much-publicized ABC series debuted on January 9, 2006 and was quickly canceled. Aidan Quinn's NBC series *The Book of Daniel* was canceled after only four episodes, while ABC's *Bob Patterson,* starring Jason Alexander, was canceled after five—as was Jason Bateman's CBS show *Some of My Best Friends.*

GAME 33

11. The star of *Boy Meets World* is the brother of which show's star?

a. *The Wonder Years*
b. *Family Matters*
c. *Smallville*
d. *Family Ties*

GAME 33 Q10 ANSWER b
Stars Hollow—a small town populated by friendly but quirky people—is supposed to be in Connecticut, about thirty miles from Hartford. In truth, all of the external shots of the town are filmed on the Warner Brothers Studio backlot "Midwest Street" set, which was originally built for the 1946 movie *Saratoga Trunk.*

GAME 53

11. Which detective series starred Susan St. James and Rock Hudson?

a. *McMillan and Wife*
b. *The Avengers*
c. *Scarecrow and Mrs. King*
d. *Diagnosis Murder*

GAME 53 Q10 ANSWER b
The show, which ran from 1972 to 1977, starred Karl Malden as veteran police detective Mike Stone and Michael Douglas, Jr. as his rookie partner Steve Keller. When Douglas left the series at the start of the fourth season, he was replaced by Richard Hatch. The show was canceled the following season.

GAME 73

11. What character does Steve Buscemi play on *The Sopranos*?

a. Jimmy Altieri
b. Christopher Moltisanti
c. Carmelo Prizzi
d. Tony Blundetto

GAME 73 Q10 ANSWER b
Played by actor Bill Paxton, polygamist Bill Henrickson lives in Salt Lake City, Utah, and has three wives: Barb (Jeanne Tripplehorn), his first (and *legal*) wife; Nicki (Chloë Sevigny); and Margene (Ginnifer Goodwin), his youngest wife. Although set in Utah, HBO and the show's producers insist the characters are not meant to be Mormons.

---

3. Which 1950s show featured The Nairobi Trio?

a. *The Ed Sullivan Show*

b. *The Ernie Kovacs Show*

c. *The Tonight Show*

d. *The Jackie Gleason Show*

GAME 8 Q2 ANSWER a

Set in Chicago, Illinois, the show featured Lee Marvin as police lieutenant Frank Ballinger, who battled organized crime and corrupt officials as part of the M Squad. Although Marvin had already appeared in a number of movies when *M Squad* began airing in 1957, it took a three-year run of the series to give the actor name recognition.

---

3. Who was *Saturday Night Live's* first female host?

a. Candice Bergen

b. Betty Thomas

c. Louise Lasser

d. Gilda Radner

GAME 28 Q2 ANSWER c

SNL featured lines from Jack Handey's *Deep Thoughts*—a book of "pensive" one-line jokes, like *"The crows seemed to be calling his name, thought Caw."* The lines were read live by Handey, who never appeared onscreen. This is not to be confused with the show's "Daily Affirmations with Stuart Smalley," a segment starring Al Franken.

---

3. Which of the following shows was *not* set in San Francisco?

a. *Dharma and Greg*

b. *Eight Is Enough*

c. *Party of Five*

d. *Full House*

GAME 48 Q2 ANSWER c

Neil Patrick Harris starred as the genius teenage doctor who also faced the problems of a normal teenager on this hit ABC series (1989–1993). Each episode ended with Doogie at the computer, typing in his diary. The show's co-creator Steven Bochco partially modeled the character after his own father, who was himself a child prodigy violinist.

---

3. Jean and Lionel Hardcastle are the main characters in which British TV comedy?

a. *Father Ted*

b. *As Time Goes By*

c. *Keeping Up Appearances*

d. *Are You Being Served?*

GAME 68 Q2 ANSWER a

This hilarious Dudley Moore/Peter Cook show ran for three seasons—the first two in 1965 and 1966, and the third in 1970. For his first appearance in 1965, Lennon read passages from his first book *In His Own Write*. In 1966 (sporting a moustache and glasses), he appeared as Dan the Doorman opposite Peter Cook in a skit about nightclubs.

Answers are in right-hand boxes on page 191.

10. Which of the following shows had the shortest run?

a. *Some of My Best Friends*

b. *Emily's Reasons Why Not*

c. *The Book of Daniel*

d. *Bob Patterson*

GAME 13 Q9 ANSWER d
Filmed on Mokuleia Beach on the island of Oahu at a cost of over $10 million, the pilot episode of this TV phenomenon is one of the most expensive in ABC history. Most of the show's post-pilot episodes are filmed in a secluded area of the island's North Shore. *Lost* has inspired a cult following of die-hard fans called "Losties" or "Lostaways."

10. In what fictional town do the *Gilmore Girls* live?

a. Capeside

b. Stars Hollow

c. Sunnydale

d. Bayside

GAME 33 Q9 ANSWER c
Treat Williams played Andy Brown during *Everwood's* 2002–2006 run, receiving two Screen Actors Guild Award nominations for the role. Tom Amandes played rival physician Harold Abbott; and Scott Wolf played Jake Hartman, yet another physician. Gregory Smith portrayed Brown's musically talented but angst-ridden son, Ephram.

10. Which ABC series introduced us to Michael Douglas, Jr.?

a. *Barnaby Jones*

b. *The Streets of San Francisco*

c. *San Francisco Beat*

d. *Kojak*

GAME 53 Q9 ANSWER b
Veteran actor Lionel Stander played the gravel-voiced butler, cook, and chauffeur who "took care of" self-made millionaire Jonathan Hart (Robert Wagner) and his gorgeous wife Jennifer (Stephanie Powers). The couple, who also owned a dog named Freeway, were amateur sleuths in this ABC series, which ran from 1979 to 1984.

10. In the first season of HBO's *Big Love*, how many wives does Bill Henrickson have?

a. Two

b. Three

c. Four

d. Five

GAME 73 Q9 ANSWER a
Since a great white shark terrorized a seaside community in the 1975 film *Jaws*, the public has remained curious about sharks. In 1988, the Discovery Channel aired *Shark Week* as a way to educate people with all sorts of shark facts. In recent years, more than 20 million viewers have tuned in to watch the *Shark Week* programs.

GAME 8

4. Which "Joan" starred on the 1950s sitcom *I Married Joan*?

a. Joan Blondell
b. Joan Crawford
c. Joan Davis
d. Joan Plowright

GAME 8 Q3 ANSWER b

This classic Ernie Kovacs skit involved three gorillas wearing derby heats and overcoats, mechanically miming to the tune "Solfeggio." The head gorilla, played by cigar-chomping Kovacs, conducted the other musicians as they moved like wind-up toys. Edie Adams, Kovacs' wife, was often the piano-playing female simian of the group.

GAME 28

4. What was the name of the announcer/newscaster on *Second City TV*?

a. Edith Prickly
b. Guy Caballero
c. Earl Camembert
d. Johnny Larue

GAME 28 Q3 ANSWER a

The daughter of famed ventriloquist Edgar Bergen, Candice Bergen hosted *SNL* on November 8, 1975, a few weeks after the show's debut. She would go on to host the show a total of five times— three times during the show's first two seasons, and twice more during the '80s, while starring in the CBS hit sitcom *Murphy Brown.*

GAME 48

4. On which series did Ken Curtis played Festus Haggen?

a. *Gunsmoke*
b. *Wagon Train*
c. *Bonanza*
d. *Rawhide*

GAME 48 Q3 ANSWER b

Dharma and Greg, the Salinger Family (*Party of Five*), and the Tanners (*Full House*) all resided in San Francisco. On *Eight Is Enough,* the Bradford Family lived in Sacramento, California. The popular ABC series, which ran from 1977 to 1981, was based on the real life of Tom Braden, a father of eight who wrote a book with the same name.

GAME 68

4. Which British sitcom focused on misadventures at Grace Brothers Department Store?

a. *Are You Being Served?*
b. *Keeping Up Appearances*
c. *One Foot in the Grave*
d. *Red Dwarf*

GAME 68 Q3 ANSWER b

This BBC sitcom ran from 1992 to 2005, and starred Geoffrey Palmer and Oscar-winning actress Judi Dench. On the show, the characters had met briefly and fell in love during the Korean War. When a letter that Lionel wrote to Jean was never delivered, each assumed the other had lost interest. Years later, they met again and got married.

GAME 13

9. Where was the pilot episode of *Lost* filmed?

a. Malta

b. Australia

c. Cyprus

d. Hawaii

GAME 13 Q8 ANSWER c
It was only natural that Scott Baio, known best to TV fans as Chachi from *Happy Days* and the star of *Charles in Charge*, would appear on this show. After all, his *Happy Days* costar Ron Howard was one of its producers. Henry "Fonzie" Winkler also appeared on this critically acclaimed show as the character Barry Zuckerkorn.

GAME 33

9. Who played Dr. Andy Brown on *Everwood*?

a. Tom Amandes

b. Scott Wolf

c. Treat Williams

d. Gregory Smith

GAME 33 Q8 ANSWER a
Loosely based on Jane Austen's novel *Emma*, the 1995 film concerned pampered but good-natured teen Cher Horowitz who, along with best friend Dionne, decided to give a makeover to unhip classmate Tai Fraser. The spinoff TV show, which debuted in 1996, continued the tale of Cher and friends.

GAME 53

9. Which TV detective show featured the loyal servant and sidekick Max?

a. *Charlie's Angels*

b. *Hart to Hart*

c. *McMillan and Wife*

d. *Remington Steele*

GAME 53 Q8 ANSWER b
Falk played the disheveled, seemingly dimwitted Lieutenant Philip Columbo. Each episode let audiences witness a murder, and then let them sit back and watch the bumbling detective lull even the shrewdest murderer into a false sense of security before outwitting him or her. The show ran from 1971 to 1979 on NBC, and was revived in 1989 on ABC.

GAME 73

9. Which cable network is known for its popular *Shark Week* series?

a. Discovery Channel

b. The Travel Channel

c. Animal Planet

d. National Geographic

GAME 73 Q8 ANSWER b
Based on a 1999 British TV show with the same name, *Queer as Folk* aired on Showtime in the US and Canada from 2000 to 2005. On the show, Sharon Gless—two-time Emmy winner for her work on *Cagney & Lacey*—played Debbie Novotny, a woman whose brother died of AIDS and whose son, Michael, was gay.

GAME 8	**5. Who played Bret Maverick's brother Bart on the 1950s TV series?** **a.** Jack Kelly **b.** Ronald Reagan **c.** Roger Moore **d.** Richard Boone	**GAME 8 Q4 ANSWER c** *I Married Joan* starred Joan Davis as the scatterbrained wife of community judge Bradley Stevens (Jim Backus). The show tried, but failed, to match *I Love Lucy* in ratings, but still ran from 1952 to 1955, possibly due to the rapport between Davis, Backus, and actress Beverly Wills—Joan's real-life daughter, who played her sister.
GAME 28	**5. Which TV variety show featured the spoof "As the Stomach Turns"?** **a.** *The Carol Burnett Show* **b.** *The Tonight Show* **c.** *Donny & Marie* **d.** *Sonny & Cher Show*	**GAME 28 Q4 ANSWER c** Eugene Levy portrayed the dimwitted *SCTV* news anchor on this Canadian sketch comedy show. An actor, director, producer, and writer, Levy is known for his work in movies, which have included *Splash, National Lampoon's Vacation, American Pie,* and the Christopher Guest mockumentaries *Waiting for Guffman, Best in Show,* and *A Mighty Wind.*
GAME 48	**5. Which show's main character was Anthony Blake?** **a.** *The Fall Guy* **b.** *The Magician* **c.** *The Incredible Hulk* **d.** *The Equalizer*	**GAME 48 Q4 ANSWER a** Curtis played Marshall Matt Dillon's (James Arness's) scruffy, backwoods deputy for eleven seasons of the show's incredible twenty-year run (633 episodes!). Arness and Milburn Stone, who had the role of Dodge City's Doctor Galen "Doc" Adams, were the only regular cast members to be on the CBS program all twenty seasons.
GAME 68	**5. Which actress played Purdey in *The New Avengers?*** **a.** Susannah York **b.** Honor Blackman **c.** Joanna Lumley **d.** Diana Rigg	**GAME 68 Q4 ANSWER a** This BBC series ran from 1972 to 1985 and was named #20 in a 2004 "Britain's Best Sitcom" poll. In addition to spoofing Britain's obsession with class distinctions, the show also relied on sexual stereotypes—especially those of the menswear department head Mr. Wilberforce Humphries (played by John Inman).

8. Who played attorney Bob Loblaw on FOX network's *Arrested Development*?

a. Henry Winkler
b. Tom Bosley
c. Scott Baio
d. Donny Most

Comedian and Emmy Award-winning actor Chris Rock narrates this series, which was inspired by his own childhood experiences. Although Rock has six siblings in real life, his TV namesake (played by Tyler James Williams) is the oldest of three kids. Both hilarious and touching, the show follows Chris while growing up in Brooklyn during the 1980s.

---

8. In what show, based on an acclaimed movie, are Cher and Dionne the main characters?

a. *Clueless*
b. *Troop Beverly Hills*
c. *That's So Raven*
d. *Gilmore Girls*

The Wonder Years ran from 1988 to 1993, with Fred Savage playing young Kevin Arnold, while the voiceover of an older Kevin (provided by Daniel Stern) offered perspective. Covering social issues, historic events, and typical teen concerns as well, the show enjoyed a spot in the Nielsen Top Ten for two of its six years.

---

8. What is the rank of Peter Falk's title character on *Columbo*?

a. Captain
b. Lieutenant
c. Sergeant
d. Chief

Brothers Frank (Stevenson) and Joe (Cassidy) Hardy were teenage sleuths in this ABC show based on the book series. Starting in 1977, episodes alternated with those of young female detective Nancy Drew (Pamela Sue Martin and Janet Louise Johnson), also based on a book series. In 1978, *Nancy Drew* was canceled. *The Hardy Boys* followed in '79.

---

8. Which Showtime series featured *Cagney & Lacey* star Sharon Gless?

a. *Soul Food*
b. *Queer as Folk*
c. *Family Business*
d. *The L Word*

Debuting in 2004, *Inside Dish* was the third of cooking-show superstar Rachael Ray's four programs on the Food Network. Celebrities who have appeared on the show include Tony Danza, Daisy Fuentes, and *NYPD Blue* star Dennis Franz. In September 2006, Ray's syndicated TV talk show *The Rachael Ray Show* first hit the airwaves.

6. Which legendary hero did Guy Williams play in a prime-time TV series?

a. Philip Marlowe

b. The Lone Ranger

c. Zorro

d. Superman

GAME 8 Q5 ANSWER a
The show, which ran from 1957 to 1960, starred James Garner as Bret Maverick and Roger Moore as cousin Beau Maverick. Although *Maverick* had to compete with the immensely popular *Ed Sullivan Show*, it quickly captured an enthusiastic audience and made James Garner a household name.

6. The Fly Girls dance troupe was part of which 1990s variety show?

a. *In Living Color*

b. *Mad TV*

c. *MTV Unplugged*

d. *The Man Show*

GAME 28 Q5 ANSWER a
The Emmy-winning show debuted in 1967 and ran eleven seasons. Burnett and her ensemble cast, including Harvey Korman, Vicki Lawrence, and Tim Conway, offered an endless supply of hilarious sketches. "As the Stomach Turns" (a parody on soap operas) and "Went With the Wind" (a spoof on *Gone With the Wind*) were among the classic skits.

6. What was the original name of the law firm in *The Practice*?

a. Donnell, Frutt, and Young

b. Young and Associates

c. Donnell and Young

d. Donnell and Associates

GAME 48 Q5 ANSWER b
Bill Bixby played magician Anthony "Tony" Blake, who used his talents as an illusionist to solve crimes and help people who were in trouble. Bixby also co-directed the CBS series and even learned to perform magic for the role, so trick photography wasn't used. When the series ended in 1974, Bixby even went on to host some NBC specials on magic.

6. Who was *not* one of the four lead characters in the British sitcom *The Young Ones?*

a. Rick

b. Hyacinth

c. Neil

d. Vyvyan

GAME 68 Q5 ANSWER c
A former model, Lumley's first film break came as a Bond girl in the 1969 feature film *On Her Majesty's Secret Service* starring George Lazenby as James Bond. While fellow British actresses Honor Blackman and Diana Rigg were also Bond girls, they both starred in the original *Avengers* TV series—one after the other.

7. How many siblings does Chris have on *Everybody Hates Chris*?

a. None

b. Two

c. Five

d. Seven

GAME 13 Q6 ANSWER b
In the '90s, Ripa won three Soap Opera Digest Awards for her work as Hayley Vaughan on *All My Children*. In 2001, she became the new cohost on *Live with Regis and Kelly*. On *Hope & Faith*, Ripa was able to parody her soap-star years by playing the role of Faith Fairfield opposite former *Murphy Brown* star Faith Ford.

7. Which TV show centered on the remembered childhood of Kevin Arnold?

a. *Family Matters*

b. *Growing Pains*

c. *The Wonder Years*

d. *Brooklyn Bridge*

GAME 33 Q6 ANSWER b
Creator Joss Whedon wrote the script for the 1992 movie, but was upset when the director turned it into a broad comedy. Years later, Whedon had the chance to produce a TV series with the central concept of "high school as horror movie," and in 1997, the first episode of *Buffy the Vampire Slayer* aired. The show ran for seven seasons.

7. Shaun Cassidy and Parker Stevenson starred which series?

a. *Alias Smith and Jones*

b. *MacGruder and Loud*

c. *The Hardy Boys*

d. *Remington Steele*

GAME 53 Q6 ANSWER a
Adrian Monk is the brilliant San Francisco detective, whose obsessive-compulsive disorder is heightened by his irrational fears (germs, needles, and milk head the list). *Monk* debuted in 2002 on the USA Network. Originally, ABC was to carry the series, starring Michael Richards; but when Richards backed out, so did ABC.

7. Who visits the kitchens of American celebrities on the Food Network's *Inside Dish*?

a. Rachael Ray

b. Jill Cordes

c. Giada De Laurentiis

d. Paula Deen

GAME 73 Q6 ANSWER c
Before earning an Emmy for his portrayal of the fiery, fast-talking agent Ari Gold in the HBO series *Entourage*, Jeremy Piven played writer Jerry Capen for the fictitious *Larry Sanders Show*. Piven has also appeared in a number of movies and TV shows, including *Ellen, Seinfeld, Coach,* and *Chicago Hope.*

7. Which of the following was an aspect of the '50s quiz show *The $64,000 Question*?

a. Blindfolds

b. Celebrity contestants

c. Big wheel

d. Isolation booth

GAME 8 Q6 ANSWER c

Born Armando Catalano, Guy Williams had appeared in several movies before being cast as aristocrat Don Diego de la Vega, who operated in secret as Zorro. The popular show, which ran from 1957 to 1959 and ended only because of a financial dispute between Disney and the network, led to an epidemic of "Z" graffitiing all across America.

---

7. What was Tracy Ullman's catchphrase at the end of her show?

a. "Cheerio"

b. "See ya' next time"

c. "Go home! Go home!"

d. "Hi-dee-ho"

GAME 28 Q6 ANSWER a

This house dance troupe for FOX network's *In Living Color* (1990–1994) helped launched the careers of Jennifer Lopez, who was a Fly Girl for two seasons, and Rosie Perez, who choreographed the edgy, energetic dancers. The show itself furthered the career of Jim (credited as James) Carrey—the original cast's only male Caucasian.

---

7. Which series took place in an inner-city California high school?

a. *My So-Called Life*

b. *Welcome Back, Kotter*

c. *Dangerous Minds*

d. *The Paper Chase*

GAME 48 Q6 ANSWER d

When this Emmy-winning ABC legal drama first aired in 1997, it focused on the Boston law firm of Donnell and Associates. Eventually, it became Donnell, Young, Dole and Frutt, and by the end of the series in 2004, it was Young, Frutt and Berluti. The show spun off the series *Boston Legal*, starring James Spader and William Shatner.

---

7. On *Fawlty Towers*, who was the well-meaning but confused waiter from Barcelona?

a. Vargas

b. Santiago

c. Manuel

d. Gomez

GAME 68 Q6 ANSWER b

Rounding out the four young male college students who shared a flat in North London was Mike Thecoolperson (played by British actor Christopher Ryan). Although it only ran in the UK from1982 to 1984, this edgy punk-rock sitcom became a major cult favorite in the US after being aired on MTV (and later on Comedy Central).

---

6. Which former soap star played an out-of-work soap actress on *Hope & Faith*?

a. Julia Barr

b. Kelly Ripa

c. Barbara Kearns

d. Sarah Michelle Gellar

6. Which popular TV series was based on a film of the same name?

a. *Everwood*

b. *Buffy the Vampire Slayer*

c. *Degrassi*

d. *Veronica Mars*

6. Tony Shaloub stars in *Monk* as an ex-cop who suffers from:

a. OCD

b. Insomnia

c. Sleepwalking

d. Flat feet

6. Actor Jeremy Piven played a writer on which cable series?

a. *Arli$$*

b. *Curb Your Enthusiasm*

c. *The Larry Sanders Show*

d. *Entourage*

8. What was the first song that Rick Nelson sang on *The Adventures of Ozzie and Harriet*?

a. "Hello, Mary Lou"
b. "Be-Bop Baby"
c. "I'm Walkin'"
d. "Travelin' Man"

GAME 8 Q7 ANSWER d
For increased drama, the show was hosted by actor Hal March rather than a broadcaster. Contestants picked a subject category and were then asked a question in that category, earning money that doubled as the challenges grew in difficulty. Players could stay until they made a mistake, quit, or won (up to $64,000).

8. Which character appeared on both *Saturday Night Live* and *SCTV*?

a. Ed Grimley
b. Master Thespian
c. Lisa Loopner
d. Beldar Conehead

GAME 28 Q7 ANSWER c
FOX network's three-time Emmy-winning *Tracy Ullman Show* aired from 1987 to 1990. The half-hour variety program featured sketch comedy and musical numbers that were choreographed by Paula Abdul. The show was also responsible for the successful spinoff *The Simpsons*.

8. On which series was the title character a nurse?

a. *Rhoda*
b. *Maude*
c. *Alice*
d. *Julia*

GAME 48 Q7 ANSWER c
Annie Potts took on Michelle Pfeiffer's film role as dedicated inner-city teacher LouAnne Johnson in this one-season ABC series. *My So Called Life* took place at Three Rivers High School in Pittsburgh; *Welcome Back, Kotter* was set at James Buchanan High School in Brooklyn; and *The Paper Chase* took place at Harvard Law School.

8. Who was *not* a sister of Hyacinth Bucket on the Britcom *Keeping Up Appearances*?

a. Flora
b. Violet
c. Rose
d. Daisy

GAME 68 Q7 ANSWER c
Manuel was played by actor Andrew Sachs, whose family fled persecution in Nazi Germany during WWII and sought refuge in England when he was only eight years old. Although Sachs and *Fawlty Towers* star John Cleese shared great comic timing, there was one instance when Cleese accidentally hit him in the head with a real metal pan!

GAME 13

5. On which show did a teenager talk to God?

a. *Crossing Jordan*
b. *Joan of Arcadia*
c. *Life As We Know It*
d. *Beautiful People*

GAME 13 Q4 ANSWER a

Joey (Matt LeBlanc) lived with his nephew Michael, who wanted to get away from his overprotective mother (and Joey's sister), Gina, played by Emmy-winning *Sopranos* star Drea de Matteo. Christina Ricci, Lucy Liu, and Jay Leno can be counted among the show's guest stars, but none of LeBlanc's former Friends costars ever appeared on the show.

GAME 33

5. Which teen show was set at the fictional University of New York when it debuted in 1998?

a. *Boy Meets World*
b. *Saved by the Bell*
c. *Moesha*
d. *Felicity*

GAME 33 Q4 ANSWER c

From 1990 to 1994, Shannen Doherty portrayed Brenda Walsh, the show's original lead female character. Although her departure from *90210* was reportedly bitter, Aaron Spelling, the show's creator, soon cast her in another series, *Charmed*—which she left after three years.

GAME 53

5. Which show's title character was tormented by the dogs Zeus and Apollo?

a. *Mannix*
b. *Harry O*
c. *Jake and the Fat Man*
d. *Magnum, PI*

GAME 53 Q4 ANSWER a

Robert Blake played the offbeat Tony Baretta—a streetwise undercover cop with the pet cockatoo. The show's theme song included Baretta's famous line, "Don't do the crime if you can't do the time," a line he delivered to his girlfriend's killer in an early episode. The character was also fond of saying "You can take that to the bank."

GAME 73

5. *Inside the Actor's Studio* airs on which cable network?

a. Bravo
b. American Movie Classics
c. The Learning Channel
d. Discovery Channel

GAME 73 Q4 ANSWER d

When the owner of Fisher & Sons Funeral Home dies, son Nate (Peter Krause) reluctantly joins his brother David (Michael C. Hall) to run the family business. Each episode of this drama opens with the death of someone who ends up at Fisher's. The show won a number of Emmy, Golden Globe, and SAG Awards during its run (2001-2005).

GAME 8

9. Which 1950s TV sitcom took place at Madison High School?

a. *Our Miss Brooks*
b. *Leave It to Beaver*
c. *Mister Peepers*
d. *Love That Bob*

GAME 8 Q8 ANSWER c
Rick bugged his father to let him sing on their show, and finally, Ozzie relented. On April 10, 1957, in an episode entitled "Rick the Drummer," Rick sang Fats Domino's "I'm Walkin'." The song almost immediately zoomed to # 4 on the charts, and soon, every episode of the show ended with a song performed by son Ricky.

GAME 28

9. Who popularized the catch-phrase, "The devil made me do it"?

a. Richard Pryor
b. Eddie Murphy
c. Goldie Hawn
d. Flip Wilson

GAME 28 Q8 ANSWER a
While he was with *SCTV*, comedian Martin Short created the triangle-playing nerdy character of Ed Grimley, who wore his pants miles above his waist, had an giant cowlick, and was obsessed with Pat Sajak and *Wheel of Fortune*. After appearing on *SNL*, Grimley became a cartoon character on *The Completely Mental Misadventures of Ed Grimley*.

GAME 48

9. Who was Brandy's fairy godmother in the TV movie *Cinderella*?

a. Bernadette Peters
b. Whitney Houston
c. Whoopi Goldberg
d. Toni Braxton

GAME 48 Q8 ANSWER d
On this NBC show, Diahann Carroll starred as Julia Baker, a nurse and single mother whose pilot husband had been killed in Vietnam. The show ran from 1968 to 1971 and was considered groundbreaking because it portrayed a black woman in a non-stereotypical role. Previously, black lead actors were typically cast as servants.

GAME 68

9. Which Monty Python member was the first person in the first skit of the first show to air on BBC-TV?

a. John Cleese
b. Graham Chapman
c. Eric Idle
d. Michael Palin

GAME 68 Q8 ANSWER a
Patricia Routledge plays Hyacinth, whose sisters are named after flowers. Violet (Anna Dawson) is married to an accountant, while Daisy (Judy Cornwell) and lazy husband Onslow (Geoffrey Hughes) live with the flirtatious sister Rose (Shirley Stelfox the first season, Mary Millar thereafter) and the sisters' father.

4. On *Joey*, when Joey Tribbiani moved to Hollywood, he lived with:

a. His nephew

b. His brother

c. His best friend

d. His cousin

GAME 13 Q3 ANSWER d
This NBC drama is *not* the first time Caan has played a Vegas tough guy. In the 2002 comedy *Honeymoon in Vegas,* he played a gambler who tries to steal Sarah Jessica Parker away from fiancé Nicolas Cage. In 2004, CBS aired a new Vegas-based show with Rob Lowe called *Dr. Vegas*—it lasted one season.

4. Who left the cast of *Beverly Hills, 90210* in 1994, halfway through the show's run?

a. Luke Perry

b. Tori Spelling

c. Shannen Doherty

d. Jason Priestley

GAME 33 Q3 ANSWER b
Jen (Michelle Williams) was a *Dawson's Creek* regular throughout the show's 1998–2003 run. In the final episode, she collapsed while attending a wedding, and died from an incurable heart defect. On the upside, Pacey (Joshua Jackson) and Joey (Katie Holmes) ended up together while staying friends with Dawson (James Van Der Beek).

4. What was the name of Tony's pet cockatoo in the 1970s series *Baretta*?

a. Fred

b. Joe

c. Jed

d. Bill

GAME 53 Q3 ANSWER c
A NYU Tisch School graduate, Kristen Bell plays Mars, the teenage daughter of a private eye. She is a student by day and her dad's assistant by night. Bell made her Broadway debut in 2001 as Becky Thatcher in *The Adventures of Tom Sawyer.* She also appeared as a scam artist posing as a prostitute on HBO's *Deadwood.*

4. The quirky Fisher family is the focus of which HBO series?

a. *Deadwood*

b. *The Wire*

c. *The Shield*

d. *Six Feet Under*

GAME 73 Q3 ANSWER c
Named "Cooking Teacher of the Year" by *Bon Appétit* magazine in 2004, Alton Brown actually worked behind the camera as a cinematographer in the 1980s and early 1990s before graduating from the New England Culinary Institute in 1997. Two years later, he produced and hosted a show called *Good Eats,* which became his first big success.

10. In the early 1950s, who was known as Mr. Television?

a. Jack Benny
b. Milton Berle
c. Red Skelton
d. Sid Caesar

GAME 8 Q9 ANSWER a
Our Miss Brooks began as a radio show in 1948 and moved to television in 1952, making a star out of Eve Arden, who played wisecracking English teacher Connie Brooks until the show's cancellation in 1956. Younger people may remember Arden's later role as Principal McGee in the 1978 film *Grease*.

10. Why did CBS cancel *The Smothers Brothers Comedy Hour*?

a. Low ratings
b. Fighting between the brothers
c. The demand for higher wages
d. Controversial material

GAME 28 Q9 ANSWER d
That phrase, along with "What you see is what you get," was made famous by Geraldine Jones, a feisty, flirty black woman—both created and played by Flip Wilson. *The Flip Wilson Show* (1970–1974) was the first successful network variety series with a black host. Earlier, Nat "King" Cole hosted a show, but it was unable to attract sponsors.

10. What was the name of the saloon/restaurant on *Walker, Texas Ranger*?

a. *Melville's*
b. *CD's*
c. *The Regal Beagle*
d. *The Brick*

GAME 48 Q9 ANSWER b
This third version of the musical, written for TV by Richard Rogers and Oscar Hammerstein II, aired in 1997 and starred Grammy-winning R&B singer Brandy. Bernadette Peters played the wicked stepmother, and Whoopi was Queen Constantina. Earlier TV versions had Julie Andrews (1957) and Leslie Ann Warren (1965) cast as Cinderella.

10. What was the name of the family on the BBC series *Upstairs, Downstairs?*

a. Bellamy
b. Blackmore
c. Beacham
d. Burton

GAME 68 Q9 ANSWER d
This one-of-a-kind, extremely popular show ran from 1969 to 1973. In the first episode "Whither Canada?," which aired on October 5, 1969, actor Michael Palin played a wizened old man who trudged through water towards the camera and gasped "It's . . ." before the opening credits cut him off and the show then began.

3. James Caan plays which character on *Las Vegas*?

a. Mike Cannon

b. Danny McCoy

c. Casey Manning

d. Ed Deline

The series stars Kiefer Sutherland as agent Jack Bauer. After five nominations in a row, he finally won a Best Actor Emmy for this role in 2006. His father, Donald Sutherland, also earned a 2005 Emmy nomination for his work in the TV miniseries *Human Trafficking*.

---

3. Which character died on the final episode of *Dawson's Creek*?

a. Joey

b. Jen

c. Dawson

d. Jack

A comedy-drama, *The O.C.* premiered in 2003 and was an immediate hit, appealing to critics and viewers alike, much as *Beverly Hills, 90210* did in the '90s. The show centers on the lives of young adults and their families growing up in the affluent area of Orange County, California.

---

3. Who plays the title role in the CW series *Veronica Mars*?

a. Julia Stiles

b. Kate Beckinsale

c. Kristen Bell

d. Amber Tamblyn

Jameson Parker and Gerald McRaney were PI brothers AJ and Rick Simon on this series, which ran from 1981 to 1988. The characters were opposites—AJ was neat and refined; Rick lived in jeans and cowboy-boots. Poor ratings caused the show's near cancellation, but when it was rescheduled after *Magnum, PI,* the ratings increased dramatically.

---

3. Which Food Network host is the commentator for *Iron Chef America*?

a. Marc Silverstein

b. Justin Gunn

c. Alton Brown

d. Gordon Elliot

Actor Willie Garson played Stanford Blatch, one of Carrie's (Sarah Jessica Parker's) most loyal friends and confidantes. Because of his gay "galpal" role, Garson, a professed heterosexual, claims that he is often approached by women who want him to be their gay best friend—shopping for clothes and bitching about men together!

---

11. Who hosted the popular *Your Show of Shows*?

a. Bob Hope
b. Ed Sullivan
c. Sid Caesar
d. George Burns

GAME 8 Q10 ANSWER b
Texaco Star Theater propelled Milton Berle to the #1 spot in the Nielsen ratings and is credited with doubling the sale of TV sets in America. So popular was the Tuesday night show that some theaters and restaurants closed for an hour during Mr. Television's program, knowing that they would get little business if they stayed open.

11. Whose TV comic routine included two seagulls named Gertrude and Heathcliff?

a. Sid Cesar
b. Jonathan Winters
c. Red Skelton
d. Jackie Gleason

GAME 28 Q10 ANSWER d
Appearing at a time of social and cultural change, the show premiered in 1967 and was hosted by comedic brothers Dick and Tommy Smothers. It jabbed at such staid institutions as organized religion and the presidency, and pushed the envelope with anti-Vietnam sketches. CBS, with its primarily conservative viewers, canceled the show in 1969.

11. What high school did Cory attend on *Boy Meets World*?

a. Woodrow Wilson
b. Thomas Jefferson
c. John Adams
d. Harry S. Truman

GAME 48 Q10 ANSWER b
CD Parker (Noble Willingham) owned the bar and grill on this CBS series starring Chuck Norris as Cordell Walker, a Dallas-based member of the Texas Rangers. Melville's was the name of the restaurant above the bar on *Cheers*; the Regal Beagle was the local pub on *Three's Company*; and Mel's Diner was the setting for *Alice*.

11. Which actress played Basil's wife Sybil in the BBC series *Fawlty Towers*?

a. Joan Collins
b. Prunella Scales
c. Connie Booth
d. Gilly Flower

GAME 68 Q10 ANSWER a
This critically acclaimed mid-1970s drama was set in London during the Edwardian era of the early twentieth century. The show explored the separate yet joined lives of the masters who lived upstairs and their servants situated downstairs. *Upstairs, Downstairs* won three Emmys for Outstanding Drama Series in 1974, 1975, and 1977.

2. Which FOX series won the 2003 Golden Globe award for Best Drama?

a. *24*

b. *Alias*

c. *The West Wing*

d. *Without a Trace*

After his divorce, uptight Alan Harper (Jon Cryer) moves into the Malibu bachelor pad of his lazy, womanizing brother, Charlie (Charlie Sheen). Alan's young son, Jake (Angus T. Jones), often stays there on weekends. The Emmy-nominated CBS comedy, which debuted in 2003, can best be summed up by its tagline: "Two adults. One kid. No grown-ups."

---

2. Which show is set in the California town of Newport Beach?

a. *Smallville*

b. *Felicity*

c. *One Tree Hill*

d. *The O.C.*

Starring Claire Danes as Angela Chase, a fifteen-year-old struggling with teen angst, *My So-Called Life* ran only one season, from August 1994 to January 1995. But after the show's cancellation—which was partly due to Danes' reluctance to return for another season—the series generated a substantial cult following.

---

2. Which detective series did *not* feature a man-and-woman team?

a. *Moonlighting*

b. *Hart to Hart*

c. *Simon & Simon*

d. *Remington Steele*

James Garner played the laid-back detective in *The Rockford Files* (1975–1980). A wrongly accused ex-con, Rockford lived in a rundown motor home, which was also his office. He was often assisted by Rocky, his dad, and Angel, his former cellmate. Robert Blake had been considered for the title role, but instead was cast in *Baretta* (1975).

---

2. Who was Carrie's gay pal on HBO's *Sex and the City?*

a. Berger

b. Stanford

c. Anthony

d. Richard

Winner of eight ACE Awards, *The Hitchhiker,* which ran on HBO from late 1983 to 1991, was a series of modern morality thrillers. The thirty-minute stories were compelling, often involving characters who struggled with fears and obsessions. Each episode was introduced and concluded by the character of the Hitchhiker (Page Fletcher).

---

12. On what game show did three guests claim to be the same person?

a. *I've Got a Secret*

b. *You Bet Your Life*

c. *Masquerade Party*

d. *To Tell the Truth*

GAME 8 Q11 ANSWER c
Running from 1950 to 1954, this live sketch comedy show featured Sid Caesar and Imogene Coca. Writers for the famed TV show included Woody Allen, Neil Simon, Danny Simon, Mel Brooks, Larry Gelbart, Carl Reiner, and many others who went on to enjoy hugely successful careers on both small and big screens.

---

12. Kevin McDonald, Scott Thompson and Dave Foley were regulars on which TV comedy show?

a. *Kids in the Hall*

b. *Jackass*

c. *Talk Soup*

d. *Dennis Miller Live*

GAME 28 Q11 ANSWER c
The Red Skelton Show premiered on NBC in 1951. Canceled in its second season, the show was picked up by CBS, and aired from 1954 to 1970. Most of Skelton's TV repertoire of characters came from his radio show. For TV, he developed Freddie the Freeloader, a hobo who never spoke, and who enabled Skelton to exhibit his pantomime skills.

---

12. What was the name of the local hangout on *The Single Guy*?

a. The Bagel Cafe

b. Central Perk

c. McGinty's Pub

d. Rob's

GAME 48 Q11 ANSWER c
Rules posted in the John Adams High School cafeteria read: "No loud talking, no reading, no shooting." Ben Savage (younger brother of *Wonder Years* star Fred Savage) played Cory Matthews in this ABC series. When the show was canceled in 2000 after seven seasons, the Disney Channel picked it up.

---

12. Helen Mirren's detective character on the British miniseries *Prime Suspect* is:

a. Lynda La Plante

b. Jean Darblay

c. Jackie Malton

d. Jane Tennison

GAME 68 Q11 ANSWER b
Born Prunella Margaret Rumney Illingworth in 1932, Scales remains well-known for playing wife to John Cleese's often-manic Basil Fawlty in *Fawlty Towers* both in the 1975 and the 1979 series. Her first big role came as Lydia Bennet in the 1952 BBC miniseries production of Jane Austen's *Pride and Prejudice*.

GAME 13	**1.** On *Two and a Half Men*, what is the name of John Cryer's son? **a.** Jerry **b.** Jake **c.** Jack **d.** Jay	The answer to this question is on: **page 206, top frame, right side.**
GAME 33	**1.** Who was the young star of *My So-Called Life*? **a.** Alyson Hannigan **b.** Neve Campbell **c.** Emily VanCamp **d.** Claire Danes	The answer to this question is on: **page 206, second frame, right side.**
GAME 53	**1.** Which private eye lived in a trailer in Malibu? **a.** Thomas Magnum **b.** Dan Tanna **c.** Barnaby Jones **d.** Jim Rockford	The answer to this question is on: **page 206, third frame, right side.**
GAME 73	**1.** What was the first original weekly TV series aired on a national cable network? **a.** *Brothers* **b.** *Dream On* **c.** *The Hitchhiker* **d.** *The Sopranos*	The answer to this question is on: **page 206, bottom frame, right side.**

GAME 9

TV of the 1960s

Turn to page 211
for the first question.

GAME 29

Twilight Zones

Turn to page 211
for the first question.

GAME 49

Family Fun

Turn to page 211
for the first question.

GAME 69

Classic Sitcoms "Easy"

Turn to page 211
for the first question.

GAME 8 Q12 ANSWER d

Originally hosted by Bud Collyer, *To Tell the Truth* debuted in 1956, and was originally called *Nothing But the Truth*. Four celebrities questioned the guests, trying to determine who was telling the truth and who was bluffing. After the celebrities cast their votes, the host would say, "Will the real _____ please stand up?"

GAME 28 Q12 ANSWER a

The Kids in the Hall featured the Canadian sketch comedy group with the same name. The name came from legendary Jack Benny, who, if a joke failed, would say he had gotten it from "the kids in the hall," referring to the studio's young writers. The show, produced by *SNL's* Lorne Michaels, featured gay characters and themes.

GAME 48 Q12 ANSWER a

This two-season, mid-1990s NBC series starred Jonathan Silverman as bachelor Jonathan Elliot, a struggling New York writer. Bad timing might have caused the show's lack of enthusiasm among viewers. With the success of *Seinfeld* and *Friends,* audiences seemed to have reached a saturation point with "single-in-the-city" themed programs.

GAME 68 Q12 ANSWER d

Real-life police detective Jackie Malton was the inspiration for the Jane Tennison character as written in the *Prime Suspect* miniseries by screenwriter Lynda La Plante. Since 1991, Helen Mirren has played Tennison in seven separate miniseries to date. Jean Darblay was the name of the female inspector in the early 1980s BBC series *Juliet Bravo*.

GAME 13

TV of the 2000s

Turn to page 208
for the first question.

GAME 33

Teen Shows

Turn to page 208
for the first question.

GAME 53

Calling All Sleuths

Turn to page 208
for the first question.

GAME 73

Cable TV Shows

Turn to page 208
for the first question.

GAME 12 Q12 ANSWER a
The hit show, which ran from 1991 to 1996, focused on the very close but very different Reed sisters—Alex (Swoosie Kurtz), Georgie (Patricia Kalember), Teddy (Sela Ward), and Frankie (Julianne Phillips). Before his role on *ER*, George Clooney was cast as Teddy's boyfriend. Swoosie Kurtz was the only sister to appear in every episode.

GAME 32 Q12 ANSWER d
CSI: Crime Scene Investigation, which premiered on CBS in 2000, is set in Las Vegas, Nevada. The *CSI: Miami* spinoff debuted in 2002, and *CSI: NY* first aired in 2004. While the shows have been criticized for their use of graphic violence, they have also been credited with making CBS the most-watched network on US television.

GAME 52 Q12 ANSWER a
When Apu's wife, Manjula, gives birth to Anoop, Gheet, Nabendu, Poonam, Pria, Sandeep, Sashi, and Uma, it's big news across Springfield. Local companies begin sending them free gifts, but the gifts are taken back when someone in Shelbyville gives birth to nine. To date, *The Simpsons,* which debuted in 1989, is the longest-running American sitcom.

GAME 72 Q12 ANSWER c
From 1957 to 1963, *Have Gun—Will Travel* followed the adventures of Paladin, played by Richard Boone. Well educated, cultured, and a former army officer, Paladin, a champion-for-hire, dressed in black, kept a derringer under his belt, and on both his calling cards and holster, sported chess knight emblems.

GAME 9

1. On what 1964–1966 music variety series was teen idol Bobby Sherman a regular?

a. *Shindig!*

b. *Hullabaloo*

c. *Music Scene*

d. *Where the Action Is*

The answer to this question is on:

page 213, top frame, right side.

GAME 29

1. Which of the following does *not* describe the fifth dimension that is Twilight Zone?

a. Vast as space

b. Timeless as infinity

c. Between light and shadow

d. Where fear is a friend

The answer to this question is on:

page 213, second frame, right side.

GAME 49

1. Which TV family is mismatched with its sitcom?

a. Petrie/*My Three Sons*

b. Stevens/*Bewitched*

c. Huxtable/*Cosby Show*

d. Keaton/*Family Ties*

The answer to this question is on:

page 213, third frame, right side.

GAME 69

1. What does Rob Petrie do in the opening credits of *The Dick Van Dyke Show*?

a. Throws a ball to Richie

b. Trips over an ottoman

c. Drinks coffee with Laura

d. Argues with Buddy

The answer to this question is on:

page 213, bottom frame, right side.

GAME 12

12. Which 1990s NBC series was set in Winnetka, Illinois?

a. *Sisters*

b. *Hearts Afire*

c. *Evening Shade*

d. *Can't Hurry Love*

GAME 12 Q11 ANSWER c

During the ABC show's twelve-year run, Andy Sipowicz (Dennis Franz) was partnered with four different actors. David Caruso was the first, leaving the show in 1994 after only one season. Jimmy Smits followed, and stayed with the show until 1998. Former child star Rick Schroder was next and later replaced by Mark-Paul Gosselaar in 2001.

GAME 32

12. Which of these cities is *not* a setting for a *CSI* show?

a. New York

b. Las Vegas

c. Miami

d. Los Angeles

GAME 32 Q11 ANSWER a

Most people don't realize that the long-running *Candid Camera* began as a 1940s radio show called *Candid Microphone*. Creator Allan Funt—Peter Funt's dad—then experimented with a visual version by producing theatrical short films also called *Candid Microphone*. The first show titled *Candid Camera* appeared in 1951.

GAME 52

12. Which *Simpsons* character became father to octuplets?

a. Apu Nahasapeemapetilon

b. Krusty the Klown

c. Santa's Little Helper

d. Moe Szyslak

GAME 52 Q11 ANSWER b

The other siblings in this Emmy-winning series were John Boy, Erin, Ben, and Jim Bob. Based on the book *Spencer's Mountain* by Earl Hamner, Jr., *The Waltons* followed the lives of John and Olivia Walton, their seven children, and John's parents as they struggled to maintain a decent life in their Virginia mountain home during the Great Depression.

GAME 72

12. What was the emblem of TV's gentleman-turned-gunfighter Paladin?

a. Scales of justice

b. Derringer

c. Chess piece

d. Sword

GAME 72 Q11 ANSWER a

Running from 1958 to 1963 on ABC, *The Rifleman* starred Chuck Connors as Lucas McCain, a widower, father, and veteran of the Civil War. McCain lived in the New Mexico Territory with his son, Mark, played by Johnny Crawford, and earned his nickname by using a modified Winchester rifle with a rapid-fire mechanism.

---

2. In a popular 1960s sitcom, on whom did Zelda Gilroy have a never-ending crush?

a. Beaver Cleaver

b. Dobie Gillis

c. Rick Nelson

d. Dennis Mitchell

GAME 9 Q1 ANSWER a
Shindig! was one of two rock-and-roll shows that aired in the mid-1960s, the other being *Hullabaloo. Shindig!* featured many of the top names in pop music performing their latest hits, while dancers staged elaborate production numbers. Other regulars included The Righteous Brothers and Glen Campbell.

2. In the original *Outer Limits* intro, which TV feature was *not* mentioned?

a. The vertical

b. The horizontal

c. The color

d. The volume

GAME 29 Q1 ANSWER d
At the beginning of the original episodes, creator Rod Serling would further describe the fifth dimension as "the middle ground between science and superstition. . . . between the pit of man's fear and the summit of his knowledge. These are the dimensions of the imagination. . . in an area which we call . . . The Twilight Zone."

2. On *All in the Family,* why do Mike and Gloria move to California?

a. To open a pizza parlor

b. To join a commune

c. Mike is offered a job

d. Gloria is offered a job

GAME 49 Q1 ANSWER a
The Dick Van Dyke Show (starring Mary Tyler Moore and Dick Van Dyke) centered on the lives of Rob and Laura Petrie and their son Robbie. *My Three Sons* starred Fred MacMurray as widower Stephen Douglas, who is left to raise his boys—Mike, Robbie, and Chip—first with the help of their maternal grandfather "Bub," and then with their Uncle Charlie.

2. What was the profession of the main character in the *The Bob Newhart Show*?

a. Dentist

b. Innkeeper

c. Veterinarian

d. Psychologist

GAME 69 Q1 ANSWER b
While Van Dyke's fall over the ottoman is the image that viewers remember, a second version of the credits—filmed along with the first one—showed the actor sidestepping the furniture. During the last four seasons of the series, the two openings were used randomly. The first season used an entirely different opening sequence.

GAME 12

11. During the 1990s on *NYPD Blue*, which actor was *not* partnered with Andy Sipowicz?

a. Rick Schroder

b. David Caruso

c. Mark-Paul Gosselaar

d. Jimmy Smits

GAME 12 Q10 ANSWER b
From its ironic use of Frank Sinatra's "Love and Marriage" as its theme song to its mockery of the "perfect" American family, this show has been described as one of the most offensive (and popular) TV shows of the 1990s. Once a high school football star, Al Bundy (played by Ed O'Neill) made a living by putting shoes on other peoples' feet.

GAME 32

11. When *Candid Camera* returned in 1998, who co-hosted it with Peter Funt?

a. Suzanne Somers

b. Whoopi Goldberg

c. Nancy McKeon

d. Eva LaRue

GAME 32 Q10 ANSWER c
Buffy Anne Summers was played by Sarah Michelle Gellar throughout the 1997–2003 run of the show. Initially, Gellar won the role of Cordelia Chase, one of Buffy's classmates at Sunnydale High. But after many auditions, creator Joss Whedon realized that he'd found his slayer, and the part of Cordelia Chase went to Charisma Carpenter.

GAME 52

11. Of the following, who was *not* a sibling on *The Waltons*?

a. Mary Ellen

b. Emma

c. Elizabeth

d. Jason

GAME 52 Q10 ANSWER c
Bradford wrote a column for a Sacramento newspaper while maintaining a paternal eye on his eight children—David, Mary, Joanie, Susan, Nancy, Elizabeth, Tommy, and Nicholas. In *TV Guide's* June 20, 2004 issue, the character "Tom Bradford" ranked #33 in the magazine's list of "50 Greatest TV Dads of All Time."

GAME 72

11. Which of these TV Western heroes was also a single parent?

a. The Rifleman

b. The Gunfighter

c. The Virginian

d. Maverick

GAME 72 Q10 ANSWER d
At first, James Garner was the only Maverick in the series, playing Bret. Then the studio hired Jack Kelly to play brother Bart, and Kelly rotated with Garner as the series lead. When Garner left the show over a contract dispute, Roger Moore was hired to play Cousin Beau, whose accent was explained by years spent living in England.

GAME 9

3. What 1960s TV series featured the characters Cinnamon Carter and Rollin Hand?

a. *Peyton Place*

b. *I Spy*

c. *Mission: Impossible*

d. *Gunsmoke*

GAME 9 Q2 ANSWER b

In *The Many Loves of Dobie Gillis,* busybody Zelda was played by Sheila James—who in 2006 became a member of the California State Senate. Although Zelda was hopelessly in love with Dobie (Dwayne Hickman), Dobie was attracted to the wealthy and beautiful Thalia Menninger (Tuesday Weld), as well as to a string of other beautiful women.

GAME 29

3. What words did Dr. Sam Beckett say at the end of each *Quantum Leap* episode?

a. "Here we go again"

b. "Oh boy"

c. "Leaping lizards"

d. "Not again"

GAME 29 Q2 ANSWER c

During the opening narration of this sci-fi series (1963–1965), the "Control Voice" would speak as the picture became snowy. It told viewers not to adjust their TV sets; that "they" were controlling the vertical, horizontal, volume, and focus. It then told them to sit quietly for the next hour—they were about to experience . . . *The Outer Limits.*

GAME 49

3. Where did "Fresh Prince" Will Smith live before moving to Bel-Air?

a. Detroit

b. Philadelphia

c. Cleveland

d. St. Louis

GAME 49 Q2 ANSWER c

Season Eight was the last for both Rob Reiner (Mike "Meathead" Stivic) and Sally Struthers (Gloria Bunker Stivic) to appear as regular members of the *All in the Family* cast. At the end of that season, the couple moved to Santa Barbara, where the perpetually unemployed Mike took a job as a college professor.

GAME 69

3. Who was in charge of the POW camp that housed *Hogan's Heroes*?

a. Hans Schultz

b. Albert Burkhalter

c. Wilhelm Klink

d. Major Hochstetter

GAME 69 Q2 ANSWER d

In this sitcom, which aired from 1972 to 1978, Newhart played Chicago psychologist Robert Hartley. A later Bob Newhart show, simply titled *Newhart* (1982 to 1990), cast the actor-comedian as Dick Loudon, an author of do-it-yourself books who moves to Vermont to operate an inn.

10. Where did Al Bundy work on the FOX series *Married . . . with Children*?

a. Clothing store
b. Shoe store
c. Hardware store
d. Furniture store

GAME 12 Q9 ANSWER d
Played by Tom Skerritt, Jimmy Brock was married to Dr. Jill Brock, played by Kathy Baker. The show, which also featured actors Don Cheadle and Lauren Holly, ran from 1992 to 1996 on CBS and won fourteen Emmys. *Martial Law; Walker, Texas Ranger;* and *Dr. Quinn, Medicine Woman* were all CBS series in the '90s.

---

10. What was Buffy's last name in *Buffy the Vampire Slayer*?

a. Winters
b. Rosenberg
c. Summers
d. Chase

GAME 32 Q9 ANSWER b
When Things Were Rotten, which aired for only half a season on ABC, was a parody of the Robin Hood legend. The cast included Richard Gautier as Robin, Bernie Kopell as Alan-a-Dale, Misty Rowe as Maid Marian—and Dick Van Patten as Friar Tuck. The show's cancellation permitted Van Patten to move on to the highly successful *Eight Is Enough.*

---

10. What was Tom Bradford's occupation in *Eight Is Enough*?

a. Magazine editor
b. Photojournalist
c. Newspaper columnist
d. Book editor

GAME 52 Q9 ANSWER b
When their parents were killed by a drunk driver, the five Salinger siblings were left to fend for themselves and stay together as a family on this FOX Network drama. The show, which aired from 1994 to 2000, helped launch the careers of several cast members, including Jennifer Love Hewitt, Neve Campbell, Matthew Fox, and Scott Wolf.

---

10. Which TV Western featured British actor Roger Moore?

a. *Paladin*
b. *The Big Valley*
c. *Bonanza*
d. *Maverick*

GAME 72 Q9 ANSWER a
The first "adult" TV Western produced by Warner Brothers, *Cheyenne* featured Clint Walker as Cheyenne Bodie, a former frontier scout who drifted through the Old West from one adventure to another, without any known motivation. Some episodes were actually remakes of Warner Brothers movies, with the character of Cheyenne inserted in the plot.

GAME 9	**4. In 1963, who had a TV show bearing her name?** a. Loretta Young b. Patty Duke c. Betty Grable d. Mary Tyler Moore	**GAME 9 Q3 ANSWER c** Carter and Hand were played by Barbara Bain and Martin Landau, who were married in real life. Their children include producer Susan Landau Finch and actress Juliet Laundau, who is best known for portraying the demented vampire Drusilla in the long-running series *Buffy the Vampire Slayer.*

GAME 29	**4. The TV show *Tales from the Crypt* was based on a 1950s:** a. Radio program b. Comic book series c. Short story d. Novella	**GAME 29 Q3 ANSWER b** "Oh boy" became the show's signature final line as Sam (Scott Bakula) leapt into the past —and into a new body—at the end of each episode. It was originally an ad-lib by Bakula, who, as scientist Dr. Sam Beckett, tried to "set things right that once went wrong" after making each leap. The NBC show ran five seasons (1989–1993).

GAME 49	**4. Who joined the cast of *Eight Simple Rules* as a regular after John Ritter's death?** a. Burt Reynolds b. Tom Skerritt c. James Garner d. Gerald McRaney	**GAME 49 Q3 ANSWER b** On this NBC sitcom, which ran from 1990 to 1996, William "Will" Smith was a streetwise inner-city Philadelphia teen who was headed for obvious trouble. In an effort to keep him on the right path and maintain good old-fashioned values, his mother sent him to live with rich relatives—the Banks family—in Bel Air, California.

GAME 69	**4. On *M*A*S*H*, with whom did Hot Lips have a long-standing affair?** a. Frank Burns b. Trapper John McIntyre c. Henry Blake d. Hawkeye Pierce	**GAME 69 Q3 ANSWER c** Played by Werner Klemperer, Colonel Wilhelm Klink was a patriotic but bumbling bureaucrat. Easily manipulated by Hogan (Bob Crane) and his fellow prisoners of war, Klink was actually an unwitting aid to the Allies' spying and sabotage efforts. For that reason, Hogan was always worried that Klink would be transferred out of the camp.

GAME 12

9. In which drama did Midwestern sheriff Jimmy Brock lay down the law?

a. *Martial Law*

b. *Walker, Texas Ranger*

c. *Dr. Quinn, Medicine Woman*

d. *Picket Fences*

GAME 12 Q8 ANSWER c
In the early '80s, Flaherty was a regular on the Canadian comedy shows *Second City TV* and *SCTV Network 90*. *The Kids in the Hall* was a five-man Canadian comedy troupe, and their show was produced by fellow Canadian and *SNL* creator Lorne Michaels. In 1996, they made a feature film called *Brain Candy*.

GAME 32

9. *When Things Were _____* was a 1975 TV sitcom created by Mel Brooks.

a. Swell

b. Rotten

c. Sad

d. Great

GAME 32 Q8 ANSWER d
Beals' character, Bette Porter, is an Ivy League-educated woman of mixed race. And, in fact, Jennifer Beals—perhaps best known as Alex in the 1983 movie *Flashdance*—was born to a black father and an Irish-American mother, and pursued a degree in American Literature at Yale University.

GAME 52

9. On *Party of Five*, the family ran Salingers, a:

a. Deli

b. Restaurant

c. Coffee shop

d. Pizza parlor

GAME 52 Q8 ANSWER a
Nick Moore (Scott Valentine) looked and sounded very much like Sylvester Stallone at the height of his *Rambo* years. Though he was ultimately accepted and loved by the Keaton family, Nick was initially a threat to father Steven Keaton (Michael Gross), who, although once staunchly liberal, had become ever more conservative over the years.

GAME 72

9. In the series *Cheyenne*, what was the last name of the title character?

a. Bodie

b. Beaumont

c. Smith

d. Miller

GAME 72 Q8 ANSWER b
Created at a time when TV Westerns were losing ground to spy series, CBS's *Wild Wild West* fused Western elements with those of espionage, comedy, and even science fiction. The show told the story of two Secret Service agents, played by Robert Conrad and Ross Martin, whose mission was to protect President Ulysses S. Grant.

GAME 9

5. Peggy Lipton played a key role in what 1960s police drama?

a. *Mannix*

b. *Man From U.N.C.L.E.*

c. *Adam-12*

d. *Mod Squad*

GAME 9 Q4 ANSWER b

Created as a vehicle for rising star Patty Duke, *The Patty Duke Show* ran from 1963 to 1966. In this highly popular program, Duke played look-alike cousins Patty and Cathy Lane, who both lived with Patty's parents in Brooklyn Heights, New York. The dual role challenged not only the show's star, but also the special effects of the time.

GAME 29

5. William Shatner played a rattled airplane passenger in which *Twilight Zone* classic?

a. "Nightmare at 20,000 Feet"

b. "The Last Flight"

c. "Odyssey of Flight 33"

d. "On the Wing"

GAME 29 Q4 ANSWER b

The episodes for this Emmy-nominated HBO series were based on EC Comics' *The Vault of Horror, The Haunt of Fear, Shock SuspenStories,* and *Tales from the Crypt* by William Gaines. Hosted by a ghoulish puppet—a decaying corpse called the Crypt Keeper—the show featured horror stories with genuine dilemmas, twist endings, and lots of humor.

GAME 49

5. Which popular 1950s sitcom featured brothers David and Ricky?

a. *Adventures of Ozzie and Harriet*

b. *Father Knows Best*

c. *The Real McCoys*

d. *Make Room for Daddy*

GAME 49 Q4 ANSWER c

Ritter starred on the ABC sitcom as patriarch of the Hennessey family. In 2003, after filming a few second-season episodes, Ritter collapsed on the set and died later that day. James Garner, who played the father of Cate Hennessey (Katey Sagal), became a regular cast member shortly after. Ritter earned a posthumous Emmy nomination for his role.

GAME 69

5. What was Fred Sanford's occupation on *Sanford and Son*?

a. School janitor

b. Gas station owner

c. Junk dealer

d. Short-order cook

GAME 69 Q4 ANSWER a

Larry Linville played pompous Frank Burns (described on the show as a "medical moron") from 1972 to 1977. When Hot Lips got married, Frank was heartbroken and began to exhibit dark and unstable behavior. Linville felt the character had gone as far as it could go, and ultimately Frank Burns was written out of the series at Linville's request.

GAME 12

8. Which performer did *not* appear on *The Kids in the Hall*?

a. Dave Foley

b. Bruce McCulloch

c. Joe Flaherty

d. Mark McKinney

GAME 12 Q7 ANSWER d
Known in the '80s as the star of the CBS series *Magnum, P.I.*, Selleck reinvented himself in the '90s as the suave doctor Richard Burke—who almost romances Monica (Courteney Cox) away from Chandler (Matthew Perry). Brad Pitt, Ben Stiller, and Bruce Willis all appeared on *Friends* during its popular ten-season NBC run.

GAME 32

8. Which character does Jennifer Beals play on the Showtime series *The L Word*?

a. Tina Kennard

b. Dana Fairbanks

c. Alice Pieszecki

d. Bette Porter

GAME 32 Q7 ANSWER a
Moviegoers are familiar with actor and director Wahlberg, who appeared in a number of successful films, including *Boogie Nights, Three Kings, The Perfect Storm,* and *The Italian Job.* Wahlberg was also an original member of the pop group New Kids on the Block, but quit before the group became successful.

GAME 52

8. Who was Mallory Keaton's artist boyfriend on *Family Ties*?

a. Nick

b. Jack

c. Rick

d. Mike

GAME 52 Q7 ANSWER b
After the family cleans out the attic, both Greg (Barry Williams) and Marcia (Maureen McCormick) battle for the room as their own. Although Greg gives in, his younger brothers don't want him back in their room, so they devise a plan to make Marcia realize what a hassle the extra flight is. Greg eventually gets the room.

GAME 72

8. Which 1960s Western featured a special train fitted with bizarre weapons and devices?

a. *The Outlaws*

b. *The Wild Wild West*

c. *Bat Masterson*

d. *A Man Called Shenandoah*

GAME 72 Q7 ANSWER c
When *Bonanza* debuted in 1959 on NBC, the first show began with the cast riding toward the camera on horseback, singing lyrics to the *Bonanza* theme song. This opening was quickly replaced with the famous burning map of the Ponderosa ranch and an instrumental version of the show's theme.

GAME 9

6. Starting in 1965, *Petticoat Junction* shared some characters with what other show?

a. *Green Acres*

b. *Wild Wild West*

c. *Mayberry RFD*

d. *Beverly Hillbillies*

GAME 9 Q5 ANSWER d

The series cast Lipton as detective Julie Barnes. The premise was that Barnes, Pete Cochran (Michael Cole) and Linc Hayes (Clarence Williams III), were troubled but "hip" young investigators who had been given the chance to fight crime as an alternative to incarceration.

GAME 29

6. Which of the following TV shows does *not* involve supernatural communication?

a. *Ghost Whisperer*

b. *Psych*

c. *Joan of Arcadia*

d. *Tru Calling*

GAME 29 Q5 ANSWER a

In this famous episode, Emmy-winning actor William Shatner plays a recently released sanitarium patient. While flying home, he looks out the window and sees a gremlin-like monster who is about to bring down the plane. Twenty years later, in *Twilight Zone: The Movie,* John Lithgow plays the same role in an updated version of the story.

GAME 49

6. Which TV series was first to include a working mom?

a. *The Many Loves of Dobie Gillis*

b. *Julia*

c. *One Day at a Time*

d. *Alice*

GAME 49 Q5 ANSWER a

The real-life Nelson family (Ozzie, Harriet, David, and Ricky) starred in *The Adventures of Ozzie and Harriet,* which began its fourteen-year run on ABC in 1952. The show embodied a wholesome, gently humorous look at a "typical" American family. Previously, the show, which was Ozzie's idea, had enjoyed ten years as a popular radio show.

GAME 69

6. In the opening credits of *The Mary Tyler Moore Show,* what did Mary toss into the air?

a. Her purse

b. Her scarf

c. Her hat

d. Her briefcase

GAME 69 Q5 ANSWER c

Fred was played by comic Redd Foxx, whose real name was John Sanford, and whose real-life brother was Fred Sanford. Although Foxx's name always conjures the image of junk-dealing Fred, Foxx first gained fame for his raunchy nightclub act, and was one of the first black comics to play to white audiences on the Las Vegas Strip.

Answers are in right-hand boxes on page 223.   **221**

GAME 12

7. Which actor played one of Monica's boyfriends on *Friends*?

a. Brad Pitt
b. Ben Stiller
c. Bruce Willis
d. Tom Selleck

GAME 12 Q6 ANSWER c
Actor Chris Burke (who actually has Down syndrome) starred as Charles "Corky" Thatcher in this family-oriented ABC drama. In addition to dealing realistically and sensitively to issues of mental retardation, the show also featured a character (played by Chad Lowe) who was HIV positive. In 1993, Lowe won an Emmy for the role.

GAME 32

7. On which producer's experiences is the HBO series *Entourage* based?

a. Mark Wahlberg
b. Steven Bocho
c. David E. Kelly
d. Aaron Sorkin

GAME 32 Q6 ANSWER b
Harry Morgan may be best known for portraying Officer Bill Gannon on *Dragnet 1967,* and Colonel Sherman T. Potter on *M*A*S*H*. But Baby Boom viewers may remember first seeing Morgan play Pete Porter in the 1954–1959 comedy *December Bride*.

GAME 52

7. Who got the attic as a bedroom on *The Brady Bunch*?

a. Bobby
b. Greg
c. Marcia
d. Jan

GAME 52 Q6 ANSWER d
Detective Phil Fish (Abe Vigoda) from the sitcom *Barney Miller,* was the main character in this short-lived spinoff. The New York cop and his wife, Bernice (Florence Stanley), became foster parents to some rowdy, street-smart kids. During the early days of the series, Fish's character made occasional appearances at *Barney Miller's* 12th Precinct.

GAME 72

7. Which Western's opening credits began with a burning map?

a. *Gunsmoke*
b. *Wagon Train*
c. *Bonanza*
d. *Rawhide*

GAME 72 Q6 ANSWER a
Deadwood's Albert Swearengen was the proprietor of the popular Gem Saloon. He was also the *de facto* head of the town of Deadwood, which he ruled through various criminal endeavors. As eccentric as he was violent, Swearengen was given to having long conversations with a cardboard box that contained the severed head of a Sioux chief.

---

7. In what series was Moon-doggie a recurring character?

a. *My Three Sons*

b. *Hawaiian Eye*

c. *Gidget*

d. *Surfside Six*

GAME 9 Q6 ANSWER a
Both shows took place in or near Hooter-ville, and frequently shared characters Newt Kiley (Kay E. Kuter) and Eb Dawson (Tom Lester). While *Petticoat Junction* was canceled in 1970 due to falling ratings, *Green Acres* was canceled in 1971 simply because CBS wanted stories that appealed to a younger urban audience.

7. In a famous *Twilight Zone* episode, the phrase "To Serve Man" refers to:

a. A cookbook

b. Female robots

c. Alien servants

d. Behavior modification

GAME 29 Q6 ANSWER b
The police in *Psych* "think" Shawn (James Roday) is a psychic, but in reality, he simply has a very keen eye for detail. In *Ghost Whisperer*, Melinda (Jennifer Love Hewitt) talks to the dead. Joan (Amber Tamblyn) speaks with God in *Joan of Arcadia*. And in *Tru Calling*, Tru (Eliza Dushku) works in a morgue, where corpses often ask for her help.

7. *Arrested Developmment's* George Bluth, Sr. did *not* do which of the following?

a. Join the Blue Man Group

b. Invent the Cornballer

c. Fake his death

d. Enter the Witness Protection Program

GAME 49 Q6 ANSWER a
Although the advent of TV working mothers didn't occur until the late '60s/early '70s—when shows like *Julia, Alice,* and *One Day at a Time* saw single mothers working to make ends meet—Dobie's mom, Winnie Gillis (Florida Friebus) was actually the first. Throughout the series (1959–1963), she worked in the family grocery store.

7. What did Jeannie do when using her magic on *I Dream of Jeannie*?

a. Whistled

b. Waved a wand

c. Twitched her nose

d. Blinked and nodded

GAME 69 Q6 ANSWER c
The show's famous opening montage was created by Reza Badiyi, who also designed the opening montage for *Hawaii Five-0*. So legendary was Mary Richard's cap toss that in 2002, it was immortalized by a statue in downtown Minneapolis, Minnesota—the city where the show's action took place.

6. Which early '90s series featured a family member with Down syndrome?

a. *A Different World*

b. *Empty Nest*

c. *Life Goes On*

d. *Sibs*

GAME 12 Q5 ANSWER c
Fighting loudly about everything from bras and water picks to marble ryes and Korean ex-girlfriends, Frank and Estelle Costanza (Jerry Stiller and Estelle Harris) are exactly the kind of parents who could create a nut like George (Jason Alexander). George's character was based on the life of *Seinfeld* co-creator Larry David.

6. Which of the following series did *not* feature actor Harry Morgan?

a. *December Bride*

b. *Bat Masterson*

c. *M*A*S*H*

d. *Dragnet*

GAME 32 Q5 ANSWER d
Monday Night Football made its ABC debut in 1970, and ran on that network until 2005, broadcasting a total of 555 games before the show moved to ESPN. Its first game—a September 21 match between the New York Jets and the Cleveland Browns—garnered 33 percent of the viewing audience.

6. The title character of which 1970s show was a foster parent?

a. *Chico and the Man*

b. *Quincy, M.E.*

c. *Newhart*

d. *Fish*

GAME 52 Q5 ANSWER c
Oldest Ingalls daughter Mary (Melissa Sue Anderson) goes blind after a bout with scarlet fever, and is sent to a school for the blind in Iowa. There she meets and falls in love with teacher Adam Kendall (Linwood Boomer), who is also blind. When Adam opens his own school, Mary joins him and they eventually marry.

6. Which character did Ian McShane play on the HBO series *Deadwood*?

a. Al Swearengen

b. Cy Tolliver

c. Doc Cochran

d. Seth Bullock

GAME 72 Q5 ANSWER b
Despite his name, The Virginian—played by James Drury, and given no other name during the show's run—lived in Medicine Bow, Wyoming, where he struggled to maintain an orderly lifestyle on the Shiloh Ranch. Running from 1962 to 1971 on NBC, this was the first Western to air in ninety-minute installments.

8. Which TV show was revived in 1967 after an eight-year hiatus?

a. *Gunsmoke*

b. *Dragnet*

c. *Ozzie and Harriet*

d. *Wagon Train*

GAME 9 Q7 ANSWER c

Moondoggie was Gidget's boyfriend both in the 1965 series and in the earlier Gidget movies. The TV show *Gidget*, as well as the three movies that preceded it, were all based on the 1957 novel *Gidget, The Little Girl With the Big Ideas*, in which author Frederick Kohner shared the adventures of his surfing daughter Kathy.

8. Which filmmaker's TV debut was the pilot episode of *Rod Serling's Night Gallery*?

a. Robert Zemeckis

b. Rob Reiner

c. George Lucas

d. Steven Spielberg

GAME 29 Q7 ANSWER a

The highly advanced alien Kanamits come to earth and begin to solve man's biggest problems—sickness, hunger, war. But when code breakers translate one of the Kanamits' books, with its harmless title "To Serve Man," they discover it is a cookbook (and realize the aliens' true intentions). The episode is based on a short story by Damon Knight.

8. Which of the following shows did *not* have an adopted family member?

a. *Webster*

b. *My Three Sons*

c. *Full House*

d. *Diff'rent Strokes*

GAME 49 Q7 ANSWER d

Patriarch of the highly dysfunctional (and hilarious) Bluth family, George Sr (Jeffrey Tambor) was involved with fraud, grand theft, and treason (he built model homes for Saddam Hussein). He was also a "serial poisoner," intimidating teachers of his children and grandchildren with poison muffins. The Emmy-winning FOX series ran from 2003 to 2006.

8. What was unique about *The George Burns & Gracie Allen Show*?

a. Burns spoke directly to viewers

b. Allen sang her dialogue

c. It was unscripted

d. It was two hours long

GAME 69 Q7 ANSWER d

Creator Sidney Sheldon hoped (in vain) that *I Dream of Jeannie* would be as successful as ABC's *Bewitched*, which also blended magical characters with mere mortals. The genie idea was inspired by the 1963 movie *The Brass Bottle*, which starred Tony Randall, Burl Ives (as the genie), and genie-to-be Barbara Eden.

5. Who are George Costanza's parents on *Seinfeld*?

a. Leroy and Maxine

b. Morty and Helga

c. Frank and Estelle

d. Leo and Lylah

GAME 12 Q4 ANSWER b
NBC hired Conan O'Brien as its new late-night host after David Letterman moved to CBS to compete against Jay Leno's *Tonight Show*. Former writer for *The Simpsons*, O'Brien used his devilish wit to build a strong fan base. His emcee performance at the 2006 Emmys was considered one of the best in the show's history.

5. Which of the following shows could you *not* have seen in 1960?

a. *Mister Ed*

b. *The Andy Griffith Show*

c. *Rocky and Bullwinkle*

d. *Monday Night Football*

GAME 32 Q4 ANSWER c
Canadian-born Lorne Michaels began his career as a writer for CBC radio in Toronto, but after moving to Los Angeles in 1968, he wrote for both *Rowan & Martin's Laugh-In* and *The Beautiful Phyllis Diller Show*. Michaels is perhaps best known for creating the Emmy Award-winning *Saturday Night Live*.

5. Which member of the *Little House on the Prairie* family lost her sight?

a. Carrie

b. Laura

c. Mary

d. Caroline

GAME 52 Q4 ANSWER a
The show, co-created by Dick Clark, centers on the life of Jack and Helen Pryor and their four kids, as they face the cultural and political changes of the '60s and '70s. Daughter Meg becomes a dancer on *American Bandstand,* and each episode features partially recreated versions of musical acts that originally appeared on the real *Bandstand*.

5. Where did *The Virginian* live?

a. Laramie

b. Medicine Bow

c. Tombstone

d. Dodge City

GAME 72 Q4 ANSWER c
James Arness was a good choice to play *Gunsmoke's* larger-than-life Marshall Matt Dillon. Standing six feet and seven inches tall, Arness was a World War II hero, and is said to have been the first soldier sent off his landing craft at Anzio so that the depth of the water could be assessed before the rest of the soldiers left the craft.

9. Which television character from the 1960s was a medical doctor?

a. Owen Marshall

b. Steve Douglas

c. Julia Baker

d. David Zorba

GAME 9 Q8 ANSWER b

Created by actor and producer Jack Webb, who played Sergeant Friday, *Dragnet* was first a radio show that ran from 1949 to 1957. The first run of the TV show was 1951 to 1959, and the second was 1967 to 1970. So beloved was *Dragnet* that when Webb died in 1982, the chief of the LAPD retired badge 714: Friday's badge number.

---

9. Which Eagles' song has a similar theme to the *Outer Limits* episode titled "The Guests"?

a. "Hotel California"

b. "Desperado"

c. "Life in the Fast Lane"

d. "New Kid in Town"

GAME 29 Q8 ANSWER d

Created by *Twilight Zone's* Rod Serling, the show was set in a dark gallery. Each episode told three stories, and each story was based on one of the gallery's nightmarish paintings. The show's 1969 pilot helped launch the career of Steven Spielberg, who, in his first industry job, directed legendary actress Joan Crawford in one of the film's segments.

---

9. Which of the following is *not* one of the sons on *Home Improvement*?

a. Brian

b. Mark

c. Randy

d. Brad

GAME 49 Q8 ANSWER c

Bob Saget starred on *Full House* as a widower raising three daughters. Emanuel Lewis was *Webster*, who was adopted by George and Catherine (Alex Karras and Susan Clark). On *My Three Sons*, the Douglas family adopted Ernie (Barry Livingston). The Drummonds adopted brothers Arnold (Gary Coleman) and Willis (Todd Bridges) on *Diff'rent Strokes*.

---

9. Where did Janet of *Three's Company* work?

a. A dress shop

b. A flower shop

c. A gift shop

d. A chocolate shop

GAME 69 Q8 ANSWER a

George Burns—who played himself on the show—often broke the "fourth wall," stepping away from the action of the sitcom and chatting directly with the home audience. Burns would use these monologues to tell jokes and make wry comments about the actions of the other characters.

---

4. In 1993, which network debuted *Late Night with Conan O'Brien*?

a. CBS

b. NBC

c. FOX

d. ABC

GAME 12 Q3 ANSWER c
Twin sisters Ashley and Mary-Kate Olsen were born in 1986 on Friday the 13th. Due to work limits set by child labor laws, the twins took turns playing the youngest of Bob Saget's three daughters on *Full House*. This popular ABC family sitcom also starred John Stamos and Candace Cameron, younger sister to Kirk Cameron of *Growing Pains* fame.

---

4. Which producer wrote monologues for *Laugh-In* as one of his first TV jobs?

a. James L. Brooks

b. Larry David

c. Lorne Michaels

d. Norman Lear

GAME 32 Q3 ANSWER d
Before Jack Benny was a comedian, he was a violinist. He began studying the instrument at age six, and was playing in local bands at fourteen. Benny quit school when he learned he could make a living playing the violin in vaudeville. Although he eventually became a great comedian, the violin always remained his trademark.

---

4. In what city does the Pryor family live in *American Dreams*?

a. Philadelphia

b. Boston

c. Detroit

d. Pittsburgh

GAME 52 Q3 ANSWER b
The show revolved around widowed mom Shirley Partridge (Shirley Jones), who formed a band with her five kids—Keith, Laurie, Danny, Chris, and Tracy. They toured the country in a colorful school bus. David Cassidy, who played Keith, is Jones' real-life stepson. The show was inspired by The Cowsills, a singing family of the 1960s.

---

4. Which actor starred in the longest-running TV Western series?

a. James Garner

b. Clint Walker

c. James Arness

d. Lorne Greene

GAME 72 Q3 ANSWER a
Throughout *Dr. Quinn's* 1993–1998 run, storekeeper Loren Bray was played by Orson Bean. Although Bean has acted in several television shows, appeared on stage and in film, and also authored a number of books, he is perhaps best known as a long-time panelist on the game show *To Tell the Truth*.

GAME 9

10. Which 1960s TV series starred Bruce Lee?

a. *Kung Fu*
b. *Land of The Lost*
c. *Green Hornet*
d. *Hong Kong*

GAME 9 Q9 ANSWER d
Played by Sam Jaffe, Dr. David Zorba was Ben Casey's mentor on the medical drama *Ben Casey*. Running on ABC from 1961 to 1966, the show competed against *Dr. Kildare*, which was broadcast during the exact same years. The two highly successful series sparked a number of shows dealing with the medical profession.

GAME 29

10. *Twilight Zone's* "Time Enough at Last" episode deals with which sci-fi theme?

a. Alien invasion
b. Time travel
c. Mutation
d. Nuclear holocaust

GAME 29 Q9 ANSWER a
While the lyrics to the song and plot of the 1964 *Outer Limits* episode are eerily similar, the song's true inspiration can't be verified. In this episode, an alien is disguised as a gothic mansion to observe humanity through its guests, who are not able to leave. At the Hotel California, guests can "check out" but they "can never leave."

GAME 49

10. Which series featured a hip, promiscuous grandmother named Mona Robinson?

a. *Growing Pains*
b. *Family Ties*
c. *Who's the Boss*
d. *The Cosby Show*

GAME 49 Q9 ANSWER a
Home Improvement starred Tim Allen as Tim Taylor, family man and host of the fictional TV show *Tool Time*. He and wife, Jill (Patricia Richardson), lived in the Detroit suburb of Royal Oak with their three mischievous sons. The Emmy-winning ABC comedy first aired in 1991 and enjoyed an eight-season run.

GAME 69

10. What was the name of Samantha's mother on *Bewitched*?

a. Endora
b. Esmeralda
c. Hepzibah
d. Tabitha

GAME 69 Q9 ANSWER b
Janet Wood (Joyce DeWitt) worked at the Arcade Flower Shop, and was fond of the plants that adorned her apartment. In fact, in the first few seasons of the show, the opening credits showed her accidentally pouring water on roommate Chrissy Snow (Suzanne Somers) as she watered a plant. Chrissy, by the way, worked as a temporary typist.

3. The Olsen twins played Michelle Tanner on which sitcom?

a. *The Wonder Years*

b. *Growing Pains*

c. *Full House*

d. *Major Dad*

GAME 12 Q2 ANSWER c
Although the series took place in Cicely, Alaska, the show was actually filmed in Roslyn, Washington. Featuring an assortment of eccentric characters, *Northern Exposure* took off after debuting on CBS as a summer replacement series in 1990. It also launched the careers of Janine Turner and *Sex and the City's* John Corbett.

3. What was the subject in which Jack Benny won $64 on *The $64,000 Question*?

a. American history

b. Comics

c. Boxing

d. Violins

GAME 32 Q2 ANSWER a
Laura and Rob, played by Mary Tyler Moore and Dick Van Dyke, were the main characters in *The Dick Van Dyke Show*. *The Adventures of Ozzie and Harriet* featured real-life husband and wife Ozzie and Harriet Nelson. And Archie and Edith—Carroll O'Connor and Jean Stapleton—headed the cast of *All in the Family*.

3. How many kids were in *The Partridge Family*?

a. Four

b. Five

c. Six

d. Seven

GAME 52 Q2 ANSWER d
Stephen Collins stars as Eric Camden, a Protestant minister who lives in suburban LA with his family. The series premiered in 1996 on the WB Network and its original series finale aired in spring of 2006. The final episode received such high ratings, the show was renewed by the CW Network and began its eleventh season in fall of 2006.

3. Who ran the general store in *Dr. Quinn, Medicine Woman*?

a. Loren Bray

b. Jake Slicker

c. Hank Claggerty

d. Horace Bing

GAME 72 Q2 ANSWER b
Airing on NBC from 1957 to 1962, and on ABC from 1962 to 1965, *Wagon Train* followed the adventures of people migrating from Missouri to California. The show was so popular that when Gene Roddenberry pitched *Star Trek* to network executives, he referred to his series as "a *Wagon Train* to the stars."

GAME 9

11. Who played Dr. Richard Kimble, the hero of the 1960s series *The Fugitive*?

a. Chris Elliott

b. Lloyd Bridges

c. Robert Stack

d. David Janssen

GAME 9 Q10 ANSWER c

Inspired by the success of the *Batman* TV series, ABC launched *The Green Hornet* in 1966. But despite interest in martial arts master Bruce Lee, who played the Green Hornet's trusty sidekick Kato, the show was canceled after one season. Afterwards, Lee opened his own Jeet Kune Do school, and eventually, he became a cult movie star.

GAME 29

11. Which of the following TV miniseries was *not* based on a book by Stephen King?

a. *Salem's Lot*

b. *The Shining*

c. *Rose Red*

d. *The Tommyknockers*

GAME 29 Q10 ANSWER d

Burgess Meredith plays a book-loving banker who never has time to read. When he sneaks into the bank vault to read, a jolt knocks him out. He awakens to find that he is the sole survivor of an H-bomb. Ironically, when he makes his way to the library and surrounds himself with the books he now has time to read, his glasses fall and break.

GAME 49

11. How many children did Florida and James have on the CBS sitcom *Good Times*?

a. Two

b. Three

c. Four

d. Five

GAME 49 Q10 ANSWER c

Katherine Helmond played the mother of ad executive Angela Bower (Judith Light) on this ABC sitcom (1984–1982). Tony Danza starred as Brooklyn widower Tony Micelli, who took a job as Angela's housekeeper in upscale Connecticut to give his daughter a better life. Helmond also played Ray Romano's mother-in-law on *Everybody Loves Raymond*.

GAME 69

11. What did Andy and Opie carry during the opening credits of *The Andy Griffith Show*?

a. A baseball and bat

b. Groceries

c. Hunting rifles

d. Fishing poles

GAME 69 Q10 ANSWER a

Played by Agnes Moorehead, Endora disapproved of daughter Samantha's mortal husband, Darrin, and many *Bewitched* episodes revolved around Endora's using magic to make life difficult for her son-in law. At the end of each episode, though, Darrin would always affirm his love for his wife despite the problems caused by witchcraft.

GAME 12

2. In which fictional Alaskan town was *Northern Exposure* set?

a. Soldotna

b. Big Delta

c. Cicely

d. Roslyn

GAME 12 Q1 ANSWER d
Patinkin's performance as Dr. Jeffrey Geiger, a "brilliant but often difficult" surgeon, aired about a decade before Hugh Laurie's Golden Globe-winning performance as *House's* "brilliant but often difficult" Dr. Gregory House. In 2005, Patinkin returned to TV in the CBS crime show *Criminal Minds*.

GAME 32

2. Which of these is *not* a classic sitcom couple?

a. Ralph and Winnie

b. Laura and Rob

c. Ozzie and Harriet

d. Archie and Edith

GAME 32 Q1 ANSWER b
In 1988, the ABC show *Head of the Class* broke new ground when it filmed an entire episode in the Soviet Union. The episode, which concerned an academic meet, ended with the American and Russian teams attending a concert in Gorky Park, listening to a song sung by American David Pomeranz and Russian rock star Alexander Manilin.

GAME 52

2. What TV show tells the story of the Camden family?

a. *Sister, Sister*

b. *Moesha*

c. *Felicity*

d. *7th Heaven*

GAME 52 Q1 ANSWER a
Sondra (Sabrina LeBeauf) was the Huxtable family's fourth daughter—a role almost landed by Whitney Houston. Bill Cosby, the sitcom's star and co-creator, modeled the TV family after his own. *The Cosby Show* (1984–1992) is one of two TV shows that have been #1 in the Nielsen Ratings for five consecutive seasons. *All in the Family* is the other.

GAME 72

2. What was the starting point of the *Wagon Train* caravan?

a. Texas

b. Missouri

c. Georgia

d. North Carolina

GAME 72 Q1 ANSWER d
Originally owned and trained by Glenn Randall, Sr., Buttermilk was offered to Dale Evans because her first movie horse looked too much like Roy Rogers' horse, Trigger. Dale rode Buttermilk in all but six of *The Roy Rogers Show* episodes that aired from 1951 to 1957.

GAME 9

12. Who was the narrator of the early 1960s TV crime drama *The Untouchables*?

a. Orson Welles
b. Walter Winchell
c. William Conrad
d. Rod Serling

GAME 9 Q11 ANSWER d
It is believed that the plot of *The Fugitive*, in which Dr. Richard Kimble is falsely accused of his wife's murder, was based on the real-life case of Dr. Samuel Sheppard. Unlike Kimble, who eluded incarceration, Sheppard was convicted of his wife's murder and served almost a decade in prison before the conviction was overturned.

GAME 29

12. Which of the following TV series is based on a real-life story?

a. *Medium*
b. *Profiler*
c. *Supernatural*
d. *Bones*

GAME 29 Q11 ANSWER c
Rose Red was a 2002 "original" TV miniseries written by King. In it, a team of parapsychologists unleashes the spirit of the former owner of a decrepit mansion, and uncovers the horrifying secrets of those who lived there. Other original TV miniseries scripted by King include *The Golden Years* (1991) and *Storm of the Century* (1999).

GAME 49

12. What was Carl Winslow's occupation on *Family Matters*?

a. Police officer
b. Fireman
c. Candy shop owner
d. Sanitation worker

GAME 49 Q11 ANSWER b
Florida (Esther Rolle) and James (John Amos) lived in inner-city Chicago with their kids—JJ, Thelma, and Michael. The writers' focus on JJ (Jimmie Walker), whose "Dy-no-mite" became a '70s catchphrase, caused tension with the cast, especially Rolle and Amos, who were upset with JJ's increasingly silly antics and negative stereotypical behavior.

GAME 69

12. In the theme song to *Gilligan's Island*, what was Gilligan called?

a. Trusted mate
b. Brave sea dog
c. Mighty sailing man
d. Crusty old salt

GAME 69 Q11 ANSWER d
The show's distinctive whistled theme song—"The Fishin' Hole" by Earle Hagen and Herbert Spencer—played over the idyllic scene. The credit sequence was filmed at California's Franklin Canyon Lake, which also served as a location for episodes of *Combat*, *Bonanza*, and *Star Trek*, as well as the film *On Golden Pond*.

GAME 12	1. For which show did Mandy Patinkin win a Best Actor Emmy in 1995? a. *Father Murphy* b. *Hunter* c. *Mad About You* d. *Chicago Hope*	The answer to this question is on: **page 232, top frame, right side.**
GAME 32	1. What school show was the first American sitcom to shoot an episode in Moscow? a. *Square Pegs* b. *Head of the Class* c. *Room 222* d. *A Different World*	The answer to this question is on: **page 232, second frame, right side.**
GAME 52	1. Which of the following was *not* a daughter on *The Cosby Show*? a. Emily b. Rudy c. Vanessa d. Denise	The answer to this question is on: **page 232, third frame, right side.**
GAME 72	1. What was the name of Dale Evans' horse on *The Roy Rogers Show*? a. Nellybelle b. Buttercup c. Bullet d. Buttermilk	The answer to this question is on: **page 232, bottom frame, right side.**

GAME 10

TV of the 1970s

Turn to page 237
for the first question.

GAME 9 Q12 ANSWER b
Newspaper and radio commentator Walter Winchell is credited with inventing the gossip column at the *New York Evening Graphic*. When Winchell narrated *The Untouchables* for five seasons, beginning in 1959, it was felt that his highly recognizable voice lent credibility to the ABC show. In return, Winchell was paid $25,000 per episode.

GAME 30

Suspense and High Drama

Turn to page 237
for the first question.

GAME 29 Q12 ANSWER a
"She sees what others can't." *Medium* is based on the life of research medium Allison Dubois, who, since childhood, has tried to make sense of her dreams and visions of dead people. For her portrayal of Dubois, actress Patricia Arquette earned a 2005 Emmy for Outstanding Lead Actress in a Drama Series.

GAME 50

Good Night and Good Luck

Turn to page 237
for the first question.

GAME 49 Q12 ANSWER a
Initially, the focus of this *Perfect Strangers* spinoff was to be on the Winslow family, but midway through the first season, nerdy next-door neighbor Steve Urkel (Jaleel White) was introduced. The character was supposed to appear only once, but audience response was overwhelming, and Urkel became a regular member of the cast.

GAME 70

Classic Sitcoms "Tougher"

Turn to page 237
for the first question.

GAME 69 Q12 ANSWER c
Although called a mighty sailing man in the theme song, Gilligan (Bob Denver) was actually responsible for the shipwreck of the *S.S. Minnow*, having thrown an anchor overboard without a line attached during a storm. Nevertheless, his big heart and innocent nature made the bumbling first mate lovable throughout the series' 1964 to 1967 run.

GAME 12
TV of the 1990s

*Turn to page 234
for the first question.*

GAME 11 Q12 ANSWER c
Harmon was a member of the *St. Elsewhere* staff, another mid-'80s NBC show with a powerhouse ensemble cast. Around that time, he also nearly stole Cybill Shepherd away from Bruce Willis in the 1987–1988 season of ABC's *Moonlighting*. In the 1990s, Harmon again played a doctor in the CBS hospital drama *Chicago Hope*.

GAME 32
GRAB BAG

*Turn to page 234
for the first question.*

GAME 31 Q12 ANSWER b
With Andy Griffith playing the title role of Ben Matlock, this legal drama ran from 1986 to 1992 on NBC, and from 1992 to 1995 on ABC. A folksy, cantankerous, yet skilled defense attorney, Matlock had a keen sense of fashion and always appeared in court wearing a gray suit. The Crown Victoria he drove was also gray.

GAME 52
Big Family TV

*Turn to page 234
for the first question.*

GAME 51 Q12 ANSWER c
Burghoff originated the role of Radar O'Reilly in the film version. Wayne Rogers' role as John McIntyre was played by Elliot Gould in the film, while Loretta Swit's Margaret "Hot Lips" Hoolihan was performed by Sallie Kellerman. Major Frank Burns, played by Larry Linville in the TV series, was portrayed by Robert Duvall in the movie version.

GAME 72
More Westerns

*Turn to page 234
for the first question.*

GAME 71 Q12 ANSWER d
"Those Were the Days" was written by Lee Adams and Charles Strouse, and sung on-camera by *All in the Family* stars Jean Stapleton and Carroll O'Connor, with Stapleton playing the piano accompaniment. Norman Lear, the show's creator, claims that the piano song introduction was originally developed as a cost-cutting measure.

GAME 10	1. Which of the following is *not* the first name of one of Mr. Kotter's Sweathogs? a. Freddie b. Vinnie c. Gabe d. Arnold	The answer to this question is on: **page 239, top frame, right side.**
GAME 30	1. Which mystery series began each episode with a silhouette of its host? a. *Masterpiece Theatre* b. *Tales from the Crypt* c. *Night Gallery* d. *Alfred Hitchcock Presents*	The answer to this question is on: **page 239, second frame, right side.**
GAME 50	1. Chet Huntley and David Brinkley were first paired in 1956 to host coverage of: a. Polish labor riots b. Political conventions c. The Winter Olympics d. Suez Canal crisis	The answer to this question is on: **page 239, third frame, right side.**
GAME 70	1. What was the name of Sanford's son on *Sanford and Son*? a. Lionel b. Lawrence c. Lamont d. Lassiter	The answer to this question is on: **page 239, bottom frame, right side.**

12. Which of the following actors was *not* a regular on *Hill Street Blues*?

a. Daniel J. Travanti
b. Ed Marinaro
c. Mark Harmon
d. Veronica Hamel

GAME 11 Q11 ANSWER c
On average, three 1969 Dodge Chargers were used during each week of filming. *Not* so easy to replace were John Schneider and Tom Wopat as Bo and Luke Duke. When they left the show after a contract dispute in 1982, their characters were replaced with look-alikes Coy and Vance Duke. By 1983, Bo and Luke were back on the show.

---

12. On *Matlock*, what was the title character's trademark piece of clothing?

a. Wingtip shoes
b. A gray suit
c. A flamboyant tie
d. Red suspenders

GAME 31 Q11 ANSWER d
The Practice, which featured Kelli Williams as Lindsay Dole and Dylan McDermott as Bobby Donnell, ran from 1997 to 2004 on ABC, telling the story of partners and associates at a Boston law firm. The show spawned the spinoff *Boston Legal*, starring James Spader and William Shatner.

---

12. Which *M*A*S*H* regular was the only one to reprise his/her role from the movie?

a. Wayne Rogers
b. Loretta Swit
c. Gary Burghoff
d. Larry Linville

GAME 51 Q11 ANSWER d
As the irascible, irreverent, and absolutely brilliant diagnostician Dr. Gregory House, British actor Hugh Laurie leads a team of young experts, who help him solve mysterious cases at fictional Princeton-Plainsboro Teaching Hospital. The Emmy-winning show debuted in 2004 on FOX. In 2006, Laurie earned the Golden Globe for Best Actor in a Drama.

---

12. What car is mentioned in the *All in the Family* theme song "Those Were the Days"?

a. Buick
b. Oldsmobile
c. Chevy
d. La Salle

GAME 71 Q11 ANSWER a
Created by Joe Connelly and Bob Mosher—writers who had worked on the popular *Amos 'n' Andy* program—*Leave It to Beaver* took place in the vaguely midwestern town of Mayfield. (The name of the state was never mentioned.) The sitcom ran for 234 episodes, airing from 1957 to 1963.

GAME 10

2. Who supplied the voice of Charlie on *Charlie's Angels*?

a. William Daniels
b. John Forsythe
c. Alan Thicke
d. Robert Sutton

GAME 10 Q1 ANSWER c
On *Welcome Back, Kotter,* which ran from 1975 to 1979, the Sweathogs included Freddie "Boom Boom" Washington (Lawrence Hilton-Jacobs), Vinnie Barbarino (John Travolta), and Arnold Horshack (Ron Palillo). Gabe was the first name of teacher Mr. Kotter, and of Gabe Kaplan, the actor who played him.

GAME 30

2. Which series saw British actor Edward Woodward battling bad guys?

a. *The Equalizer*
b. *The Avengers*
c. *The Defenders*
d. *The Naturalizer*

GAME 30 Q1 ANSWER d
Hitchcock began each show with a dry, rather formal introduction of the evening's story, which typically had elements of suspense, comedy, and irony. He then led into a commercial with amusing, but disparaging comments about the sponsor. For European audiences, he made separate intros in which his comments belittled Americans.

GAME 50

2. Who gave the first televised report of the assassination of John F. Kennedy?

a. Frank McGee
b. Chet Huntley
c. Walter Cronkite
d. Mike Wallace

GAME 50 Q1 ANSWER b
After covering the '56 political conventions, the pair was asked later that year to host a new NBC news program (to replace *Camel News Caravan* with John Cameron Swayze). Chet Huntley (in New York) and David Brinkley (in Washington, DC) co-anchored the show, called *The Huntley-Brinkley Report,* which ran until 1970.

GAME 70

2. The debut episode of *All in the Family* made television history when viewers heard:

a. Flushing toilets
b. Racial epithets
c. Obscenities
d. Bedroom noises

GAME 70 Q1 ANSWER c
Demond Wilson played Lamont Sanford thoughout the run of *Sanford and Son,* from 1972 to 1977. Afterwards, Wilson did further television work before becoming a minister in 1984. Eventually, the actor-turned-minister founded Restoration House, a center that provides spiritual guidance and vocational training for former prison inmates.

---

11. On *The Dukes of Hazzard* what type of car was the General Lee?

a. Chevrolet Camaro
b. Ford Pinto
c. Dodge Charger
d. Pontiac GTO

GAME 11 Q10 ANSWER b
The character of Mama Thelma Harper, played by Vicki Lawrence, was first seen in a recurring skit called "The Family" on the award-winning *Carol Burnett Show*, which ran on CBS from 1967 to 1978. *Mama's Family* debuted on NBC in 1983 and featured future *Golden Girls* Betty White and Rue McClanahan as Thelma's daughters.

11. Lindsay and Bobby were an item on which popular drama?

a. *Boston Legal*
b. *Once and Again*
c. *Judging Amy*
d. *The Practice*

GAME 31 Q10 ANSWER a
Running from 1999 to 2005, *Judging Amy* starred Amy Brenneman as Amy Gray, a New York attorney who, after a divorce, returns to her Hartford, Connecticut home to become a family court judge. The series also featured stage and screen actress Tyne Daly as Gray's mother, Maxine McCarty Gray.

11. The title character of *House* is a physician specializing in:

a. Neonatal surgery
b. Plastic surgery
c. Accident victims
d. Infectious diseases

GAME 51 Q10 ANSWER a
Arkin, son of actor Alan Arkin, was with the series for its full run (1994–2000). During *Chicago Hope's* first season, it aired on Thursdays against *ER*, which was the clear ratings winner. The show moved to Mondays, where it performed well; but cast changes and the decision of creator-writer David E. Kelly to leave, led to its eventual cancellation.

11. What suburban town was the setting for *Leave It to Beaver*?

a. Mayfield
b. Springfield
c. Riverdale
d. Fernwood

GAME 71 Q10 ANSWER c
The role of *My Favorite Martian's* Tim O'Hara—the young man who finds and befriends Martian "Uncle Martin" (Ray Walston)—was Bill Bixby's big career break. The sitcom ran from 1963 to 1966, and led to starring roles in other high-profile shows—namely, *The Courtship of Eddie's Father* (1969–1972) and *The Incredible Hulk* (1977 to 1982).

3. Jack Albertson was The Man. Who played Chico?

a. Ernest Thomas
b. Raul Julia
c. Lou Diamond Phillips
d. Freddie Prinze

GAME 10 Q2 ANSWER b
In 1976, John Forsythe began a thirteen-year role as the mysterious millionaire Charles Townsend on *Charlie's Angels*. Because his character never appeared on-screen, but was only heard, Forsythe wasn't required on the show's set. Nevertheless, during the show's run, he was the highest-paid actor on television.

---

3. What chart does the *Without a Trace* team reconstruct to help in its search?

a. Simulated Scenario
b. Vanishing Point
c. Day of Disappearance
d. Personal Profile

GAME 30 Q2 ANSWER a
Woodward played former spy Robert McCall, who, in an effort to atone for past sins, offered his services to people in trouble who had nowhere to turn. His newspaper ad read "Got a problem? Odds against you? Need help? Call the Equalizer." Due to the show's popularity, Woodward was often approached on the street by people who asked for his help.

---

3. News journalist Anderson Cooper is the son of which well-known socialite?

a. Doris Duke
b. Lilly Pulitzer
c. Gloria Vanderbilt
d. Abby Rockefeller

GAME 50 Q2 ANSWER c
Many Americans clearly remember CBS Evening News anchor Walter Cronkite trying to maintain composure while breaking the news of Kennedy's death on November 22, 1963. After silently reading the wire, Cronkite removed his glasses, looked into the camera, and told the viewing audience of the tragedy. Parts of this broadcast appear in the film JFK.

---

3. What was "Reverend" Jim's last name on the classic sitcom *Taxi*?

a. Rieger
b. Cabby
c. Ignatowski
d. Banta

GAME 70 Q2 ANSWER a
After *All in the Family's* January 1971 premiere, it took American audiences a few months to adjust to the blunt, outrageous humor of the show—not to mention the audible flushing of the Bunkers' upstairs toilet. But by the second season, the series had become television's number-one program, and it held that position for five years.

GAME 11

10. Which series was set in the Midwestern suburb of Raytown?

a. *Knots Landing*

b. *Mama's Family*

c. *Perfect Strangers*

d. *Riptide*

GAME 11 Q9 ANSWER c
Dallas producers killed off Bobby Ewing at the end of the 1984–1985 season. Then, in a move that rivaled the 1980 "Who Killed JR?" cliffhanger, the 1986 season finale ended with Pam Ewing (Victoria Principal) finding Bobby alive in the shower. Viewers waited all summer to learn that the entire season was only Pam's dream.

GAME 31

10. What was the lead character's last name on *Judging Amy*?

a. Gray

b. Cassidy

c. Potter

d. Hoobler

GAME 31 Q9 ANSWER b
Born in 1964, Mariska Hargitay is the daughter of Hollywood legend Jayne Mansfield and Mr. Universe Mickey Hargitay. In 2006, Hargitay won an Emmy (Outstanding Lead Actress in a Drama Series) for her portrayal of Detective Olivia Benson in NBC's *Law & Order: Special Victims Unit*.

GAME 51

10. Which *Chicago Hope* character was played by Adam Arkin?

a. Dr. Aaron Shutt

b. Dr. Daniel Nyland

c. Dr. Jeffrey Geiger

d. Dr. Phillip Walters

GAME 51 Q9 ANSWER d
In addition to Howie Mandel, *St. Elsewhere* helped launch the careers of a number of young actors, including Denzel Washington, Alfre Woodard, Helen Hunt, Mark Harmon, Bruce Greenwood, David Morse, and Ed Begley, Jr. During its run from 1982 to 1988, the show and its cast earned multiple Emmy nominations and won thirteen.

GAME 71

10. What was Tim O'Hara's occupation on *My Favorite Martian*?

a. Accountant

b. Lawyer

c. Reporter

d. Pilot

GAME 71 Q9 ANSWER b
Played by Carolyn Jones throughout *The Addams Family's* 1964–1966 run, Morticia was the daughter of Hester Frump, who was portrayed by Margaret Hamilton—*The Wizard of Oz's* Wicked Witch of the West. Pale, elegant, and artistic, Morticia was always able to drive husband Gomez Addams wild simply by speaking in a foreign language.

4. Which 1970s cop show starred Jack Lord?

a. *Hawaii Five-O*

b. *Chips*

c. *Streets of San Francisco*

d. *Starsky and Hutch*

GAME 10 Q3 ANSWER d
Running on NBC from 1974 to 1978, *Chico and the Man* was the first television series set in a Mexican-Amerian neighborhood. Jack Albertson played Ed Brown, the owner of a run-down garage; and Freddie Prinze played the Chicano street kid Chico Rodriguez who, despite initial protests from Brown, worked at the garage.

---

4. Who made Leland Palmer kill his daughter on *Twin Peaks*?

a. Black Tom

b. Bob

c. The Giant

d. Phillip Gerard

GAME 30 Q3 ANSWER c
Headed by agent Jack Malone (Anthony LaPaglia), this special FBI missing persons unit uses a Day of Disappearance chart to detail each minute in the twenty-four hours prior to a person's disappearance. The show, which premiered in 2002, includes a fifteen-second spot in each episode, asking the public for help in finding a real missing person.

---

4. Who once co-anchored *NBC Nightly News* with Tom Brokaw?

a. Roger Mudd

b. John Chancellor

c. Floyd Kalber

d. John Hart

GAME 50 Q3 ANSWER c
Anderson Hays Cooper, son of writer Wyatt Cooper and railroad heiress Gloria Vanderbilt, has long been a TV journalist as well as news anchor on ABC and CNN. His on-site reports have included such events as the Vietnam War, Hurricane Katrina, and the 2005 Iraq elections. He earned his first Emmy for coverage of Princess Diana's funeral.

---

4. Which character was *not* one of Beaver's friends on *Leave It to Beaver*?

a. Larry Mondello

b. Eddie Haskell

c. Whitey Whitney

d. Gilbert Bates

GAME 70 Q3 ANSWER c
Portrayed by Christopher Lloyd, *Taxi's* Reverend Jim Ignatowski was a gentle but confused soul, whose spaced-out behavior was attributed to extensive use of recreational drugs in the '60s. Jim's eccentricities included living in a condemned building and sharing his living room with a racehorse.

GAME 11

9. Which *Dallas* character dreamed the entire 1985–1986 season?

a. Miss Ellie Ewing

b. Sue Ellen Ewing

c. Pam Ewing

d. JR Ewing

GAME 11 Q8 ANSWER a

Played by actress Tannis Vallely, this character was a twelve-year-old genius who hadn't had time to grow up. Running on ABC from 1986 to 1991, *Head of the Class* starred Howard Hesseman (best known as rock DJ Johnny Fever in *WKRP in Cincinnati*) until 1990, when he left and was replaced by Irish comic Billy Connolly.

GAME 31

9. Which *Law & Order* actress is the child of an American actress/sex symbol?

a. Jill Hennessey

b. Mariska Hargitay

c. Michelle Hurd

d. Elisabeth Röhm

GAME 31 Q8 ANSWER c

E.G. Marshall, perhaps best known for his Emmy-winning performance in the film *12 Angry Men*, portrayed defense lawyer Lawrence Preston, while future *Brady Bunch* dad Robert Reed played his son. The show ran from 1961 to 1965, with the father-and-son team specializing in hopeless cases.

GAME 51

9. Which medical drama had comedian Howie Mandel playing Dr. Wayne Fiscus?

a. *Dr. Kildare*

b. *Chicago Hope*

c. *ER*

d. *St. Elsewhere*

GAME 51 Q8 ANSWER a

Dr. Bailey (Chandra Wilson) and her no-nonsense, tough-love attitude, earned the disparaging nickname from her resident interns. The Emmy Award-winning medical drama, which debuted in 2005, centers on the professional and personal lives of a group of surgical interns at fictional Seattle Grace Hospital.

GAME 71

9. What was Morticia Addams' maiden name on *The Addams Family*?

a. Munster

b. Frump

c. Craven

d. Goth

GAME 71 Q8 ANSWER d

After being rejected, the powerful Blue Djin had banished Jeannie (Barbara Eden) to a tiny but plush bottle. But while Jeannie wouldn't marry the Blue Djin, she was more than eager to spend her life with Captain Tony Nelson (Larry Hagman)—the astronaut who unwittingly set her free after finding her bottle on a beach.

GAME 10

5. On *The Rockford Files*, who played Jim Rockford's father?

a. Stuart Margolin
b. Joseph Cotton
c. Noah Beery, Jr.
d. Robert Loggia

GAME 10 Q4 ANSWER a
Born John Joseph Patrick Ryan, the actor who would play *Hawaii Five-O's* Steve McGarrett wanted a name that would fit on a movie marquee. Although he first wished to be called Jack Ryan, another actor of that name already belonged to Actor's Equity, so he chose Jack Lord instead.

GAME 30

5. On *The Fugitive*, what event allowed Kimble to escape police custody?

a. A flood
b. A tornado
c. A train accident
d. A car wreck

GAME 30 Q4 ANSWER b
Bob was an evil spirit that haunted Laura Palmer and possessed humans. In this two-season TV series, which first aired in 1990, FBI agent Cody Cooper (Kyle MacLachlan) investigated the murder of Palmer in the fictional town of Twin Peaks. During the investigation, Cooper became involved with the townspeople and their problems.

GAME 50

5. Of the following, who covered the 1991 Gulf War from Baghdad?

a. Bill Zimmerman
b. Daniel Schorr
c. Wolf Blitzer
d. Peter Arnett

GAME 50 Q4 ANSWER a
Roger Mudd—Emmy-winning TV journalist, broadcaster, and political reporter—has also hosted NBC's *Meet the Press* and served as anchor for *CBS Evening News*. He has also been primary anchor for The History Channel. When Mudd retired from full-time broadcasting in 2004, he continued working on documentaries for The History Channel.

GAME 70

5. What was Sue Ann Nivens' "professional" name on *The Mary Tyler Moore Show*?

a. The Happy Homemaker
b. The Creative Cook
c. The Giddy Gardener
d. The Daring Decorator

GAME 70 Q4 ANSWER b
Played by Ken Osmond, Eddie Haskell was a friend of Beaver's older brother, Wally. Eddie was known for being overly (and insincerely) polite to his friends' parents. Then, as soon as the parents' backs were turned, Eddie would instigate trouble, all the while insuring that his friends, and not he, would be blamed if they were caught.

---

8. Which character was the youngest student on *Head of the Class*?

a. Janice Lazarotto
b. Lori Applebaum
c. Aristotle McKenzie
d. Sarah Nevins

For his excellent work on this popular NBC cop show that made it hip for men *not* to wear socks with loafers, Olmos earned a Golden Globe and an Emmy. He later received an Oscar nomination for his role as real-life teacher Jaime Escalante in the 1988 film *Stand and Deliver*.

---

8. What series starred E.G. Marshall and Robert Reed as a father-and-son defense team?

a. *Perry Mason*
b. *Jake and the Fatman*
c. *The Defenders*
d. *Law & Order*

Before appearing in *Judd, for the Defense,* Carl Betz spent eight years playing Dr. Stone, Donna Stone's husband, on *The Donna Reed Show*. Unlike the rather bland Dr. Stone, Clinton Judd was a flamboyant character, supposedly based on high-profile lawyers such as F. Lee Bailey and Percy Foreman. The show ran from 1967 to 1969.

---

8. Which *Grey's Anatomy* character is nicknamed "The Nazi"?

a. Dr. Miranda Bailey
b. Dr. Richard Webber
c. Dr. Alex Karev
d. Dr. Preston Burke

Dr. John Becker (Ted Danson) ran a Manhattan clinic. The cantankerous Becker was a good doctor who spent most of his time annoyed with the world (in an effort to keep his kindhearted side under wraps). Danson, who may be best known as Sam Malone from the major hit sitcom *Cheers,* returned to TV in 2006 as a psychiatrist in ABC's *Help Me Help You*.

---

8. On *I Dream of Jeannie*, why was Jeannie sealed in her bottle for 2,000 years?

a. She abused her magic
b. She goofed up a spell
c. It happens to all genies
d. She refused to marry

The role of *WKRP's* disk jockey, Dr. Johnny Fever, had originally been intended for Richard Libertini. But when Libertini was not available, Hugh Wilson, *WKRP's* creator, thought of Howard Hesseman, whom he knew from Hesseman's recurring role of Mr. Plager on *The Bob Newhart Show*.

---

6. What was the name of the *Six Million Dollar Man*?

a. Hulk Hogan

b. Peter Parker

c. Jesse Ventura

d. Steve Austin

GAME 10 Q5 ANSWER c
Noah Beery, Jr. was born into a family of actors. His father, Noah Beery, Sr., had a lengthy film career; and his uncle, Wallace Beery, was a well-known character actor. Although he appeared in dozens of films, including *Red River,* Noah Beery, Jr. is probably best known for playing Jim Rockford's father, Joseph "Rocky" Rockford.

---

6. David Suchet plays which Agatha Christie character in the PBS *Mystery!* series?

a. Tommy Beresford

b. Superintendent Battle

c. Mr. Parken Pyne

d. Hercule Poirot

GAME 30 Q5 ANSWER c
David Janssen starred as Dr. Richard Kimble, the man falsely convicted for his wife's murder. The 1960 series had Americans glued to their sets as they watched Kimble always stay just one step ahead of Lieutenant Gerard. Bill Raisch, who played the one-armed killer of Kimble's wife, had actually lost his arm during WWII.

---

6. What event prompted the beginnings of ABC's Nightline with Ted Koppel?

a. Moon landing

b. Challenger explosion

c. Munich Olympics massacre

d. Iran hostage crisis

GAME 50 Q5 ANSWER d
Americans were glued to their TVs as CNN journalist Peter Arnett, along with colleagues Bernard Shaw and John Holliman, brought continuous coverage of the war live from Baghdad. Shortly after the war's onset on January 17, 1991, Arnett, who remained there for five weeks, became the sole reporter from the "other side."

---

6. What was Dr. Huxtable's medical specialty on *The Cosby Show*?

a. Forensics

b. Psychiatry

c. Dentistry

d. Obstetrics

GAME 70 Q5 ANSWER a
Betty White's Sue Ann Nivens was the host of WJM-TV's *Happy Homemaker* show—a women's program that offered household tips and hints. Although seemingly sweet and helpful, Sue Ann was actually rather nasty and sex-obsessed, and was especially interested in bedding the station's producer, Lou Grant (Ed Asner).

---

7. Who played Lieutenant Martin Castillo on *Miami Vice*?

a. Jimmy Smits

b. Dennis Farina

c. Edward James Olmos

d. Robert Hegyes

GAME 11 Q6 ANSWER c
Debuting in 1984 and lasting two seasons, this CBS series told the story of conservative attorney Harrison K. Fox (John Rubinstein), whose job was always complicated by the misadventures of his father, Harry (Jack Warden), who was a con artist and private eye. The show's pilot episode featured Joyce Van Patten in a guest role.

7. In which series did the star of *Judd, for the Defense* also play a major role?

a. *The Donna Reed Show*

b. *Father Knows Best*

c. *Family*

d. *Leave It to Beaver*

GAME 31 Q6 ANSWER d
Running from 1997 to 2002, *Ally McBeal* was a notable series in many ways. It was the first hour-long comedy in American history, and it used vivid fantasy sequences—including musical numbers—to show the characters' thoughts, hopes, and fears. Some say it also pioneered a new genre called *dramedy,* or comedy-drama.

7. In what city did the CBS sitcom *Becker* take place?

a. Philadelphia

b. Boston

c. Los Angeles

d. New York City

GAME 51 Q6 ANSWER a
Chad Everett has played numerous leading and supporting roles both in films and on TV, but he may be best known for his role as the *Medical Center* surgeon. When the CBS hit series ended its seven-year run in 1976, it tied with *Marcus Welby, MD* (which ran during the same period) as the longest-running TV medical drama up to that point.

7. Which *WKRP* star was a patient of Dr. Hartley on *The Bob Newhart Show*?

a. Gordon Jump

b. Tim Reid

c. Howard Hesseman

d. Frank Bonner

GAME 71 Q6 ANSWER a
In an episode that continued *Friends'* tradition of disastrous Thanksgivings, Christina Applegate played Rachel's (Jennifer Aniston's) "evil sister" Amy. She showed up unexpectedly and pretty much ruined the Thanksgiving celebration in Monica's (Courteney Cox's) and Chandler's (Matthew Perry's) apartment.

7. What was the name of Angie Dickinson's character in *Police Woman*?

a. Chris Cagney

b. Leanne Anderson

c. Julie Barnes

d. Jaime Sommers

GAME 10 Q6 ANSWER d
Based on the novel *Cyborg* by Martin Caidin, *The Six Million Dollar Man* starred Lee Majors as astronaut Steve Austin. When Austin is severely injured in a crash, his right arm, both his legs, and his left eye are replaced by bionic parts that give him superhuman strength, speed, and vision.

---

7. Which of the following characters was *not* a *Prison Break* escapee?

a. Theodore Bagwell

b. Brad Bellick

c. Fernando Sucre

d. Charles Patoshik

GAME 30 Q6 ANSWER d
In 1980, this PBS program began airing British-produced mysteries to American audiences. Agatha Christie's keenly observant Miss Marple and the fastidious Hercule Poirot are the show's commonly featured sleuths. Suchet offers a brilliant portrayal of Poirot in the TV role, while Peter Ustinov played the detective in several movies.

---

7. Who joined Dan Rather in 1993 as co-anchor of the *CBS Evening News*?

a. Judy Woodruff

b. Jane Pauley

c. Connie Chung

d. Diane Sawyer

GAME 50 Q6 ANSWER d
In November 1979, four days after Americans were taken hostage at the US Embassy in Tehran, ABC created the show to keep the country updated. It was first called *The Iran Crisis—America Held Hostage: Day 4* (then *Day 5,* and so on). When the crisis ended in 1981, *Nightline* remained as ABC's late-night news program. Koppel left the show in 2005.

---

7. On *The Dick Van Dyke Show*, for which fictional TV show did Van Dyke's character write?

a. *The Rob Petrie Show*

b. *The Alan Brady Show*

c. *The Jerry Halper Show*

d. *The Buddy Sorrell Show*

GAME 70 Q6 ANSWER d
Obstetrician/gynecologist Heathcliff Huxtable (Bill Cosby) and his attorney wife, Clair (Phylicia Rashad), raised TV's first upper-middle class African-American family on *The Cosby Show*. While some praised the series, calling it a symbol of hope and progress, others criticized it for failing to acknowledge race-related problems.

GAME 11

6. What 1980s series focused on a San Francisco attorney?

a. *Hart to Hart*
b. *Spenser: For Hire*
c. *Crazy Like a Fox*
d. *Night Court*

GAME 11 Q5 ANSWER b
Appearing on *21 Jump Street* with Johnny Depp and Peter DeLuise (son of comic actor Dom DeLuise), Richard Grieco played cop-turned-detective Dennis Booker. The show was canceled after one season, but Grieco went on to portray Bugsy Siegel in the 1991 film *Mobsters,* also starring Christian Slater and Patrick Dempsey.

GAME 31

6. Judge Whipper Cone slammed her gavel on which courtroom series?

a. *L.A. Law*
b. *Perry Mason*
c. *The Practice*
d. *Ally McBeal*

GAME 31 Q5 ANSWER b
Lee Majors played one of Owen Marshall's assistants in the critically acclaimed 1971–1974 show, which centered on a lawyer practicing in a small California town. Paul Michael Glaser was *not* in the show, but his *Starsky and Hutch* costar David Soul was, playing another of Marshall's assistants.

GAME 51

6. Who starred as Dr. Joe Gannon on *Medical Center*?

a. Chad Everett
b. Richard Boone
c. Vince Edwards
d. Michael Cole

GAME 51 Q5 ANSWER b
Dr. Carter (Noah Wyle) said goodbye to the show at the end of its eleventh season with 248 episodes under his belt. Although the last appearance of Dr. Lewis (Sherry Stringfield) was in the show's twelfth season, Stringfield had left the show from 1996 to 2001. Wyle's *ER* performances earned him several SAG Awards and Emmy nominations.

GAME 71

6. Who won an Emmy for her performance in a *Friends* 2002 Thanksgiving special?

a. Christina Applegate
b. Alexis Arquette
c. Catherine Bell
d. Jennifer Grey

GAME 71 Q5 ANSWER b
In the very first Gleason-Carney-Meadows-Randolph *Honeymooners* episode —1952's "The New Bowling Ball"— Ralph (Jackie Gleason) gets his new bowling ball stuck on his thumb. But after finally getting it off with the help of Alice (Audrey Meadows) and Ed (Art Carney), he finds that his thumb is too swollen to allow him to bowl.

Answers are in right-hand boxes on page 253.

GAME 10

8. Who sang the theme song "Keep Your Eye on the Sparrow" for the show *Baretta*?

a. Sammy Davis, Jr.

b. John Sebastian

c. Mike Post

d. Roberta Flack

GAME 10 Q7 ANSWER b
From 1974 to 1978, on NBC, Sergeant Leanne "Pepper" Anderson was an agent in the Criminal Conspiracy Unit of the LAPD. Pepper, as Dickinson's character was called, often had to work undercover, posing as everything from hookers and teachers to waitresses and nurses.

GAME 30

8. Which of the following code names was *not* used by Sydney Bristow in *Alias*?

a. Bluebird

b. Freelancer

c. Phoenix

d. Evergreen

GAME 30 Q7 ANSWER b
Brad Bellick is a corrections officer captain at Fox River who believes the purpose of a prison is punishment, not rehabilitation. The other escapees led by Michael Scofield (Wentworth Miller) and brother Lincoln Burrows (Dominic Purcell) were Benjamin Franklin, David Apolskis, and John Abruzzi. *Prison Break* premiered on FOX in 2005.

GAME 50

8. What was Walter Cronkite's signature sign off?

a. "Good night, and good luck."

b. "That's part of our world tonight."

c. "And that's the way it is."

d. "Good night, and good news."

GAME 50 Q7 ANSWER c
Connie Chung's journalistic career has included stints with NBC, CBS, ABC, CNN, and MSNBC. When she joined Rather in '93, she became the second woman (Barbara Walters was first) to co-anchor a national news program on a major network. In '95, Chung joined ABC to co-host *20/20* and begin independent interviews, which became her trademark.

GAME 70

8. By the time *I Dream of Jeannie* came to an end, Jeannie had managed to:

a. Lose her powers

b. Join the Air Force

c. Get a new master

d. Marry her master

GAME 70 Q7 ANSWER b
Carl Reiner, creator of the series, based much of the story line on his own experiences as a writer for *Your Show of Shows*. Reiner himself played Alan Brady; Richard Deacon played Mel Cooley, the show's producer; and Morey Amsterdam and Rose Marie portrayed Buddy Sorrell and Sally Rogers, Rob Petrie's (Van Dyke's) fellow writers.

GAME 11

5. *Booker,* which debuted in 1989, was a spinoff of which show?

a. *Knight Rider*
b. *21 Jump Street*
c. *Hunter*
d. *L.A. Law*

GAME 11 Q4 ANSWER d
Airing on CBS from 1982 to 1990, *Newhart* had Bob running a bed and breakfast. The show may be best remembered for the recurring brother characters Larry, Darryl, and their *other* brother Darryl. In the series finale, Newhart woke up next to his former sitcom wife Suzanne Pleshette, only to realize that the entire series had been a dream.

GAME 31

5. Who costarred with Arthur Hill on ABC's *Owen Marshall: Counselor at Law?*

a. Burt Reynolds
b. Lee Majors
c. Ryan O'Neal
d. Paul Michael Glaser

GAME 31 Q4 ANSWER c
Crooner Mel Torme appeared in nine episodes of *Night Court* during its 1984–1992 run on NBC. Besides idolizing Torme, quirky, good-humored Judge Harold T. Stone—played by Harry Anderson—loved movies and fashions from the forties. He was also a skilled magician.

GAME 51

5. Which of *ER's* original doctors appeared in the most consecutive seasons?

a. Dr. Susan Lewis
b. Dr. John Carter
c. Dr. Peter Benton
d. Dr. Mark Greene

GAME 51 Q4 ANSWER b
The series, which ran from 1961 to 1966, followed the life of a young medical intern and his older surgeon-mentor Dr. Leonard Gillespie (Raymond Massey). The show helped make Chamberlain a teen idol in the '60s. The actor went on to appear on stage, in films, and in TV miniseries, including *The Thorn Birds, Shogun,* and *Centennial.*

GAME 71

5. Which classic sitcom character played on a bowling team called The Hurricanes?

a. Rob Petrie
b. Ralph Kramden
c. George Jefferson
d. Ricky Ricardo

GAME 71 Q4 ANSWER d
When *Welcome Back, Kotter* debuted in 1975, educators feared that the "Sweathogs" would celebrate juvenile delinquency or that Gabriel Kaplan's depiction of a teacher would be inappropriate, while an ABC affiliate worried that Kotter's integrated classroom would cause problems in schools with less racial equality. But all fears proved unfounded.

9. Who played Newhart's wife in *The Bob Newhart Show*?

a. Julia Duffy
b. Suzanne Pleshette
c. Mary Frann
d. Virginia Quinn

GAME 10 Q8 ANSWER a
Baretta aired on ABC from 1975 to 1978, starring Robert Blake as Detective Tony Baretta, an unconventional, streetwise cop who was also a master of disguise. The show's memorable theme song, "Keep Your Eye on the Sparrow," was written by Dave Grusin and Morgan Ames.

9. In the *Murder, She Wrote* pilot, where does Jessica Fletcher find the dead body?

a. In the pool
b. In the garden
c. In her car
d. On a train

GAME 30 Q8 ANSWER d
During the show's first season, Sydney (Jennifer Garner) had the code name "Bluebird" at the SD-6 and "Freelancer" at the CIA. In season four, her code name at the APO was "Phoenix." "Evergreen" was Nadia's code name. For her role as agent Bristow, Garner took home the 2002 Golden Globe for Best Actress in a TV Series Drama.

9. Of the following, who cohosted a program with Barbara Walters?

a. Hugh Downs
b. Dan Rather
c. Peter Jennings
d. Charles Gibson

GAME 50 Q8 ANSWER c
For nearly 20 years, Cronkite ended the *CBS Evening News* with this phrase. His successor, Dan Rather, used "That's part of our world tonight," while Edward R. Murrow signed off with "Good night, and good luck." As for "Good night and good news," that was the farewell of newsman Ted Baxter (Ted Knight) on *The Mary Tyler Moore Show*.

9. What did Murphy Brown name her baby?

a. Eldin
b. Quayle
c. Avery
d. Marvin

GAME 70 Q8 ANSWER d
When Captain Tony Nelson (Larry Hagman) first stumbled upon Jeannie (Barbara Eden), he was engaged to the general's daughter. But Jeannie fell in love with Tony at first sight, and one of her initial acts was to break up the engagement. Five years later, Tony and Jeannie were wed.

4. Which Bob Newhart sitcom is from the 1980s?

a. *The Bob Newhart Show*

b. *Bob*

c. *George and Leo*

d. *Newhart*

This show, which ran on NBC from 1986 to 1991, was *not* the first time Hemsley played a man of the cloth. In the George Hamilton 1979 vampire spoof *Love at First Bite*, Hemsley did a cameo as a frightened reverend while his *Jeffersons* costar Isabel Sanford also appears in a cameo as an ill-tempered judge.

4. Which jazz vocalist was the object of the judge's admiration on *Night Court*?

a. Tony Bennett

b. Louis Armstrong

c. Mel Torme

d. Frank Sinatra

Harry Hamlin played Michael Kusak—the firm's top litigator and the love interest of Grace Van Owen (Susan Dey of *Partridge Family* fame)—from 1986 to 1991. During that period, Hamlin was named *People* magazine's Sexiest Man Alive. In 2004, Hamlin began a recurring role in the television series *Veronica Mars*.

4. Who played the lead character on *Dr. Kildare*?

a. Robert Wagner

b. Richard Chamberlain

c. Tab Hunter

d. Troy Donahue

As a hand drew the five symbols, the voice of elderly Dr. Zorba (Sam Jaffe) would pronounce, "man, woman, birth, death, infinity." Starring Vince Edwards as the young idealistic surgeon in the title role, *Ben Casey*, which aired from 1961 to 1966, rivaled the medical drama *Dr. Kildare*, which ran during the same period.

4. After which president was the *Welcome Back, Kotter* high school named?

a. Grover Cleveland

b. Millard Fillmore

c. Teddy Roosevelt

d. James Buchanan

Portrayed by Steve Landesberg, Detective Arthur Dietrich began working with Barney Miller (Hal Linden) in 1976, after Detective Fish (Abe Vigoda) left the station. Highly intellectual and something of a know-it-all, Dietrich was found particularly irritating by fellow police officer Ron Harris (Ron Glass).

10. In which 1970s series did George Peppard play the title role?

a. *Harry O*
b. *Dan August*
c. *Hawkins*
d. *Banacek*

GAME 10 Q9 ANSWER b
The popular NBC series cast Bob as Chicago psychologist Robert Hartley, and Suzanne Pleshette as his somewhat sarcastic wife, Emily. Julia Duffy played the spoiled maid Stephanie in Newhart's later show, simply titled *Newhart,* and Mary Frann was cast as his wife, Joanna, in that same series. Virginia Quinn is Newhart's real-life wife.

10. In the first season of *24*, who killed Jack Bauer's wife?

a. Victor Drazen
b. Jamey Farrell
c. Nina Myers
d. David Palmer

GAME 30 Q9 ANSWER a
The episode took place at a costume party, where a detective is found dead in the swimming pool. Although a Broadway star and active in TV since the 1950s, Lansbury achieved her greatest fame for her portrayal of the show's mystery writer/amateur sleuth Jessica Fletcher—a part that was first offered to Jean Stapleton and Doris Day.

10. Which newscaster wrote the autobiography *Anchorwoman*?

a. Jane Pauley
b. Jessica Savitch
c. Debra Norville
d. Katie Couric

GAME 50 Q9 ANSWER a
Walters has been paired with Hugh Downs twice in her career. In 1974, she was appointed his cohost on *Today*—NBC's morning news and talk show. In 1979, they began hosting the ABC newsmagazine *20/20* together. (From 1999 to 2002, she was the show's solo host.) Back in 1976, she co-anchored the *ABC Evening News* with Harry Reasoner.

10. What was the name of the town drunk on *The Andy Griffith Show*?

a. Otis
b. Opie
c. Goober
d. Emmett

GAME 70 Q9 ANSWER c
In the 1991–1992 season of *Murphy Brown,* Murphy (Candice Bergen) had a baby boy whom she named Avery. Soon after, then-Vice President Dan Quayle criticized the show for letting the main character have an out-of-wedlock child. *Murphy Brown's* response was a special episode celebrating the diversity of American families.

GAME 11

3. *Jeffersons* star Sherman Hemsley played Deacon Ernest Frye on which sitcom?

a. *That's My Bishop*
b. *Brotherly Love*
c. *Amen*
d. *They Call Me Reverend*

GAME 11 Q2 ANSWER a
From 1980 to 1984, Tarkenton cohosted ABC's *That's Incredible!* along with John Davidson and Cathy Lee Crosby. This show, along with sister reality shows *Those Amazing Animals* and *Ripley's Believe It or Not*, was produced by ABC in response to the success of NBC's *Real People* in 1979.

GAME 31

3. Which of these actors was the first to leave the series *L.A. Law*?

a. Jill Eikenberry
b. Harry Hamlin
c. Susan Dey
d. Susan Ruttan

GAME 31 Q2 ANSWER a
Elliot portrayed Captain Harmon "Harm" Rabb, Jr., while Bell played Lieutenant Colonel Sarah "Mac" MacKenzie. The final episode of *JAG* found the two characters being assigned to different posts. They decided to marry, and a coin was tossed to see who would give up their career, but the audience never learned the outcome.

GAME 51

3. What was drawn on a blackboard at the start of each *Ben Casey* episode?

a. A skeleton
b. An AMA symbol
c. Life symbols
d. A skull and crossbones

GAME 51 Q2 ANSWER c
The popular drama saw older physician Welby mentoring his young assistant Steven Kiley (James Brolin). The show won many Emmys, including Best Dramatic Series (1970). A doctor once told Young, "You're getting us all in hot water. Our patients say we're not as nice to them as Dr. Welby is to his patients." Young replied, "Maybe you're not."

GAME 71

3. Which character was *not* an original member of the *Barney Miller* crew?

a. Phillip Fish
b. Ron Harris
c. Arthur Dietrich
d. Nick Yemana

GAME 71 Q2 ANSWER a
Actor-writer Harry Shearer provides voices for a large array of characters on this long-running animated sitcom, including not only Mr. Burns, Principal Skinner, and Ned Flanders, but also Smithers, Dr. Hibbert, and many others. But the character of Apu, proprietor of the Kwik-E-Mart, is voiced by Hank Azaria.

GAME 10

11. Who played Dr. Kiley opposite Robert Young's *Marcus Welby, M.D.*?

a. Lyle Waggoner
b. James Brolin
c. Chad Everett
d. Steve Forrest

GAME 10 Q10 ANSWER d
The light-hearted series *Banacek* ran from 1972 to 1974, and featured Peppard as Thomas Banacek, a freelance investigator who solved theft cases for insurance companies. David Janssen starred in *Harry O*; Burt Reynolds played the title role in *Dan August*; and James Stewart headed the cast of the short-lived *Hawkins*.

GAME 30

11. From which country did the *Lost* plane take off before it crashed?

a. England
b. Australia
c. Iraq
d. France

GAME 30 Q10 ANSWER c
Myers, who once had an affair with Jack, was a double agent. Each season of this innovative show has 24 episodes that represent one day—24 heart-pounding hours—with LA's Counter Terrorist Unit. *24* has received a number of Emmys, including Best Drama Series and Best Cast. Kiefer Sutherland earned a Best Actor Emmy for his role as Agent Jack Bauer.

GAME 50

11. Who is the first solo female anchor of a weekday nightly news show on a "Big 3" network?

a. Jane Pauley
b. Connie Chung
c. Katie Couric
d. Barbara Walters

GAME 50 Q10 ANSWER b
After starting as a local broadcaster in Philadelphia, Jessica Savitch went on to become a weekend anchor for *NBC Nightly News*. In October 1983, while apparently under the influence of drugs and/or alcohol, she "slurred" a live 43-second *NBC News Update*, which ended her career. A few weeks later, she was killed in a car accident.

GAME 70

11. Who played Samantha's cousin Serena on *Bewitched*?

a. Linda Evans
b. Agnes Moorehead
c. Louise Lasser
d. Elizabeth Montgomery

GAME 70 Q10 ANSWER a
Played by Hal Smith, Otis Campbell was Mayberry's "town drunk." Extremely well behaved and responsible for a man who went on drinking binges, Otis had a key to the front door of the courthouse and would lock himself in a jail cell whenever he was inebriated, and stay there until he was once again sober.

Answers are in right-hand boxes on page 259.

2. Which show did former NFL quarterback Fran Tarkenton cohost?

a. *That's Incredible!*

b. *Real People*

c. *Those Amazing Animals*

d. *Ripley's Believe It or Not*

GAME 11 Q1 ANSWER b
Actress Allyce Beasley played Maddie's (Cybill Shepherd's) secretary at the Blue Moon Detective Agency. In addition to answering the office phone in rhyme, Miss DiPesto fell for office temp Herbert Viola (played by Curtis Armstrong of *Revenge of the Nerds* fame).

2. Who played David James Elliott's ongoing love interest on the legal drama *JAG*?

a. Catherine Bell

b. Zoe McLellan

c. Kim Delaney

d. Isabella Hofmann

GAME 31 Q1 ANSWER c
Raymond Burr played the title role in the 1957–1966 show *Perry Mason,* with William Hopper playing private investigator Paul Drake and Barbara Hale portraying secretary Della Street. In 1973, an attempt was made to recreate the popular series, with Monte Markham taking the title role, but *The New Perry Mason* ran for only one season.

2. Who played ABC's *Marcus Welby, MD* from 1969 to 1976?

a. Buddy Ebsen

b. Adam West

c. Robert Young

d. Hugh Beaumont

GAME 51 Q1 ANSWER d
Miami plastic surgeons Christian Troy (Julian McMahon) and Sean McNamara (Dylan Walsh) are at the center of this FX network drama, which premiered in 2003. Deemed the highest-rated new cable series, the show's edgy plotlines, graphic surgical scenes, and sexual depictions have gotten much criticism from groups like the Parents Television Council.

2. Which *Simpsons* character is *not* voiced by Harry Shearer?

a. Apu

b. Mr. Burns

c. Principal Skinner

d. Ned Flanders

GAME 71 Q1 ANSWER c
Cloris Leachman played Timmy's mom, Ruth Martin, for one season—1957 to 1958—before being replaced by June Lockhart, who had previously appeared in the 1945 film *Son of Lassie.* It would be more than a decade before Leachman was cast as Mary Richards' busybody neighbor, Phillis Lindstrom, on *The Mary Tyler Moore Show.*

12. In what Minnesota town did NBC's *Little House on the Prairie* take place?

a. *Willow Grove*

b. *Maple Grove*

c. *Walnut Grove*

d. *Oak Grove*

12. Who replaced Martin Landau on *Mission: Impossible* as the new master of disguises?

a. Leonard Nimoy

b. Sam Elliot

c. Greg Morris

d. Peter Graves

12. Who replaced anchor Peter Jennings on ABC's *World News Tonight*?

a. Aaron Brown

b. Charles Gibson

c. Dan Harris

d. John Roberts

12. Who produced *Maude, The Jeffersons, Sanford and Son,* and *Good Times*?

a. Grant Tinker

b. Norman Lear

c. Aaron Spelling

d. Larry Gelbart

GAME 10 Q11 ANSWER b
This medical drama, which aired from 1969 to 1976, focused on the conflict between Dr. Welby's unconventional way of treating patients and Dr. Kiley's more orthodox approach. The twist was that Dr. Kiley was the younger of the two. The formula worked, because after its first season, *Marcus Welby, M.D.* ranked #1 in the Nielsen ratings.

GAME 30 Q11 ANSWER b
After the plane left the Sydney airport, it was torn apart in midair before crashing on a Pacific island. *Lost* garnered twelve Emmy nominations after its premier in 2004 and won six—including Outstanding Drama Series. A large ensemble cast and the cost of filming (primarily in Hawaii) has made it one of the most expensive shows on television.

GAME 50 Q11 ANSWER c
Katie Couric made broadcasting history when she left ABC to anchor *CBS Evening News* in fall of 2006. A number of female anchors, including Jessica Savitch, Jane Pauley, Connie Chung, Carole Simpson, Elizabeth Vargas, and Susan Spencer, had worked solo, but only on weekend broadcasts. Vargas had also "subbed" solo for the injured Bob Woodruff.

GAME 70 Q11 ANSWER d
In an unusual move, *Bewitched* star Elizabeth Montgomery took on the second role of Serena. Although all lines were voiced by Montgomery, various tricks were used to get both characters on the screen at once. Sometimes, the star's stand-in, Melody Thomas, played the character with the least lines, with her hair arranged to hide her face.

Answers are in right-hand boxes on page 261.

GAME 11	**1.** Agnes DiPesto was a character on what popular 1980s ABC series? a. *Thirtysomething* b. *Moonlighting* c. *Cheers* d. *Remington Steele*	The answer to this question is on: **page 258, top frame, right side.**
GAME 31	**1.** Paul Drake and Della Street were the loyal associates of: a. Benjamin Matlock b. Owen Marshall c. Perry Mason d. Jack McCoy	The answer to this question is on: **page 258, second frame, right side.**
GAME 51	**1.** *Nip/Tuck* centers on the lives of two: a. Pediatric surgeons b. Brain surgeons c. Orthopedic surgeons d. Plastic surgeons	The answer to this question is on: **page 258, third frame, right side.**
GAME 71	**1.** Which *Mary Tyler Moore Show* costar played Ruth Martin in TV's *Lassie*? a. Joyce Bulifant b. Valerie Harper c. Cloris Leachman d. Betty White	The answer to this question is on: **page 258, bottom frame, right side.**

GAME 11

TV of the 1980s

See page 260
for the first question.

GAME 10 Q12 ANSWER c
Loosely based on the best-selling books by Laura Ingalls Wilder, *Little House on the Prairie* ran from 1974 to 1983. Set during the late 1800s, the show began with Charles and Caroline Ingalls and their three daughters moving to Walnut Grove, Minnesota, in search of a better life. Michael Landon produced, directed, and starred in the show.

GAME 31

In the Courtroom

See page 260
for the first question.

GAME 30 Q12 ANSWER a
When actress Barbara Bain was hired as part of *Mission Impossible's* first cast, she arranged for husband, Martin Landau, to make guest appearances as Rollin Hand, a master of disguise. The role was so popular, Landau was hired as a regular. When he was replaced in 1969 by Leonard Nimoy over a salary issue, Bain left the show, too.

GAME 51

Medical Shows

See page 260
for the first question.

GAME 50 Q12 ANSWER b
In April 2005, after anchoring the network's flagship news program for over twenty years, Jennings left to undergo treatment for lung cancer. Charles Gibson, Elizabeth Vargas, and Bob Woodruff all served as temporary anchors. In May 2006, Gibson left his post at *Good Morning, America* to become Jennings' permanent replacement.

GAME 71

Classic Sitcoms "Toughest"

See page 260
for the first question.

GAME 70 Q12 ANSWER b
After serving in the Army Air Force in World War II, Norman Lear became first a comedy writer and then a film director. He then tried to sell a concept for a situation comedy about a blue-collar American family—a concept that eventually resulted in his first hit series, *All in the Family*. The rest, as they say, is history.

DICK VAN PATTEN
An Entertainer's Life

Dick Van Patten, a name known and trusted across America and around the world, has been in show business since his first modeling assignment at the age of three. Few actors have had as rich a background as Van Patten or have shown such versatility. Although perhaps best known for the popular role of Tom Bradford in the long-running hit series *Eight Is Enough*, his remarkable career has also included more than six hundred radio shows, twenty-seven Broadway plays, and thirty-five feature films.

A one-time child actor billed as Dickie Van Patten, Van Patten began working on Broadway at the age of seven, when he portrayed Melvyn Douglas's son in *Tapestry in Gray.* He would appear in twelve more plays before reaching adulthood, and eventually, his roster of stage hits would include three Pulitzer Prize winners—*On Borrowed Time; The Skin of Our Teeth,* starring Tallulah Bankhead and Frederic March; and *Mister Roberts,* in which he played Ensign Pulver opposite Henry Fonda. Still other stage productions of note included *The Tender Trap, Will Success Spoil Rock Hunter?,* and *Don't Drink the Water.* Along the way, Van Patten worked with many American theater greats, including Max Reinhardt, Joshua Logan, Moss Hart, George Kaufman, George Abbott, Alfred Lunt, Elia Kazan, Martin Ritt, and Elaine May.

In 1941, Dick Van Patten and his younger sister, Joyce, made a joint film debut in *Reg'lar Fellers,* repeating their roles from the radio show of the same name. But Van Patten's next important foray into films did not take place until 1968, when he appeared along with Oscar-winner Cliff Robertson and Claire Bloom in the film *Charly.* His movie career would eventually become quite varied. In addition to taking supporting parts in the sci-fi movie classics *Soylent Green* and *Westworld,* Van Patten worked with Walt Disney Studios, starring in family favorites such as *Gus, Freaky Friday,* and *The Shaggy D.A.* He also became a part of the talented team of actors who worked with Mel Brooks. His first Mel Brooks movie was the 1977 Hitchcock parody *High Anxiety*, but perhaps his most famous film role was that of King Roland in the 1987 Mel Brooks sci-fi spoof, *Spaceballs*.

Despite Dick Van Patten's long list of stage and film credits, he is best known as a television actor. In 1949, at the beginning of television, Van Patten made the transition from stage to TV by appearing in the award-winning series *I Remember Mama*, in which he portrayed Peggy Woods' son Nels for eight years. From there, he went on to win regular roles on such TV series as *Young Dr. Malone* (1961–1962), *The Partners* (1971), *The New Dick Van Dyke Show* (1973–1974), and *When Things Were Rotten* (1975). Van Patten also had memorable guest parts on literally dozens of television shows, including *I Dream Of Jeannie*, *Sanford and Son*, *Adam-12*, *Emergency!*, *S.W.A.T.*, *McMillan & Wife*, *The Six Million Dollar Man*, *The Streets of San Francisco*, *Wonder Woman*, *Barnaby Jones*, *Maude*, *Happy Days*, *What's Happening!!*, *One Day at a Time*, *The Love Boat*, *Too Close for Comfort*, *Hotel*, *Crazy Like a Fox*, *The Facts of Life*, *Growing Pains*, *Lois & Clark: The New Adventures of Superman*, *Boy Meets World*, *Touched by an Angel*, and *Murder, She Wrote*.

Of course, Dick Van Patten will always be remembered for his portrayal of Tom Bradford—proud father of eight children in ABC's TV series *Eight Is Enough*. Running from 1977 to 1981, the show struck a chord with viewers, and the Bradfords became one of America's most-beloved TV families. Dick Van Patten's fun-loving yet sensitive portrayal of Tom Bradford later earned him a ranking in *TV Guide's* "50 Greatest TV Dads of All Time." Although the series ended in 1981, Van Patten reprised his role of Tom Bradford in the 1987 ABC-TV movie *Eight Is Enough: A Family Reunion.*

Dick Van Patten's career in the entertainment field has been so distinguished that he was honored with his own star on the Hollywood Walk of Fame. Yet his interests extend far beyond show business. Since 1989, Van Patten has had his own pet food company called Dick Van Patten's Natural Balance Pet Foods, Inc. Natural Balance makes holistic dog and cat food, as well as also

That's me and my wife, Pat, standing with our son Nels. Seated from left to right are our sons Jimmy and Vincent.

having a Zoological Division that supplies food for lions and tigers at some of the most prestigious zoos in the country, such as the San Diego Zoo, the Lincoln Park Zoo in Illinois, and the Staten Island Zoo.

When he isn't working, Van Patten can usually be found on his tennis court or at the beach swimming. He is also a horse racing enthusiast. Dick and his wife Pat, a former June Taylor dancer, have known each other since childhood and have been married for more than fifty years. They reside in the San Fernando Valley near their three sons, Nels, James, and Vincent.

JOE FRANKLIN'S GREAT ENTERTAINMENT TRIVIA

Here's the book that will put your knowledge of movies, radio, music, and television to the test. New York's famous talk- and variety-show host Joe Franklin, whose guest list over the years reads like a who's who of celebrity royalty, has drawn on his own unique knowledge and personal experiences to create the *Great Entertainment Trivia Game*. Not only is the book packed with challenging questions, it also provides lots of interesting information along with the answers.

Guaranteed fun, dozens of individual games, each with twelve questions, will both challenge and amuse. But unlike other books of this type, which reveal the answers below the questions or group them together with all of the other answers, this book cleverly formats the games in a way that allows the reader to see only one answer at the appropriate time. This way, the reader can play along. In addition to the questions, Franklin shares some of his favorite memories in fascinating insets that are peppered throughout the book.

From cover to cover, the *Great Entertainment Trivia Game* is pure entertainment. And who better to create such a book than Joe Franklin, with his decades-long involvement in the business that he so dearly loves—and that so dearly loves him.

$7.95 • 288 pages • 4 x 7-inch paperback • ISBN 0-7570-0038-X

MICKY DOLENZ' ROCK 'N ROLLIN' TRIVIA GAME

Here he comes, walking down the street . . .
For nearly forty years now, Micky
Dolenz has pleased millions of fans
throughout the world by playing a
role in rock 'n roll history as a member
of The Monkees. And in that time, he
has also played a number of other
roles—actor, director, writer, producer,
brother, husband, father, and even
radio DJ. Now he's ready to play a
brand-new role as trivia maven—and
in *Micky Dolenz' Rock 'n Rollin' Trivia*,
you're invited to play a role, too!

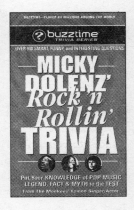

From Elvis in America to The Beatles in England; from
doo-wop to punk rock; from MTV to MP3; it's all here in one big
collection of over 900 questions hand-picked by Micky himself
to tease and please any rock 'n roll fan. Unlike other trivia books
that simply supply the answers to the questions, this book includes interesting information along with each answer. Furthermore, the answers are cleverly formatted in a way that allows
the reader to play alone or with others.

With over 65 million records sold worldwide, Micky Dolenz
remains an important part of rock 'n roll culture. But now he
wants to take a close look at rock 'n roll history, one question at
a time. Micky's ready—are you? Pick up this book and find out
for yourself.

$7.95 • 288 pages • 4 x 7-inch paperback • ISBN 0-7570-0289-7

RICK BARRY'S
SUPER SPORTS TRIVIA

Irascible, opinionated, and absolutely
brilliant, Rick Barry was named one of
the fifty greatest players to have ever
competed in professional basketball. A
natural on the court, he possessed the
physical ability, quick mind, and God-
given talent to play among the best.
Now, Basketball Hall of Famer Rick
Barry challenges all those who pride
themselves on their knowledge of
sports with his unique book of trivia.

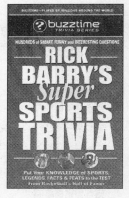

Drawing information from the history, legends, and lore of
basketball, baseball, football, boxing, hockey, auto racing, and
more, Barry has created a series of quizzes that are guaranteed to
provide hours of entertainment and fun. But unlike other trivia
books that simply supply the answers to the questions, this book
includes interesting information along with each answer—
you'll actually learn as you play! Furthermore, the answers are
cleverly formatted in a way that allows the reader to play alone
or with others. Each game is guaranteed fun—challenging, informative, and amusing.

Rick Barry's knowledge of sports results in a trivia book
with a spin that's more challenging than a curveball. If you're
ready for a game that is interesting, educational, and always fun
to play, *Rick Barry's Super Sports Trivia Game* is the way to go.

$7.95 • 288 pages • 4 x 7-inch paperback • ISBN 0-7570-0134-3

**For more information about our books,
visit our website at www.squareonepublishers.com**

FOR A COPY OF OUR CATALOG, PLEASE CALL TOLL FREE:
877-900-BOOK, ext. 100

ABOUT
BUZZTIME TRIVIA

If you are one of those people whose head is filled with obscure information, but you are never quite sure of what to do with all that knowledge, you're going to love Buzztime. Why? Because now you have a way to shine.

Buzztime is the company behind the world's largest interactive trivia game network. Go to any one of the nearly 4,000 Buzztime/NTN restaurants and sports bars located throughout North America, and you can compete against players at that location or against the thousands of other trivia buffs across the United States and Canada. Since Buzztime is the largest repository of trivia facts, you know that the questions will always be fresh, current, and stimulating. These Buzztime/NTN locations are also great places to meet people and enjoy evenings of fun and entertainment. Interested? Simply log onto www.buzztime.com for a listing of local sites.

But there's more. You can also play Buzztime trivia games on the Internet, on your television, and even on your cell phone. That's right. If you're tired of standing in long lines, waiting around at airports, or sitting in office waiting rooms with nothing to do, you can simply pick up your cell phone and place a call to connect with Buzztime games.

Many cable and satellite television packages offer Buzz-time trivia as well. Check the Buzztime website to see if the games are offered by your local service provider. But if they aren't, don't worry—the Buzztime Home Trivia System will allow you to enjoy the Buzztime experience in the comfort of your own home. And since it is a multi-user game, you can play it with your family, friends, and neighbors.

Medical researchers have determined that if you don't exercise your brain, intellectual function weakens. Why take a chance on getting flabby brain cells when you can strengthen them with a daily dose of Buzztime? Your brain will thank you for it.

For more information about Buzztime trivia games,

visit
www.buzztime.com